This is the title page for

Process Music:

songs, stories, and studies of graphic culture by Kenneth FitzGerald.

It has been given a
differently styled typographic
treatment to highlight its significance,
differentiate it from other pages,
and elaborate on standard
settings for title pages.

Onomatopee 164

This page is part of the "front matter" for «Process Music» and contains a dedication, acknowledgements, and copyright information. Further production notes are included in the colophon, at ther end of the book. «Process Music» is dedicated to my parents, Janet and Gerald Fitzgerald. Love always to Ellen, Emma, and Leaf. My thanks to these good people for commissioning, accepting and/or editing works that appear in this collection: Sue Apfelbaum, Michael Bierut, Scott Burnham, Steven Heller, John Kramer, Francisco Laranjo, Zachary Petitt, Elizabeth Resnick, Stefan Sagmeister, Kristina Lamour Sansone, Rudy VanderLans, Betsy Vardell, Armin Vit, and John Walters. My apologies to anyone I've inadvertently neglected to include in this list. Lorraine Wild was one such in my previous book for her inspiration and support so she gains a dedicated thanks here. Infinite thanks to Debbie Millman for generously providing a Prelude, plus her encouragement and friendship. Greatest thanks to Freek Lomme at Onomatopee Projects for investing in this book and guiding it to its completion. The contents of this book is ©2022 Onomatopee and Kenneth FitzGerald. This publication is licensed under a Creative Commons Attribution-NonCommercial-ShareAlike 4.0 International Licence (CC BY-NC-SA 4.0). To view a copy of this license, visit https://creativecommons.org/licenses/by-nc-sa/4.0/

First edition, 2022

ISBN 978-94-93148-77-2

Onomatopee Projects
www.onomatopee.net

This is the contents page for «Process music», another part of the book's front matter. It lists the writings included in the book and provides page numbers for direct access. Ordinarily, the contents are arranged as an ordered list, usually aligned flush left or centered. However, to continue the design concept set out on the cover — an homage to Hipgnosis' «Go 2» album design — it here has been set as continuous text, like a prose paragraph. A further conceit is that writings are presented as they would in a record album's track listing. Before the proper book contents, there is a Prelude by Debbie Millman (6), and an author's introduction (8). The collected writings are organized in four sections followed by a coda. They are: *Blues in CMYK*

13 Ways of Looking at Kenneth FitzGerald: a Prelude by Debbie Millman

(or: Why Kenneth FitzGerald is one of the most distinguished design practitioners working today)

1. In *Emigre* 66 (2004), Kenneth wrote an essay titled, "I Come to Bury Graphic Design, Not Praise It," and posed the question, "To consider how to teach or theorize about graphic design, a basic question must be answered: what is its ultimate goal?"

2. When AIGA, the Professional Association of Design (and one of the world's largest design organizations) sent out a booklet containing a 12-step guide to strategic design, Kenneth went on the record stating the brochure was another demonstration of simultaneous affirmation (we're influential!) and denial (preaching to the converted).

3. He once wrote that he believed that a broader and deeper appreciation of design can — and should — lead to its demise.

4. Kenneth declared, "Designers are widely seen as possessing an elitist æsthetic agenda insensitive to people's needs."

5. He posited that honoring Dave Eggers seemed less a pronunciation of design's significance than an expression of self-loathing.

6. These songs make Kenneth cry: "Walk Away Renee," The Left Banke; "Angel of the Morning," Merrilee Rush and the Turnabouts; "Beer and Kisses," Amy Rigby; "Misguided Angel," Cowboy Junkies; "If I Needed

You," performed by Lyle Lovett; "No Telling," Linda Thompson; "Bogie's Bonnie Belle," and "Saving the Good Stuff for You," Richard Thompson; "A Heart Needs a Home," Richard & Linda Thompson; "(Talk to Me of) Mendocino," and "Leave Me Be," Kate & Anna McGarrigle; "Miracle," Heidi Berry; "At the Beginning of Time," Jane Siberry.

7. Knowing I was a brand consultant, Kenneth suggested, "Maybe design should be left to people inspired by the nutrition labels on food packages."

8. He hates his obsessive, catastrophizing thinking but loves his blue eyes.

9. In an interview for the Perpetual Beta blog, Ian Lynam asked him: What are things that you think every designer should read in terms of edification? He replied: "Things that are antithetical to their deeply held and treasured beliefs about design."

10. In an essay titled, "Fuck All," (which was a response to Michael Rock's essay "Fuck Content") (see page 64) he stated that the author's reductive view was absurd and, "Design isn't a glossy and empty abstraction of itself. It's by and for people. Our content is, perpetually, ourselves."

11. His biggest regret is not getting his wife Ellen an engagement ring.

12. He's critical of the disconnect between advocating the free flow of information but allowing only a clique of specialists to direct it.

13. In an interview Silas Munro conducted with Martin Venezky in 2005 on Speak Up, he suggested that Kenneth FitzGerald felt that monographs were ... over.

Debbie Millman is a designer, author, educator, host of the award-winning podcast Design Matters, and an AIGA Medalist. She is also co-founder and chair of the world's first graduate program in branding at the School of Visual Arts; editorial director of Print *magazine; and the author of seven books on design and branding.*

Opening track (medley)

♪

"Why would you want to do that?"

It was Paula Scher asking, referring to an essay I'd recently posted on my blog that discussed her album cover work (see page 88). We'd just been introduced, and I was immediately put on the spot. No problem. After twenty years of writing and lecturing, I was practiced at answering at length and in *tl;dr* mode. Here the latter was called for.

I said it was because her work hadn't received any meaningful critical attention. It was presumptuous of me to dismiss the copious articles that addressed her design. And that I represented something special and desirable.

Always sensitive to how "criticism" is frequently equated with negativity, I hastily added that said attention might increase regard for her design. I refrained from detailing the mechanism of how this new esteem would be attained or what the benefit would be. Was it even possible for Paula Scher to gain more renown?

But she asked what my motive was; what was in it for me? It was a good question, ideal for a book introduction. Having often speculated on designers' unvoiced and hidden motivations, some reflexivity is only fair.

It's a luxury to be able to write a 6000-word exegesis on any design topic. The absence in design of "meaningful critical attention" is primarily rooted in pragmatic considerations. Venues are few, word limits tight,

recompense rare. For academics, some institutions will, under certain conditions, accept writing as credit toward a faculty's research obligation. In my particular situation, one major provision wasn't met, specifically that the essay failed to undergo any kind of peer review. I did earn a lesser citation credit when my article was quoted in a book.

The occasional critic of criticism has claimed self-aggrandizement to be writers' true motivation. The profession's prevalent attitude toward criticism belies this, as it's welcomed in word but shrifted-short in practice. The limits previously mentioned arise from indifference to criticism: there's no market for it. Trolling star practitioners hardly seems an effective and sustainable means of notoriety. Unless you think that *any* attention is good. I don't.

However, I knew when writing my essay that I had the means to potentially have it read by Scher and learn her reaction. This could be considered evidence for writing's efficacy as a means to a kind of repute (though, in this case, it preceded the article) as my writing isn't an adjunct to a primary status as a practitioner. But it's doubtful if the trajectory of my career is representative or replicable.

Sometimes a kind of altruism is assigned as a motive for critical writing — an effort to improve design. In retrospect, a judgement that an article contributed positively to the discipline is gratifying. But I'm more comfortable testifying the impulse is self-centered and the gain tangential. Even when commissioned, all the articles I've written first satisfied my desire to write (and do so well) and make an argument.

Overall, I'm agnostic about bettering design. There's much design work I admire that didn't and doesn't engage criticism. At the same time, criticism can and has enhanced the quality of design discourse and performance, especially in work I most admire. And it has enriched my appreciation of all of it.

Before offering understanding to an audience, writing can educe it for the writer. Writers have often presented their activity as more than descriptive. It is a method of discovery itself. Throughout my career, this has been a primary impetus. It's been my fortune that at times I've garnered tangible benefits.

I should have answered Paula Scher that I did it to sort out what I really thought about her work. The reason is the process is the result.

♫

All these texts have been subjected to some degree of emendation, mainly to ameliorate compositional quirks and clarify prose. Some sharp remarks were smoothed and snark abated. In my writing, haste and the desire to turn a phrase sometimes overrode contemplation. Original opinions, however, have been kept intact, though some now qualify as relics.

♫♫

This book contains both the first piece I ever wrote about design ("The angel is my floating point!" 1996) and the last ("(incomplete)," 2019). At the time, I thought that initial publication would be my final one. Now, the latter may be. Or not.

On the first day of my graduate study in design at Massachusetts College of Art and Design, Al Gowan, co-director of the program, challenged me to publish an article in the design press. He was a writer himself and knew me from writing for the alumni newsletter. I accepted though I hadn't given any thought about writing about design beyond what the program would demand. As time wore on, I forgot about Al's charge, even as my thesis mutated to a study of contemporary design writing. With graduation months away, I was on track to disappoint us both.

That changed when Rudy VanderLans commissioned me to review Elliott Earls' *Throwing Apples at the Sun* (see page 160) for *Emigre* magazine, prompted by a letter to the editor I'd sent him. I'd submitted it as a stalling tactic from starting my thesis document. So long frying pan. Hello, fire.

Rudy's invitation led to another then another. I also realized I had things I wanted to say unprompted, so I wrote articles about them. Except in rare instances where I agreed to write an essay while working on another, each could have been my last. This is largely how my career as a design writer played out. I fell into it, over and over—but *up* a staircase.

This collection is more of my fallout, concentrated. Imperfect analogies aside, I hope it's illuminating for and lingers with you.

This is the title page of the first section of «Process Music», called "Blues in CMYK." It presents short essays focusing on a variety of issues in graphic design. These include: the importance of metaphor and cross-disciplinary inspiration; the practice, limits, and future of design criticism; the proper context of digital technology; design education; authenticity; the threat and promise of design authorship; and more. "Singing the Surface" was originally presented as a lecture then adapted for publication in «Print» magazine, winter 2017. "11 things they don't teach you about lists of 10 things they don't teach you in design school outside of design school" was posted under the title "Learning by numbers: eleven lessons taught only in design school" on Design Observer, June 2017. "The team player" was posted at the AIGA Design Educators Community journal, February 2015. "Design's just dessert" was posted at Voice: AIGA Journal of Design, September 2009. "The printer's devil's dictionary" was a guest editorial at Speak Up, April 2006. "Implosure" was presented as a paper for the 2011 College Art Association Annual Conference panel, "What's art got to do with it? Design writing in the twenty-first century." "(incomplete)" was published in «Modes of Criticism» 4: Radical pedagogy, spring 2019. "Fuck all" was published in «Modes of Criticism» 1: Critical, uncritical, post-critical, 2015. "I believe in design" first appeared at Design Observer, March 2009. The revised and expanded version presented here was published in «Faith is trust: trust design» publication 3, Premsela, Netherlands, Institute of Design and Fashion, 2011. "Transmission" was originally posted on the Ephemeral States blog.

Singing the Surface

> *Strictly considered, writing about music is as illogical as singing about economics. All the other arts can be talked about in the terms of ordinary life and experience. A poem, a statue, a painting or a play is a representation of somebody or something, and can be measurably described (the purely æsthetic values aside) by describing what it represents.*
>
> — "The Unseen World" by H. K. M., *The New Republic*
> (p. 63, vol. 14, February 9, 1918)

Critical writers respond to creativity. Everything wrong about doing this, and everything right, can be condensed to three words. This trinity has bothered me for some time but I never fully contemplated why.

The three words conjure a ludicrous image ripe for parody: a caricature Martha Graham prancing and swooning across a bleak brick plaza at the foot of some austere, anonymous steel and glass skyscraper, tulle swirling with every grand, affected, sweeping gesture. Imagine it's an entire troupe capering about like loony fools. Modern dance meets modern design. Cue the laugh track. That's dancing about architecture.

"Writing about music is like dancing about architecture," is the full, familiar formulation of the quip in question. It has no definitive attribution, being contemporarily credited to Steve Martin, Frank Zappa, Laurie

Anderson, and, most recently, Elvis Costello. There's some evidence that each of them made at least an approximation of the jibe but not for its coinage. The distinctive personalities involved provide affirmation for each claimant. It sounds like something one of them would have said.

Attempts are ongoing to establish that provenance but likely pointless. In a December 30, 2010 *New York Times* "Freakonomics" blog post on the phrase, Garson O'Toole's quoteinvestigator.com website was credited for unearthing the earliest usage: in 1979 by actor/comedian/musician Martin Mull. At best, Mull adapted (wittily unwittingly) the *New Republic* construction above. It's the earliest example of the corollary that O'Toole could locate. Mull obviously was going for laughs, where "H.K.M." was simply making an argument.

The many permutations over time are evidence that it's a popular diss, one that's spawned a web site dedicated to establishing its originator. You can also dial up a batch of blogs titled with variations on "dancing about architecture," each centered on discussions of music. All defy their titles as they verbally promenade.

The attraction of the dig is plain. It's a clever, crisp, slightly surreal twist of language, a crowd-pleasing deflation of the stereotypical pretentiousness associated with critical commentary. It's unfortunate that the phrase is so firmly attached to music criticism: it's tailor-made for graphic design. In comparison, there's likely less patience among design practitioners for deep thought about their activity. Plus, there's graphic design's historic association with architecture.

But amusing as the remark is, it's totally phony. Snicker if you want, it can't stand scrutiny. At the center of the snark is the futility of analysis itself. As opposed to possibly just going with a gut feeling. Not only does the wisecrack stick it to writing, the writing's subject suffers collateral damage. Isn't composing a song about love, language, Montana, revenge and guilt, or ventriloquism also a performance of building boogie?

To be consistent, you can't stop at the response to the art; you must encompass and reject the work as well. (And here, and in all instances going forward, when I speak of "art" or "artists," I'm referring collectively to the disciplines of music, fine art and graphic design, along with their

respective performers.) Our established creative disciplines and many of their themes and tropes seem normal only through tradition. They are regarded as natural because they're so pervasive and established. Take that away, and all expression seems absurd. Talking about love is like daubing paint on fabric to cruelty.

Not that upstarts are universally pleased with their press but established artists well into their careers usually out-trot the comment. It's the hook of a lament on negative critical response to the musician's recent offerings. But it's not like musicians have ever waxed poetic about being a musician, right? And how many songs are there that have songwriting and performing as their subject matter? What about freestyle rap battles? Someone like Laurie Anderson should definitely know better. In her early days, she collaborated on songs with critic Lester Bangs.

If the marketplace has spoken on the issue, it has declared a constant and voracious appetite for indulging in and observation of house hoofing. Admittedly, the preponderance of what's in the music press is celebrity reporting: writing about musicians. Which, if talking to pop stars, can seem like you're talking to architecture. That there's a dearth of affective literature in any creative discipline is a given. However, there are also the exceptions that prove cavorting to constructions can be just as vital as cutting the grooves.

Similarly, graphic designers have an ambiguous relationship with their literature. Pragmatic "how to" articles abound and are happily consumed. As are showcases of and interviews with leading practitioners. A prevailing opinion among practitioners is that critical thought should be expressed through and in the work, not in portentous essays … if you must indulge in it at all.

An irony is that it's the smarter musicians that recycle the "dancing about architecture" gibe. The remark's nuance and wit are beyond most pop stars. And plenty of writing is incapable of matching the subtlety of the art it attempts to describe. Still, I've always been averse to the comment simply as an enthusiast for t and reading about and discussing the arts. Having status as a line-dancer doesn't play into my response.

Grousing about bad press is understandable. But tearing down the

entire communal, generative experience of art is overkill. If anyone needs and benefits from an architectonic gambol, it's musicians of the kind who'll fuss about dancing to architecture.

Through phrasing variations over the years, the comment will actually reach further. It's often alleged that merely talking about music is a pointless activity. How could any art survive such prohibition on conversation? That artists might idealize a passive, undiscriminating audience seems the antithesis of the creative contract.

For all their drollery, the total eight words in question comprise perhaps the most nihilistic assertion ever uttered about the imaginative experience. It does provide a service by negatively engaging essential truths about creativity in all its forms. By denying the effectual possibility of discourse, the phrase ultimately affirms its import. Yes, writing about music is like dancing about architecture. So what?

The phrase's central flaw is ridiculing the act of crossing one discipline's boundary to illuminate another. As mentioned above, this is observably contrary to most musicians' practice and creatives in all the arts. Creativity is often, maybe always, a process of directed, simple synæsthesia. This is the psychological term for the state where stimuli are cross-sensed: hearing color or tasting touch. Usually, it's the unwelcome result of physical trauma. The late neurologist Oliver Sacks described the common music/color inversion in the chapter "The Key of Clear Green" for his 2007 book *Musicophilia: Tales of Music and the Brain*.

The malady has been a constant fascination for people in many artistic disciplines. Charles Baudelaire and Arthur Rimbaud wrote poems about the synæthesic experience, works that deeply influenced musicians such as Patti Smith. Creativity manifests and experiments in the realm of the senses, so any phenomenon, especially a deranging one, is of interest and possible utility.

Creativity and culture may be regarded as activities where reality is subjected to metaphor, to a deliberate scrambling of the senses. The process is an acknowledgement that experience cannot be contained by its host medium. You may be compelled to paint a picture to celebrate words, and vice versa. Every physical means possible to the body may need to be

called to the task in a figurative pageant.

If taken literally, "dancing about architecture," suggests that music can truly be only about music. Possibly only instrumentals. In reality, as soon as language permitted, lyrics were set to song. Instrumental music has long been inspired by and titled to people, places, emotions, actions, and events. According to Anne Kilmer, professor of Assyriology at the University of California, the oldest known song dates from 1400 BCE and is a hymn to Nikal, the moon god's wife. Shall we fear the wrath of her husband, Sin ("Ferocious bull, whose horn is thick, whose legs are perfected"), for our presumption?

If we're prohibited from dancing to architecture, our culture becomes entirely insular and self-referential. If we have one at all. Silence must descend, poetry purged from our pages, if cross-art connections are prohibited.

In a commercially determined culture, art is a product. Artists must place fearsome, legally enforced claims on their "intellectual property." Poor reviews and inept commentaries threaten more than artists' pride. Livelihoods are at stake. This is felt sharply amongst graphic designers, who regard practically all design writing as PR. While fine artists and musicians dissemble about their relationship with consumer culture, graphic design crafts valentines daily.

Practically, art must be regarded a discrete possession with clearly delineated boundaries. Closing out any discussion of art also limits the event to the artist-supplied circumstance. Upon conclusion, the curtain closes swiftly and firmly, and the audience ushered out, securely gagged.

This possibility is untenable and contrary to history. And it's a foolish, self-defeating action. Countless works in all media are creative homages and progeny of a precursor. More so in our contemporary, sampling era. In fact, criticism itself may be considered a long-standing sampling activity in culture. Discourse selects elements from the artwork to construct a new work. The specific sampling analogy would be a usage of non-musical elements in a composition. While less common, this form of sampling is established and widespread.

Criticism, however, isn't usually awarded standing as an art form in

its own right. It's regarded as and frequently adopts the position of being outside of creative activity: a commentary upon it. Style and skill are desirable in commentators, yet discourse has secondary, subservient status to the art. A critic can more often be likened to parasite, or a barnacle, on the body of art. If an artist is charitable, elevation to symbiote status is possible. And this is only the formal practice of art dialogue. Colloquial criticism is just someone talking smack.

Squelching discussion is potentially hazardous economically for artists, far more than poor reviews. In reality, artists, musicians, and designers are striving to generate buzz about themselves and their work. But with potential reward, there's risk. In today's blogging landscape, the exponentially increased number of terpsichordians in the house can make you a name — or a target.

Underlying this is the certainty that art is a generative experience, not a passive one. The potency of an artwork is in its ability to provoke response, whether verbal, written, or inspired, in the same medium or in another. Discussion extends the artwork beyond its physical, chronological boundaries. This extension links it with other works, forming the complex web of associations that is culture. The network of culture is always active, dynamic, transcending the individual works.

Our relationship to art can change under this conception. The art takes precedence over the artists and becomes an independent presence. The artist is the custodian, the medium, for art. In the case of music, it's that music plays the performer.

My first encounter with this notion was from King Crimson guitarist Robert Fripp, in a joint 1981 interview with the late Joe Strummer of The Clash: "Sometimes — and this is only a theory — I think that music needs a musician to play it. That the music itself is alive, but you have to be out there to know it. And at that point it may be possible that the music is waiting to be played. So it needs a musician." (*Musician*, No. 33, June 1981)

Fripp is an idealistic but pragmatic musician that has spoken out frequently and passionately about musicians' legal and moral rights to their work. His coinage of the term "Soundscapes" for a solo aspect of his performing is pure dancing about architecture. Reflexively, I am opposed

to a conception of an abstraction as an entity one serves, whether it is "rock and roll," or "art," or "graphic design." However, Fripp links his idea to a generous, communal experience that promotes and enriches public experience.

Music also needs an audience, as does all art. Might art also perform the audience? The compulsion to witness creativity, to further sustain it through discourse, might be as profound as the creative impulse. Fan is an abbreviation of fanatic. That people bearing witness to art might struggle, stammer, thrash about, stumble over boundaries to describe the enormity and allure of the experience should draw no censure. The expression can only be as driven and occasionally messy as the art that compelled it.

The intensity of reaction to visual art, music, and literature is storied within and across each of those mediums. My special interest, however, is graphic design. Can the same be said for writing about that? If anything, graphic design's status as a prosaic activity makes it eminently discussable. Writing about graphic design is like … writing about graphic design. The challenge is making it strange.

Had the practice existed then as we now know it, "H.K.M" probably would add graphic design to the list of things that "can be measurably described (the purely æsthetic values aside) by describing what it represents." Today's graphic designers likely would agree. Graphic design is the ultimate representer. The "dancing about architecture" prohibition wouldn't seem to apply. The discipline's prosaic status is lauded within the design field and enforced within its professional literature.

However, H.K.M.'s representation of the arts is naïve and historically mistaken. As far as painting goes, he was probably thinking more Sir Lawrence Alma-Tadema than Kazimir Malevich. Writing in 1918, abstract art was just starting out and would soon definitively demolish H.K.M.'s conception of painting. The other disciplines named above were similarly straying from descriptiveness.

While realism and representation predominated prior to the early 20th century, matters weren't as apparent as thought. Impressionism, for instance, had already twisted representation into eccentric areas that transcended literality. An enormity of meaning is lost if you say that Monet was

documenting Rouen Cathedral and leave it at that. Some light fantastic is obligatory in your text to fully impart the painter's own fantastic light.

The inadequacy of literal readings extends further back in history. For centuries, paintings have contained complex symbolism and iconography. Simply detailing the apparent account presented in a painting would overlook crucial meanings. Secondary narratives of contemporary times are woven throughout ostensibly religious stories.

Art history has prosaically documented various symbologies. No fancy stepping required. Yet artists utilized the symbolization as conduits to the ineffable. To revelation. Overall, the paintings are themselves are examples of dancing about architecture. As are the poems, plays, statues... and graphic designs.

Graphic design is ready for an unrepentantly absurd, tangential literary indulgence. Similar to the dance/architecture pairing, there needs to be a linkage that's equally incongruous and evocative. For me, that association has been design/music. Writing about graphic design is for me, an exercise of singing the surface.

Graphic design is usually considered an accompanist discipline, a backing band for the content. In this context, the lyrics carry the substance. The claim is, even with the design field, that here is where meaning truly resides; the words tell you what the song is "about." Design is regarded as instrumental: it holds no content of its own.

Just as our visual proclivity is toward representation, our auditory preference is toward vocalizing. Still, instrumental music has been historically stirring and substantive. Beethoven isn't panned for his lack of librettos. On their own, the melodies hold sway. Design is instrumental: it creates a context for the content. It generates the desire to hear the words. Then becomes content in its own right.

Indicting graphic design as an activity preoccupied with surface is a charged charge. While a simple truth, to designers it's a frequent slur decrying an alleged obscuring of an underlying emptiness. Yet the surface for design resembles that of our body. Like skin, or the paper upon which graphic design is often performed, design itself is a cultural membrane composed of multiple layers. Design's fine depths emblematize subtle

strata of meaning.

The songs of graphic design are diverse, encompassing all styles, from folk immediacy to industrial impersonality. In its most popular expressions, graphic design is a 2D musical staged daily on myriad platforms. Stock companies act out most of the shows, while many others are amateur hours, occasionally enlivened by the participants' verve but plagued by flubbed lines ("did anyone think to proofread this?") and cardboard sets ("here's a marker and a pizza box lid, go crazy").

Grabbing the headlines and attention are the big budget Broadway extravaganzas. Whatever the quality, we suspend our disbelief as characters unrelentingly croon tunes with the oddest subject matter. These refrains often extol the virtues of some humdrum product or service.

At the same time, there are the airs of the audience, their invented melodies and halting, improvised performances. On one hand, formal graphic design doubts these ditties, while cycling them back into proper compositions with the other.

But it's the professional sounds of graphic design that fill the concert halls, a massed chorus dispersed throughout the world, harmonizing on ballads of people, places, possessions, participation, passions. And always, more. All pitch perfect ... by which I mean destined for the garbage can.

What are the songs of the surface? For lyrics, there's the magnificence of typefaces that embody words and compel associations and sensations. Fonts are visual madeleines, acting surreptitiously when wielded by sophisticates and laypeople alike. Their ubiquity compounds their stealth as they spell out ideals in their forms.

There are the plangent profundities of a multitude of graphic marks: rules, curves, patterns, shapes, sigils. Hues assign humors, coloring these elements, and the expanses amongst them. There is the symphony of a book, the album of a magazine. The sequencing and pacing of turned pages are no less a composition of movements and variations, than is chamber music.

The aspects of graphic design can magnify or nullify our interpretations of text and image. The arrangements of graphic elements on a page,

their juxtaposition, can release storehouses of ideas, affect beliefs on how we should manage our body politic, how we relate to and operate our technology, and interpret reality itself. That's worthy of a pop song at least. Or, more appropriately, an orgy of operas.

H.K.M. proposes that it's contra-rational to sing about economics, infamously the "dismal science." Too often, graphic design is made into the dismal art, overdetermined by commercial concerns. H.K.M.'s problem is being wrapped up about illogic when discussing the ineffable. Much of, maybe all, creativity is extra-logical. But our modern era expects "measurable description." Or silence.

This isn't to say that design writing shouldn't be exacting — just the opposite. It's a hope for writing that's adventurous and expansive when articulating graphic design, writing that will trample boundaries gladly to celebrate it, just as design scatters across page, screen, and space.

Design demands a disciplinary transubstantiation to fully portray its deceptive apparency, its manifold semblances. To talk about graphic design in voice and written word is to perform sight-readings from a different kind of sheet music.

If you know the score, please play, and sing along.

Transmission

Walt's Transmissions has a new sign, its third in as many years. It took a while for me to notice, even though I drive past twice a day on the way to and from work. The new sign was placed to the left of their garage door, posted no higher than an average person's height, on the side of a small addition to the cinder-block structure. The cab of a battered pickup truck stationed in front easily obscures the sign.

The previous two signs were positioned for maximum visibility, just below the apex of the roof. This one may have found its less prominent location not so much out of some sense of self-effacement than someone's diminished desire to climb a ladder.

Whatever the reason for its less than optimal positioning, the new sign was an encouraging move. From all appearances, the shop appeared in the process of closing: activity slowed, the number of distressed cars in the fenced-in yard decreased significantly. That latter development first seemed a positive step toward a leaner, meaner, cleaner facility. Then I noticed the shop's sign — its second — had been removed along with the junk cars. What appeared at first to be a freshening up quickly took on features of a winding down.

My interest in Walt's was largely due to its original sign, which I had delighted in. It was hand painted directly onto the building, by someone with a degree of experience or training. The letterforms were fanciful,

more in keeping with graffiti than professional sign painting. Graffiti itself was influenced by corporate logos and packaging's stylized lettering. Here was culture sampling and remixing itself. And the artist had signed the work.

Having avoided any transmission trouble with my car, I had no practical connection with Walt's. If I had the need, I would have gone elsewhere, to mechanics I already had a relationship with. As much as I treasured the sign, it didn't affect my consumer choices. It's problematic if this or any sign could provoke me to a service purchase.

While my attention to Walt's was for purely æsthetic reasons related to the sign, its replacement represented basic debates on the purpose and capacity of design. It also came to stand for our area's revitalization attempts. Long-awaited changes were underway in our borough of South Norfolk, Virginia. Many more were planned or hoped for, all to rescue a sorely neglected section of the city of Chesapeake. After decades of decay, any change seemed for the better. Even a new sign for a transmission shop.

Technically, Walt's was just over the city line and in Norfolk proper. But its proximity — a ten-minute leisurely stroll east across the railroad overpass — brought it within the scope of what I consider our locale. The quality and character of the streets and houses were consistent well beyond the borderline. Our area was a zone of "before" pictures yearning for an "after." Or, as a designated historic district, longing to return to its beneficent before.

Walt's sign entered emblematic status in its substitution. Not long after I got around to documenting my beloved sign, it was covered over with a new one. The replacement was a dully commercial product, surely promoted as able to increase visibility AND sales! In place of the eccentric lettering was the consistency of a typeface. Though in this context, was unconventional in its own right, being "Souvenir," a 1914 creation of eminent type designer Morris Fuller Benton that found its full favor in the 1970s. (I'll always think of it as the *Innervisions* type, as my first exposure to it was on the sleeve of that classic 1973 Stevie Wonder album.)

All told, the new sign was more professional. It included credit card info and a web address: indicators of an efficient and tech-savvy business.

The sign wasn't ugly. Just anonymous and bland, despite the unusual typeface. The product of a standardized process, it was unlikely to acquire any admirers.

But is that a sign's job? What's most important to the business? It's specious to claim that the original sign, by virtue of its novelty, attracted more attention. And, from that, potential customers.

Then again, is "artistic" signage what you're looking for when you're in the market for a CV joint? I want my mechanic to be like the sign: competent but with a little personality. Still, all of the original sign's information was perfectly readable. By basic rules of design, it was successful. Why replace it?

This gets us into another transmission issue: of messages by design, both perceptible and imperceptible. The design styling of the sign or any artifact modulates what's transmitted. That original graffiti-sign probably was broadcasting a message that was too "folksy" for the owner. Or, perhaps, a new owner wanted to put his stamp on the business.

From the perspective of the neighborhood, any upgrade in a local business is a good thing. The area is economically depressed, in need of bolstering its tax base and drawing people in. And while a house on that corner would be more attractive and in keeping with the largely residential nature of the block, the area is still zoned light industrial. Everything's a trade-off. As it is with the new sign. There's not much you can do to make a transmission shop "sexy" graphically. Except maybe an unusual typeface.

What you quickly encounter is the ongoing drama pitting "revitalization" against preserving a neighborhood's "character." The wrecking ball versus restoration. It's an impromptu theatre piece being staged across the country in all varieties of communities. The scorched-earth urban renovation schemes of the 1970s instigated a preservation movement that has engendered its own backlash. This was echoed in graphic design as the Modernist impulse sought to pave all visual culture with an austere Helveticascape.

Revitalization isn't an abstract topic for me, having bought a home within South Norfolk's historic district. Restrictions are placed here on what and how renovations may be made. However, in attempting to

invigorate neighborhoods, the civilian review board that approves changes often misses the spirit of the initiative for the letter. The greater goal would seem to be encouraging conscientious homeowners to buy into the area to repair and maintain properties at a reasonable common standard. Instead, residents find themselves trapped under leaking tin roofs because of the expense of replacing them with identical materials. The mandate mutates into one requiring deep pockets rather than good faith.

Were our area composed of tracts with uniform house styles from the same era, the prohibitions on contemporary additions considered not in keeping would be consistent. However, our neighborhoods and the houses themselves are mélanges. With the establishment of the historic district, an arbitrary baseline was established. Existing structures were declared acceptable, no matter their peculiar makeup.

For instance, common throughout the district are Craftsman-style bungalows retrofitted in the 1940s with brooding metal awnings. Neither historically "accurate" nor particularly attractive, the hybrids have been deemed acceptable and worthy of preservation. But we won't be allowed to screen in our front second floor porch, despite the feature's prevalence around us.

The result is mixed feelings throughout the district about the guidelines and its attempt to standardize variety. The effort is another example of how the designation of "original" has always been a moving target, a matter of interpretation rather than objective analysis. While we acknowledge that the guidelines have been for the area's betterment, the regimented, capricious application thwarts and frustrates us.

Fortunately, for most of us, graphic design isn't macro-managed on the citizenry (it's the high Modernist designers and visionary/grandiose architects/urban planners who count this as misfortune). Supervision occurs at the micro stage, within organizations. Apart from signage, graphic design occurs at an immediate, personal level. For his signs, Walt evidently worked off of his own, subjective sense of how design functioned.

Corporations have much more at stake and adopt a more strategic approach. Their situation is somewhat similar to crafting and enforcing guidelines for historic districts. They also aspire to retain graphic aspects

of their established identity — their brand — while injecting stable doses of contemporaneity.

Companies may have come to their graphic identity through happenstance. Adoption came before the rise of focus group testing of designs. However, the companies incur significant risk from deviating too far from established characteristics. It's the younger graphic designers that may chafe under the resultant regimented identity systems mandated by other designers. Much as I do under the historic district's decrees.

But it's also graphic designers — primarily older, seasoned ones — that raise a hue and cry when some iconic logo receives an update that deviates from identities fashioned by other, often legendary designers.

When Paul Rand's 1961 UPS logo (the company's third) was reworked 42 years later, numerous designers rejected the change solely due to the original being a work of the master. You don't revise Paul Rand any more than you revise Picasso.

The revision still stings logo *connoisseurs*. In "How to Ruin a Great Design" in the March 13, 2011 *The New York Times*, design critic Alice Rawsthorn categorized it as a "crime against design." "... UPS did this by replacing the wonderful "present" logo designed by Paul Rand in 1961, with a dispiritingly bland version devised by the global design group FutureBrand.

The new logo is described on FutureBrand's Web site as "a simplified dynamic curve" that expresses "the evolution of the company's services and its commitment to leading the future of global commerce." A waggish design blogger summed it up more succinctly as the "'golden combover.' Each time I see it, I yearn for its predecessor."

That "waggish design blogger" (D. Mark Kingsley) expressed his opinion on the deactivated Speak Up site, co-founded by designer, writer, and entrepreneur Armin Vit. When I asked for his current take on the UPS remake, Vit — who now comments on corporate identity at the site Brand New — took a holistic view of branding, one with healthy elements of idealism and pragmatism: "I still hate the execution of the logo, but I have come to understand how necessary it was to get rid of Rand's logo. It made business sense. It was strategic. It didn't cater to the utopian Preservation

of Classic Logos Society. It was a stab at the heart of nostalgia. But guess what? We all survived. Hundreds of corporate logos have changed since then and hundreds more will change. As long as the product or service doesn't change, or changes for the better, we just have to adjust to the changing visual landscape. We can lament it, but that doesn't move us forward."

Designers overreach when calling down cultural or commercial calamity should some prized public graphics be deleted from the landscape, or paltry ones be introduced. Ensuring the economic efficacy of particular signage and logos is impossible; too many unknown or uncontrollable factors are involved. As Vit indicates, logo redesigns can only be signifiers of a substantive change (and, we hope, improvement) in the product or service.

At the same time, culture matters. And not only to graphic designers. If society overall didn't care about such concerns, designers wouldn't exist. Faced with a potential æsthetic enhancement to the environment, why not have it? The problem, always, is individual taste ... and what it transmits.

Were any of these considerations part of Walt's deliberations when he changed his signs? The evolution was curious. The current sign, along with its casual placement, was stylistically odd. In its five lines of type, it managed to employ four different typefaces.

"SAVE MONEY W/OUR SERVICE" it now advised, and that we should "ASK FOR 'TWIN.'" Type was all CAPS. But in red, unlike the previous sign's blue.

Rather than rely on any more speculation, I took the ten-minute walk to Walt's to inquire about their signs. A young man left his work on a garaged vehicle to greet me. When informed of the reason for my visit, he identified himself as Ulysses, the artist of the original sign. He painted it when he was in high school, indulged by his dad, the "Walt" of the business' name.

I expressed my admiration for his work and asked why it was displaced. The cause had nothing to do with æsthetics or a business plan. A customer that owned a sign store found himself unable to pay his car-repair bill. Rather than get stiffed, Walt took his payment in the customer's

product. This didn't please Ulysses but he resigned himself to it. "You don't argue with your pop," he stated.

The sign was painted over and the yard cleared when Walt's lost its business license. Ulysses and his brother had recently reopened the shop on their own. They acquired the current sign to announce their reopening and serve as a placeholder. With his brother deferring, Ulysses made plans for a new airbrush painted sign.

As we chatted, a young woman yelled to Ulysses from across the street, crossed, and joined us. He was obviously pleased by her attention, though he teased her about being over-demonstrative with her call. With the shift in his focus, I thanked Ulysses for his time, said I looked forward to his new creation, and moved on. He had a new audience and message to transmit.

After a couple of months, there was another change in signage, though not what my chat with Ulysses had led me to anticipate. The minimal tacked-up sign, now faded, had shifted position to adorn a small, garden shed-like building alongside the cinderblock shop. This window-less structure had a single door in the center, over which was another sign stating "OPEN" and an arrow pointing toward the shop.

Occupying the space above the garage door was another home-made, wooden sign: red and black painted letters on white background, obviously accomplished with a stencil but with the gaps filled in. "WALT'S TRANSMISSION" stood over two phone numbers. No flourishes. Simple and functional.

Or was it? I found myself imparting a knowing, deliberate stylishness to the block lettering. Below, for the signs "STRUTS" and "BRAKES" he hadn't even bothered to go beyond the stenciling. Was I seeing a nuance, a *design brut* perhaps? Or did my admiration for the original sign have me attribute its maker an intentional æstheticization, one that didn't exist?

Just as I may have been projecting my desire onto the sign, I may have additionally ascribed a flourishing of the business. The brothers seemed to be laboring every day of the week. A car or two or three always occupied the yard, awaiting or fresh from repair. My disappointment in not experi-encing a dramatic new Ulysses creation was overridden by satisfaction that

they were making a go of it. If business was steady, their *current* signage was successful. *Post hoc ergo propter hoc*, right?

Whatever prosperity I believed I witnessed abruptly ended, at least from my perspective. The garage door closed one day and I've yet to pass when it's open, no matter the time of day or week. Then what few cars waited outside in the yard went away, as did everything that wasn't a structure or attached to it. Once more, for whatever reason, the business seemed dormant, or dead. On occasion, a small pickup truck with "REPAIR" spray-pained on the side, and a hand truck, appeared outside the shack.

Though my previous speculations on the reasons for the sign changes at Walt's were off base, I feel confident in my conjecture about what may be the last. Ulysses had priorities, and crafting creative signage wasn't high amongst them. Just get something up there. The new sign was enough ... until it wasn't enough.

However, assigning any responsibility for the business' fortunes onto the signage, especially considering the capricious routes to their crafting and installation, seems foolish, if not simply unfair. Some other cause may have shuttered Walt's. One or the other brother falling ill, finding a better job, a falling out, a legal or licensing problem. Any number of reasons were possible. Maybe it's another hiatus. Which it turned out to be.

The signs were just carried along by circumstances, rather than directing them. They projected and were projected upon. Design gives, and receives.

11 things they don't teach you about lists of 10 things they don't teach you in design school outside of design school

Dear Design Student,

Though no cognoscente of clickbait, I'll admit these "Ten Things They Don't Teach You About *X*" lists are attractive. They're absolutely abundant. Name the field and there's a decalog of lessons untaught by thousands of teachers yet breezily impartible by one (un)humble guide. You don't even have to specialize; there are even lists of ten things they don't teach you in "school."

However, the issue that arises from this bevy of lists is the notion that clueless and/or mendacious teachers are ubiquitous and deliberately holding out on students. I'm certain that the list compilers are working off their own (apparently unpleasant) experience but unfortunately, anecdote isn't evidence of much beyond being in the hands of a skilled raconteur.

With two decades of design education experience behind me (and a reader of the popular design press for even longer), I've picked through the bulging bin of designers' opinions about school enough to compile my own eleven spot of advice (no tenner tyranny!) on what practitioners aren't apprehending about education. In some particular order:

1. It's not that tough to get *a* design job.

This is usually the entirety of students' motivation: *I want to get a design job.* Truth is, that's low-hanging fruit (like mocking listicles). While

every grad isn't assured a cubicle, if you're not too choosy, you can likely claim *some* kind of design job. But the *good* ones? Well, that's a more complicated and subtle story. Be sure you're not aspiring to the lowest common denominator. Or mediocrity.

2. Design is not an industry, it *has* an industry.

For most designers, *design* and the *design profession* are synonymous. Design as a discipline extends well beyond practitioners engaging the activity as a career. Myriad one-off and occasional design artifacts, from logos to posters to signage to books, have been and are designed by individuals that don't participate in the activity beyond that specific job. On-demand printing has expanded and accelerated this reality. Like design, music and the music industry is primarily put to applied, commercial uses. It's prevalent and lucrative but not definitive. However you think of music, replace the term with "design." Still works.

3. School should not replicate the work environment.

That's what internships and part-time jobs are for. Even if we accept the premise, *which* work environment are we talking about? It's different to labor on design for IDEO as opposed to UDEO, with each equally valid. More importantly, will that work environment even be *around* in ten years — or even five? School provides the ability to understand and guide those changes. Unless the program is too busy aping the design shops of yesterday.

4. Design professionals know the design profession, not education.

As a design educator, I attend design education conferences to be informed about my profession. I also attend design conferences to be informed about design activity (which is also covered in education conferences). While I see many of my academic colleagues at conferences aimed at practitioners, the inverse is almost unheard of despite the fact that many designers teach part-time. The design education described by practitioners is one I rarely recognize and students should be wary of.

5. School serves learning, not the profession.

What university is or should be is a complicated question. But we

can say what it *isn't:* trade school. As a product of trade school myself (a college of art), I'm not running that down, just making a real distinction. Mistaking college as vocational training is easy to do, as education has been fashioned as another commodity with students as its customers. For many, school is to serve the design industry by churning out more upstart designers. But that isn't school's purpose.

6. Education shouldn't give you what you expect.

Attending school is a declaration that there's knowledge you don't already possess and lack the ability to gain on your own. Otherwise, you'd just go and do it. Introducing the unexpected, like going beyond assigning "real world" projects like punching out brochures, doesn't play well with most students. Education, though, is the time and place to indulge unexpected ideas and unanticipated actions.

7. You don't want the real world experience.

As fervently as some students clamor for a "real world" simulation, I know if I built some of my actual work experiences into class, students would revolt. Such as: the sprung surprise of a dramatically shortened deadline, acres of extra text with no increase in page count, copy arriving in dribs and drabs up to the last minute, or servers crashing with all data lost yet a firm due date. I can do that. But students, be careful what you wish for. School is totally unlike the job experience. It's regular, predictable, and controlled.

8. Professionals have their own interests at heart, not yours.

There are many generous and genuine practitioners providing worthy advice and mentorship to aspiring designers. They're a valuable resource students should take advantage of at every opportunity. This doesn't, however, preclude the pro acting in their interest first when offering guidance. That interest is maximizing the supply of suitable junior designers. For a while, your interests and tastes may align and it's win-win. But someone else needs to be thinking of and providing for your broader educational needs. And your future beyond that first job. Which may not involve design. Enter the teacher.

9. Design is not "problem solving."

This conceit is a historical artifact from the mid-20th century when design adopted the science/rational speak infecting all parts of society, particularly business. Shrewdly, design recognized a change in rhetoric was necessary to appear like sober "designocrats" and not a batch of graphic beatniks. It's a clumsy distancing from "making art," which binary-minded designers regard as the opposite. Though we're way past that era, the problem-solving trope still rolls right off designers' collective tongues. Problems are found in math, where, unlike design, there's one solution. If you're a *reductio ad absurdum* aficionado, all design *is* definable as problem solving. So are most pursuits. Consider shopping for clothes. It's a problem to be naked in the wrong context or climate. But solving it doesn't automatically lead to Rihanna's Coachella outfit or my psychedelic cat T-shirt. Design education offers relevant, practical and inspiring alternatives models for design activity.

10. Not everyone studying design may want to be a designer.

This may be the most incomprehensible reality for some students and design practitioners to confront. Someone may want to study design in the same way other students do English: without the intention of being a writer. So drilling in design firm exigencies may not be the best course, even for the dedicated design aspirants. Again, there's trade school for that. In my experience, a determination to design hasn't been a sure-fire indicator of facility or success.

11. There is no one "design"

The Modern movement gave it the old college try but couldn't homogenize design. As with the varieties of work processes mentioned above, these lists masticate a wide array of sensibilities into a bland bolus of "design." If these lists confront design's variety, it's the hoary and wrong-headed instruction that students must become chameleons. Design's essence is variety in form, intention, context, and process.

What (or who) is a student to believe?

Sadly, there seems a special estrangement that the design profession has from its professional educators. It's odd considering the dedication

and passion educators must have for a subject to teach it. We're design's biggest fans. Usually practitioners too!

So who do you trust? What's the *real* story? It isn't necessarily an either/or. What you need to do is cultivate a critical sensibility about *everything* you're taught or advised. And where can you *learn* this critical sensibility? Funny you should ask ....

The team player

I once served as a visiting critic at a small art college to review under-graduate senior graphic design projects. I individually critiqued a group of self-determined, semester-long theses that showcased students' interests and abilities. As is usually the case, all the projects achieved a level of merit in subject, concept and execution to sustain a reasonable, affirmative discussion.

Overall, it was a fairly routine, anodyne experience. The terms of en-gagement on both sides were familiar and rehearsed, trademarked even. I could make an overarching critique that as commendable as the work was, it hardly challenged my faculties. Or broke us out of what could be termed a Crit™. But to do so seems uncharitable. The work was agreeable and so was I. The students appeared satisfied and I felt I was giving the school its money's worth.

However, one meeting broke the otherwise pleasant but rote exercise. It was for a project that was distinctly more ambitious in scope and execu-tion than the others. This student offered an extensive identity system for an entire fantasy U.S. sports league. He had devised names for every team — there were at least a dozen — and designed hand-rendered logos for each.

The level of detail was impressive, as was the execution. He had mastered the particular look of contemporary pro sports graphics while

contriving his own distinct variant. It was undeniable big league design work. Any smart art director would punch his ticket.

And my subject knew it. His demeanor was one of quiet confidence, at times lapping up against but never spilling into cockiness. He wasn't particularly fluent but he wasn't inarticulate either. Every teacher or reviewer can attest that a facility with form often doesn't translate to the spoken word.

Many students and professionals insist they're mutually exclusive talents. That the work does the talking was a major reason they got into design in the first place. In Crit™, students frequently seem as if it's the first time they've encountered their own work. The nervous, inarticulate stammering better fit a scenario of a hostage situation, with subjects dragooned into explaining this graphic oddity under duress.

My reviewee didn't have to say much and, especially, he didn't feel he had to. It was all right there. The entirety of his commentary was describing his formal challenges, the stock ingredient of Crit™. The presentation only lacked a denouement, which was obviously for me to provide: the praise. In terms of practical, commercially relevant form — in other words, graphic design's near exclusive concern — the piece was beyond reproach. I might fuss about details but I knew I'd be just making taste judgments. And I knew that he knew *that*, too.

What he *didn't* know was, for me, a fatal flaw at the heart of his project. It was a concern that obviously was nowhere on his radar. My respectful silence during his prologue was due to me churning over how to phrase what was sure to be a blindsiding. When he wound down, I asked, as neutrally as I could, "Do you realize that you're employing stereotypes people could find offensive?"

At least two or three of the team names and their attendant images were recognized ethnic or racial slurs. They were also, unfortunately, prevalent identifiers in all sports from school teams, little leagues to majors. In virulence, they were along the lines of dubbing your team the "Redskins" and portraying a glowering Native American.

It was apparent there was no intentional malice on the student's part. At the most, it demonstrated that he hadn't done his research. Or that the

research he'd done only involved exploring potential representations. This is fairly common amongst students, who even when directed to explore the *meaning* of terms they employ, and consider how their images might be "read"...still collect pictures solely for formal play.

For this student, these were just what teams were named. In our back and forth, he could, and did, cite examples. I allowed he was right but it didn't change matters. What simultaneously relieved and surprised me was his ultimate plaint. I'd worried he might infer that I was calling him a racist. My points were all couched with earnest disclaimers to that effect, ones that fell on deaf ears. Not because he found them insincere but because they were irrelevant: "I thought this was going to be a graphic design critique."

To claim his comment was a complete surprise would be disingenuous. I took the visiting critic gig with an agenda founded on expanding design's single-minded absorption with matters of form and commercial viability. Here was just more evidence. I insisted to the student that this *was* a graphic design critique. He and designers everywhere were responsible for the meanings they introduced and perpetuated in society. He wasn't convinced.

Our time up, the reviewee departed, radiating a polite yet palpable frustration. What was *that* about? I'd nullified his touchdown by throwing a flag for illegal man downfield. Often, it's a struggle just to get students to concede to the necessity of criticism, even on their expected terms. Here I'd gone and turned it into a session of "Calvinball."

Design criticism is nowhere as anarchic as that. But it's the perception. Such as it exists, criticism's problem is its predictability. It's determined by an ongoing, profession-centric perspective, constrained by Modernist rationales in a permanently postmodern reality. Just as my student had patterned his suspect logos on extant examples, he'd modeled the profession's wary attitude toward criticism.

There's also a tangible sense in the field that criticism itself is not just unsportsmanlike but *turning on your own team*. It's not so much traitorous, though some can't rule that out, but undermining. Though the field celebrates design's increasing public recognition, it will probably always

feel embattled and unappreciated.

I'm always bemused by my students' reflexive feelings towards, for instance, clients. Despite the fact that the overwhelming majority is yet to *have* a client, they can readily channel a seasoned professional's jaundiced mindset about them. Of all the design lessons I want the profession to instill, *these* are ones they effortlessly absorb.

Sharp critical commentary isn't wholly absent in the field but it's almost exclusively directed at design's scrubs and role players. Going after the stars is out of bounds. Your teammates will alert to you this immediately. Or, as I've found, the luminaries might contact you directly, asking, "Why do you hate me?" The particulars of the criticism are immaterial.

The details are what *make* a criticism salient. Criticism is impersonal but much of the resistance to it is very human. It's awkward to call out your classmate or conferee. Though our roles may fluctuate from referee, coach, to player-coach, design educators are in an ideal position to advance criticism. We do it by performing it in the classroom and on the field, along with continually articulating why it's good for the sport. And, always, keeping up an exacting self-criticism. In the meantime, Go Design.

Design's just dessert

I have a prop that I use on the first day of the introductory graphic design course. It's a box of cake mix that I connect to a surplus computer keyboard and mouse. While I review the syllabus, my construction sits in the middle of the grouped tables we gather around. Sometimes, I add to the theater by setting it up piece by piece without comment after students have arrived.

To try and maintain the suspense while I plow through the course details, I'll occasionally pause, tap on the keyboard, and then frown at the box, as if witnessing an undesirable result. This still won't compel an inquiry from the students. I find their expressions generally inscrutable in their varied states of attentiveness, more so on a first day. Either through good manners or disinterest, they always wait me out to explain the contraption.

This bit of "business" is in service of two tasks. One is to simply inject some mystery and anticipation into a rote exercise: greetings, handing out sheets of paper, the ritual mispronunciation of roster names. Actually, I'm hoping to *disrupt* students' expectations of what's going to happen in class. Often that seems to be that they just sit down at a Mac and design just appears on screen.

My set up relates to this expectation, illustrating a metaphor of design activity that I find serviceable and, I hope, illuminating. Attempting to

put the computer's role into a useful context has been a struggle since its introduction. That it's "just a tool" ranks as the most popular description. Contesting this is the opinion that the device embodies a new paradigm of design visualization.

I tell students that when they look at the computer, they should visualize that box of cake mix. The machine and its attendant software are a pre-made formulation to facilitate amateurs' need to easily create something attractive. Aspiring and professional graphic designers are a secondary market. The resultant problem is that, as intended, it's relatively easy — *too* easy — to come up with something palatable.

Some ability is necessary. That cake, or that design, can't make itself. And crafting suitable design isn't as foolproof as using the cake mix, which requires just the addition of a few simple ingredients (that could also be put in the blend but are excluded so the maker gets some baking gratification), and an oven with one numbered dial. Design students need to demonstrate a facility, some creativity, beyond following predetermined steps.

I urge students to aspire to pastry chef status as graphic designers. They should select choice ingredients; carefully consider the utensils they employ, and eschew default choices. This isn't to run down cake mix product, which I often enjoy. It's a satisfactory and convenient option when you want a treat. With a little embellishment, it can be especially tasty.

So can design. While I encourage students to move beyond convenience, I also caution against elaboration for its own sake. That someone's going to enjoy garlic ice cream doesn't make it a *need* necessarily. However, there are circumstances where it's important to start from scratch or to devise a new delicacy. And students should graciously accept that some people are unable to distinguish between $10 per slice Black Forest Cake and RingDings®. Just as long as *students* sense the difference.

I conclude my rant by pointing out that the best baked cake or brownie, ultimately, in nutritional terms, isn't *good* for you. Tiramisu or Twinkie®, you're trading in empty calories and sugar rushes. In the strictest sense, these concoctions aren't even *food*. You can go without sweets and be physically healthy. You're probably healthier for cutting them out

completely. However, such comestibles are prevalent and highly desirable.

Nutritional value isn't the sole, or even primary, criterion for what people ingest. Similarly, many graphic designers don't enter the field due to their admiration for the nutritional facts label. Cake plays an æsthetic, sensuous, and symbolic role: as *culture food*. It's feeding our feelings. This is also the case for graphic design.

My equation *design = dessert* isn't that much of an incitement to students. They're largely deferential to authority and express the same mixed range of attentiveness they offer to any random topic. Certainly, my delivery is as questionable as my premise. I regularly receive as many vacant stares as gently nodding heads.

I'd be surprised and delighted if a student actively contested my framing. Resistance or refutation would demonstrate that someone had given some thought about what design's role is. Right now, students and most practitioners work from semi-comprehended, received wisdom of doing and being "good."

A restated and more nuanced definition of "good" should be on design's menu. Being a product of culture is worthy … just not how graphic design has striven to present itself. It labels itself as nourishment, essential, serious. That may be the *objective* good for life but the *subjective* makes life worth living. And not all delights lack substance. There are some pretty austere treats out there: Swiss International Style = Nilla® Wafers?

What's wrong with purveying pleasure? It only goes off the rails when you get the 24K gold-flaked cakes. Dessert and design are good for you emotionally. Purvey that idea and more people may save room for both.

Authenticity is a groove

In my twenties, I worked at a national historic site on Boston's Freedom Trail. A frequent question of visitors was "How much of the building is original?" I knew what they meant by the question but sometimes I felt waggish (or was a smarmy asshole, depending upon your view) and would answer that it was *all* original. Just not of the same era.

As with many historic buildings, it was a patchwork, a collage, having undergone many changes before being "saved." Then it underwent more adaptations, with well-meaning but naïve or poorly researched alterations over time in attempts to return it to its "original" state. At some point, they called it quits and either glossed over or foregrounded the hodgepodge state.

Questions of "originality" are close to but not quite the same as "authenticity," though they sometimes are used interchangeably. They at least go hand-in-hand: the former denoting the latter. Why I relate the example of the historic site is for this connection but also because I see the *notion* of authenticity to be like the building. The concept of authenticity is a patchwork that is — and is about being — simultaneously consistent and an artifice.

Put into a graphic design context, authenticity is also a lot like notions of "neutrality." Robin Kinross gave that concept a thorough and deserved thrashing 30 years ago in his essay "The Rhetoric of Neutrality."

Authenticity isn't as prevalent and active a design concept as neutrality was and continues to be. But it shares aspects. The primary one is that both concepts have been imported from another realm. Metaphorically, the adaptation is intriguing. Functionally, we have to question the "rightness."

Kinross outlined how the ideas of communication theory such as the Shannon-Weaver model, which described the sending of radio signals, were grafted onto design theory. This gave rise to the idea of the designer as an objective "transmitter" of "information." Kinross showed how this transplant was a product of an era with a rising, optimistic belief in technology and science. We know the critiques of this model: audiences aren't homogeneous passive receivers; designers aren't objective transmitters; and messages are abstract, active, and multiform.

Authenticity similarly was first concerned with another kind of determination: the status of an *object*. "Not false or copied; genuine." Objects can be put through an evidentiary analysis to establish veracity and value. Once again, we must make a conceptual leap to apply the concept not to the physical product *per se* but to the abstraction of the *process* that created it. Taken literally, *every* design or song is authentic on its actual face. But not, possibly, to your process requirements.

Authenticity as abstract process evaluation becomes another observer-oriented, relative experience. Like Einstein's relativity, the authenticity experience runs on separate, internally consistent, parallel measures. Instead of clocks, you have scales of sorts. Reconciling the separate spheres isn't possible. There's no overarching reality but the artifacts in question. But the perceptions differ and they're all true.

We can dip into the discrete authenticities and it seems possible to cross between them. We become sensitized to another authenticity and embrace it. Exploring the different authenticities is worthy as it will tell us things about the permutations of culture. Crafting a unified field theory, though, is something else.

The popular conception of authenticity is a role. By necessity it is a well-defined, recognizable one. As in rap-related authenticity, the features are clearly delineated. It's an act, though in a bio-pic ("based on a true story") that gestures toward the real. Authenticity is superimposed, not

arisen from the actor/performer's life. Instead of an *absence* of artifice, popular authenticity is the *ultimate* artifice. Popular authenticity then provides an imprimatur to any product of the actor. The actual "music" is irrelevant. Popular authenticity doesn't *free* music, it *kills* it.

This isn't the only paradoxical inversion of chasing popular authenticity. What do we make of an artifact like 1974's *Having Fun with Elvis on Stage*? This LP consists entirely of samples of surreally-edited, between-songs patter by the King. Is it the *most* authentic Elvis — dispense with the music altogether, it doesn't matter — or the *least*. It evidently was a commercial "ploy" by Colonel Tom Parker to evade Elvis' contract with his label.

What has driven authenticity from product to process and created a popular authenticity? Perhaps it is the result of a technologically enhanced estrangement from the musician. Recording technologies provide greater access to the product but, as popularity increases, less access to the artist. Contact is through the machinations of PR. Image-making, in the sense of a creative persona, is of the most importance. The search for "authenticity" is an attempt to negotiate the Spectacle's funhouse hall of mirrors.

Authenticity is popularly regarded as a center point, a statement of tradition and stability. Authenticity can and should be *returned to*. However, culture is not static, nor is authenticity. It must always be a state of the *new:* simultaneously a transformational agent and response. Authenticity is not comforting and secure, it is a challenge and *extreme*. It shocks the system, reboots it, and runs a fresh program. Authenticity is a breakthrough. It's an advance beyond the static role of encumbering popular authenticity to a reconfiguration.

Authenticity isn't a point, it is a *wave front*. A kind of carrier wave, transforming not transmitting the leading edge of meaning. Authenticity is not the *result*. It is the *cause*. It changes its nature depending upon the expression. Formless in itself; it's the *generator* of form. Authenticity isn't embodied within either the artifact or artist. Authenticity *makes them*, then moves on.

The printer's Devil's Dictionary

Shortly into my graduate study, I considered compiling a lexicon of common graphic design terms. I avoided defining profession-specific words like "kerning" or "corporate identity." My choices were common to design discussions everyday and everywhere, employed by clients and designers. The definitions were my own derisive views on the process.

My design career to that point had been brief and erratic. As inexperienced as I was, I knew that it wasn't just my cynical nature. I had done enough design to encounter the disconnect that's often between what a client says and what is meant. And this was something different than realizing when someone asks, "Can you make the type bigger?" it's really a call for a greater emphasis on the particular text. No, this was using a word that pointed to a meaning wholly at odds with the dictionary definition. They were code words, doubletalk. I imagined making a small volume of terms and my alternate definitions. It would be called *The Printer's Devil's Dictionary*.

My inspiration was Ambrose Bierce's classic 1911 book, *The Devil's Dictionary*. First published five years earlier as *The Cynic's Word Book* (a title the author hated), the tome is still in print today, along with a variety of web versions. It is a masterwork of what would now be called language deconstruction. Then it was simply satire. Bierce was a contemporary and friend of Mark Twain, and some consider Bierce the greater wit.

Unfortunately, if he's mentioned today, it's alongside Amelia Earhart and Jimmy Hoffa. Like them, Bierce disappeared mysteriously and his fate will likely be forever unknown.

Bierce's scathing humor spared no person, belief, or institution. Today, it can seem decidedly insensitive — and startlingly relevant. Bierce continues to spawn a number of imitators, none of which can match his acuity, word play and venom.

I didn't fancy myself anywhere near Bierce's level with my collection but it was great therapy. From my freelance days I had things like:

Audience, *n.* An army of me.

Deadline, *n.* A point in time whose arrival results not in actual demise, though its approach induces yearning for that sweet release.

Quick-and-dirty, *v.* Method of dispatch suitable to those who employ the term.

Simple, *adj.* Cheap.

Straightforward, *adj.* Designed in a manner the client's already determined.

X-acto, *n.* A cutting tool that, unlike the surgeon's scalpel, assists the wielder in embellishing the surface, rather than penetrating it.

Graduate school was where I mainlined design literature. My frustration with much of the popular discourse directed the lexicon's emphasis inward:

Art, *n.* What graphic design isn't, except when it is.

Fame, *n.* As a design usage — e.g. "famous designer" — it is an oxymoron. (See also, "design superstar.")

Over-analyze, *v.* 1. To perform even the most cursory critical study of a design artifact. 2. To analyze.

Theory, *n.* A manner of creating design inconsistent with my own, and is therefore incomprehensible and faddish.

White-space, *n.*. An area where the designer demonstrates the greatest ability by restraining from displaying any effort. Less is — and costs — more.

And like Bierce, I amended little stories, though my tales were true:

Appropriate, *adj.* An expectation fulfilled. A requirement of my

second-year graduate seminar was to write an artist's statement. The class included students from all disciplines. The professor showed interest during my oral presentations and supported my investigation. As I was exploring the rhetoric of design, I designed my statement differently than the typical artist's statement (i.e. 12 pt. Helvetica, double-spaced). I used three highly readable typefaces to weave alternate lines of three different short texts. She returned my submission with the notation that the writing was good. But it wasn't in the appropriate form. This brief, dashed-off comment essentially negated my entire graduate study. I knew I was in for a hard time. I also knew I was on the right track.

I toyed with making *The Printer's Devil's Dictionary* part of my graduate thesis document. As that tome already had two addenda and much apocrypha, I dropped it. My dictionary remained scattered notes that, over the years, were absorbed into various essays and lectures.

Since then, whenever I'm referred to as a critic, I ponder Bierce's definition:

Critic, *n*. A person who boasts himself hard to please because nobody tries to please him.

Then I recall my aborted project. It really came back when our Speak Up friends introduced *The Design Encyclopedia*. When I poke through many of "real" entries there, I insert my own, sardonic takes. Surely, I'm not alone in this.

Maybe there's still a place for *The Printer's Devil's Dictionary*. The two serious flaws of the original effort was my design experience (limited), and relying solely on my own wit (insert your own descriptive here). What if I throw it open to the world?

So, I welcome submissions to the *Dictionary*. While the temptation may be great to focus on client claptrap, doublespeak cuts both ways. A study of design gibberish might provide more enlightenment. Terms that were on my list to be "defined" ran from the profound to the mundane: *brainstorm, concept, creative, elegant, freelance, inevitable, interactive, intuitive, layout, logo, pop, rough, stock, tweak*. All these and more, plus the ones above, are up for grabs. *Style*, however, might need a rest.

Implosure

The closer you look at design, the more you see failure. I certainly
don't think design museums and critics should avoid it. Because of
design criticism's relative infancy, it has been cast as a fresh cheekier
version of art criticism; instead of writing about paintings, palaces
and sculptures, we wrote about ice cream trucks, coffee cup lids and
surfboards. But that's not enough in the age of consumerist burn-out
and environmental crisis. We don't need to justify design's importance
to the world or the art establishment: We need to look into how it works
and where it's going wrong. We need a new generation not to venerate
design, but to sniff out failure. The days of armchair design criticism are
over. As the philosopher Ludwig Wittgenstein advised, "don't look for
the meaning, look for the use."
— Peter Hall

Before we consider if art and architectural thinking have continued
relevance to design history, theory, and criticism, we might first establish
what, if any, relevance they've had so far. Despite the natural allegiances
amongst design, art, and architecture, the import of the latter two disciplines' discourse in design writing is far from given. Of art and architecture,
I will largely address the former's relationship to design thinking. Having

come to design from a career as an artist, it's been foremost on my mind and a regular topic in my critical writing.

It should be accepted that our contemporary conceptions of art and design sprout simultaneously from the European avant-garde movement of the early 20th century. Less spoken has been the inherent lack of inclusivity of other cultural sources. Graphic design history, such as it is, has acknowledged this, no matter the chronicler. For its part, art has considered its twin's existence beneath notice.

While art remains an occasional topic and reference point in design discourse, the impact of actual art theory upon design is questionable. This is an important distinction to make. Art has played a regular role in design thinking but primarily as a strawman. If not stereotyped and flogged for alleged impenetrability, design thinkers simply don't get art. A comprehensive and comprehensible regard for art thinking has not been consistently presented in design.

Discussing the potential of other disciplines and traditions entering the realm of design discourse is a welcome development and worthwhile. But we can and should say much more about art's status, or, as will be argued, it's lack of standing. In addition, while privileging art and architecture's role in design writing is reasonable, there is a far greater influence on design writing that requires challenge and closure: the design profession. The most vital and relevant agendas in design thinking haven't been masked by art history's interventions but by the profession's.

Reference to art has been constant, almost reflexive, for decades in design writing but problematic. Following their audience's proclivities, design writers have largely shied away from or shunned engaging with art thinking after the 19th century. This has been due to design writing being largely the province of practitioner/writers that are uncomfortable or unfamiliar with, and subsequently often dismissive, of contemporary art theory.

Rather than establish links with art, significant effort in design writing has been expended to declare design as a discrete activity, requiring isolation from non-design incursions. The principle tenet of the majority of definitions of graphic design generated from within the profession is that it's *not* art. Design is art's happy Other.

Sustained engagement with art thinking occurs at the fringe of design discourse where design academics have largely been relegated. But even here, the record is spotty. A significant amount of design research echoes and reinforces the commercial aspect of design activity, theorizing methods to produce more effective business applications. To find a practicing critic that is just as likely to write authoritatively on contemporary art as graphic design, we must look to someone from outside the profession like Rick Poynor.

The rejection of art as a meaningful contributor to design thinking is ironic. As previously noted, art and design are inextricably linked through that shared avant-garde origin. The European modernist strain of graphic design has been over-privileged in design history. Thoughtful, articulated graphic design activity occurred in the 19th century in the United States and elsewhere around the world. However, it is design's emphasis upon the European direction that makes art's diminution incongruous.

Since that initiation, art and design have behaved like separated-at-birth twins, closely paralleling each other in their development. Difference has come in establishing alternate marketplaces and evaluation systems. Roughly, art sells its product wholesale, design retail. Both disciplines require the patronage of substantial capital to disseminate their products. Artists are cultural activists that prefer to operate in and sustain the class of moneyed individuals that arose in the 19th century and permitted fine artists to generate artwork ahead of and to stimulate demand.

Design practitioners evolved from the avant-gardes that embraced the idea of the social utility of art and the necessity to employ the most advanced production technology. Briefly, artists sell CEOs a painting for their mansions; designers sell them an identity system for their business. The formal underpinnings and their rationales are the same. But design, tightly embracing the "speaking to the masses" ethos of avant-gardists, mutates it into the notion that design thinking was accessible and free of cerebralizations of art. More importantly, that unlike artworks, design products required no supporting explication. To be graphic design artifacts, things must need no intermediary. Design's leaders embrace utilitarianism as its selling point, and its differentiation from art.

Art increasingly and unashamedly develops an intermediary literature for itself, while design denies the necessity. It has trade journals. However, design has a secret literature that's out in the open. Books like Paul Rand's *Thoughts on Design* and his successive volumes firmly broke with the European modernists by bounding behind them to rummage through pre-20th century art history. This was in direct contradiction to the past-denying European Modernist dogma. Rand's goal was to establish a lineage of design as a discrete entity. This was ultimately taken up by other design thinkers, such as Philip Meggs in *A History of Graphic Design*.

Where art can count critics, curators, academics, and artists amongst its influential thinkers, design counts only practitioners. If you don't make design, you can't "get" design. (Type)case closed. Art's network of thinkers grew exponentially during the 20th century, creating a diverse field of attitudes and influences that's still roiling today. A hierarchy is present but art boasts an expanse of entry points to creditably contribute to its thinking.

In general terms, the graphic design field professes the desire for an active, challenging critical literature. In practice, however, when outlining the specifics of who is best situated to write about design, practitioners invariably identify practitioners. A recent example is 2009's *Graphic Design: A User's Manual* by Adrian Shaughnessy: "Ironically, the way to get respect from opinion-formers is through critical writing about contemporary design that shows self-awareness and wider cultural awareness. For this we need writers who can rise above the professional concerns of design (important as these are) and writers who can translate the often non-verbal reasoning that designers apply to their best work. And who can do this better than graphic designers?" I'm totally with Shaughnessy up to that last sentence. I ask it with a different inflection ... and don't consider it a rhetorical question.

This is not to suggest that design practitioners are incapable of comprehending other disciplines or ably incorporating outside thinking into design discourse. However, when discussing design thinking of any kind in any context, the overwhelming influence of design practitioners and practice-based thought must first be considered. What can be regarded as design thinking occurs almost exclusively in practice-based

contexts. The limited field of thought and the privileging of practice can't be underemphasized.

Design writing is overwhelmingly the province of practitioners in profession-centric forums. So if we are to contemplate design writing in the 21st century and the role of art, we must recognize that at best it's a secondary influence. And other disciplines? They fare no better. As late as 1993, we have Paul Rand proclaiming in his book *Design Form and Chaos*, that a "student whose mind is cluttered with matters that have nothing directly to do with design … is a bewildered student."

Rand was referring specifically to design education. However, the declaration may be seen as totalizing in terms of seeing design through any lens other than the professional. Or Rand's own curious, cherry-picked, pre-20th century æsthetic. Where is it more relevant than in education to engage other intellectual disciplines? (Aside: Though he refused to stoop to explicitly identifying his target, Rand was specifically critiquing the appointment of Sheila Levrant de Bretteville as director of Yale's graduate program in graphic design. Subsequent and present realities show that Rand needn't have worried. Yale's most visible and influential faculty and critics remain firmly within and supportive of a profession-centric view of design activity.)

While hankering for the cultural regard afforded art and architecture, design still is unable to get beyond pragmatism when it comes to critical writing. If anyone here has a reason why Paula Scher should give a damn about the opinion of a design writer who isn't another renowned design figure, I'd love to hear it. (And there are no design writers honored in the field that wasn't practitioners first. Well, maybe Rick Poynor, because he started a magazine.) To the profession, writing and criticism remains the province of promotion, not investigation.

An important question to ask is where will this new writing exist? If future design writing is agreeable to being unread by designers, then we're in business. The profession-centric forums are most characteristic of celebrity journalism. A writing that engages art, architecture, and the other suggested disciplines here would simply be too long for the typical design forum. The future for design writing is bright. If it's without designers.

While offering an admittedly self-serving and problematic example, my own experience attempting to directly inject contemporary art thinking into design discourse may provide an illustration. It absolutely shaped the opinions I express here.

In late 1998, I published an 8400-word essay titled "Skilling Saws and Absorbent Catalogs" in *Emigre* magazine. This article sought to directly address the joint incomprehension that art and design demonstrated when contemplating the other discipline. It was an exercise that attempted to speak to the core conceptions that each discipline had for the other, with the intention of dispelling the reflexive clichés and stereotypes widely promulgated on either side. Put simply, art and design were clueless about each other and I was here to set them both straight.

At the time, *Emigre* was arguably the foremost forum for critical design writing. More importantly, it was likely the broadest forum where a cross-section of profession-based and academics design thinkers could be engaged. In service of my theories, my article cited naturalist Edward O. Wilson, cultural historian Morse Peckham, and art critics Dave Hickey, Hal Foster, Brian O'Doherty, Benjamin Buchloh, and some designers.

In my arrogance — or naïveté if you're charitable — I thought that I might interrupt, if not exterminate the tired construction of art as a rule-free zone of personal expression, and graphic design as art's whore.

While I take great pride in the essay and received personal compliments for it over the years (and it remains on line at *Emigre*'s web site and was reprinted in their recent *Emigre no. 70* compendium), I must acknowledge that it's had zero effect on designers' consciousness, even in the small world of design writing. It's yet to be cited by anyone that I'm aware of. Meanwhile, designers and design thinkers continue to unashamedly espouse the views I consider thoroughly debunked. And artists? Why would they read a design magazine?

This can be due to many reasons, not the least of which may be that the essay simply isn't very good. Or, less judgmentally, that the attitudes I sought to counter are deeply entrenched. However articulate, accurate, or lengthy my essay might be, it's tough for just one treatise to act as a counterforce. Especially when artists' and designers' self-image is tied up

in those entrenched attitudes. It's far more than an academic issue. The short moral of the story is that writers seeking to introduce new disciplines into design must be in it for the very long haul.

Architecture has been another discipline with a sporadic presence in design thinking. Once again, it's uncertain if the ideas expressed in architectural theory have play in design. The most prominent example of architectural thought influencing design was the 1977's *Learning from Las Vegas* by Robert Venturi, Steven Izenour, and Denise Scott Brown. This book famously inspired and provided intellectual support for graphic design investigations into its vernacular, most notably at Cranbrook Academy of Art.

Architectural theory also conspicuously intruded into design thinking in the 1990s around designer Bruce Mau and architect Rem Koolhaas. Koolhaas' theorizing on the concept of "bigness" was expressed in word and form in the Mau-designed 1998 tome *S, M, L, XL.*

Practically, Koolhaus' thinking provided intellectual cover for the corpulent graphic designer monographs that dominated the design publishing landscape at the end of the last millennium. Architecture has primarily influenced design thinking by helping fuel the field's hunger for grandiosity and the moneyed culture clients necessary to realize ostentation.

These impulses were weightily on display in Mau's own 2000 cinderblock-sized book, *Life Style*. It was a showcase for another tendency of practitioner/thinkers: repackaging insight. The combination of the design profession's incuriousness and hostility towards other disciplines plus a limited attention span has allowed figures like Mau and John Maeda to be branded as deep thinkers. All while repackaging insights by more articulate thinkers.

From Mau's clumsy reworking of Brian Eno and Peter Schmidt's Oblique Strategies as "An Incomplete Manifesto for Growth" to Maeda's ongoing pronouncements that are part recycled Paul Rand epigrams and parcel sub-Shoji Hamada koans.

The lesson is that if design writing in the 21st century wants to be recognized by and affect the practice of graphic design, it must confront the branding of thinking and thinkers that occurs in the field. In one sense,

it could be encouraging to aspiring writers: the bar is low on insights. Conversely, an aspirant may be discouraged to observe that as with Mau and Maeda, mere proximity to substantive thinkers will convey a legitimacy a mere writer can never attain.

The ultimate potential of interventions from other disciplines is to compel an intellectual scrupulousness that remains largely absent in design thinking within the field. Narrow-gauge popularizations of design history abound, crowding out and disenfranchising scholarship. Criticism within or of elite practitioners is unacceptable. Reputation rather than rigor rules as the determinant of importance. If the specific themes and interests in other disciplines fail to be insinuated into design writing, we will still benefit if the thoroughness common in other literatures take root.

Unlike in design, critical writing in art plays an important role in the contemporary art world. The diversity and breadth of writing on art can only be envied by design. It also ensures that major art figures can withstand a significant amount of critical disdain. Reputation helps drive the speculative nature of the art market. However, a wholesale tide-turning of critical regard can occur and consign a formerly high-riding artist to near oblivion. And it can happen in graphic design (see: Carson, David — though it's mostly been personality-driven).

What is also enviable about art thinking is that it is expressed across a wide variety of forums, established and independent. Design writing has markedly fewer outlets, resulting in a near-heterodoxy of critical thought.

Another area where contemporary art thinking has been found was in *dot-dot-dot* magazine and its associated Dexter Sinister project (through *dot-dot-dot* cofounder Stuart Bailey). Dexter Sinister (also the name for the "Just-In-Time Workshop & Occasional Bookstore" on Ludlow Street in New York) presented "True Mirror" as part of the 2008 Whitney Biennial. Interestingly, this art project can be considered design only in a broad, almost tenuous sense. Its emphasis is upon literature and the replication/ multiplication of texts. It suggests that its acceptance into the art realm comes largely from the absence of any aspect that might commonly be considered design.

That design writing in the 21st century will engage art, architecture,

and other disciplines I consider to be a matter of inevitability. The erosion of intellectual, egotistic, and practical barriers to writing about graphic design is slow but inexorable. In other words, individuals interested in engaging modes of production in contemporary popular culture will no longer personally dismiss graphic design as worthy of examination, forums to present such writing will welcome and even commission such material, and the various evaluating structures that support and reward writing (such as tenure committees) will affirm the legitimacy of said literature.

While this is only personal speculation on my part and may be regarded as cynical, I like to think this evolution will largely be driven by art and architecture having been "mined out" by previous generations of writers. It will also be facilitated by an increasing number of artists like Ryan McGuiness who cites *Emigre* magazine as an inspiration for his work.

For most of the 20th century, design has separated itself from the wider cultural conversation, forcefully ejecting outside thinking from intruding upon design thinking. The unnatural state isn't that other disciplines might influence design thinking, it's that design could be isolated from the rest of culture.

I like to think it was an untenable exercise, and intellectual attempt to defy cultural gravity. What I hope we're witnessing is the return to a natural state of mutual attraction and interaction. At some point, the scattered elements of our culture will draw back together. Perhaps that point has already been passed.

We can and should hasten the movement onward and inward. The resulting implosion will devastate an insupportable and unstable structure. But from the debris will emerge an expansive and inspiring home for thinking that freely and meaningfully sees no barrier between design and any other thought that may inform it.

(incomplete)

*Knowledge emerges only through invention and re-invention,
through the restless, impatient, continuing, hopeful inquiry human
beings pursue in the world, with the world, and with each other.*
— Paulo Freire

(A)

Despite the prevalence of design programs within liberal arts institutions, design as an academic area of study is an uneasy situation for many
design teachers — never mind practitioners. There remains a fundamental
discomfort, if not disdain, for any progressive, critical manifestations of
design theory or production. An exposure to graphic design history is
acceptable if its function is to introduce students to canonical figures. But
any classroom exploration of design's cultural, social, political, or ecologi-
cal import is distraction.

In the U.S., the vocational-training formation of design education still
thrives in academia, reflecting the prevalent perspective in the discipline.
The quote above could have been encountered in a variety of faculty meetings, at conferences, in articles and blogs, and in the teaching statements
within tenure review packages. Churning candidates for entry-level design
jobs is how "education" is defined.

A major challenge to the functionalist model of design education

came recently from within the profession, in the AIGA report *Design Futures* (originally titled *Designer of 2025*) (2017). The document, helmed by North Carolina State University Professor Emerita Meredith Davis, is a deft summary of contemporary trends affecting design activity. While wide-ranging in its findings, the fundamental underpinning of design education remains preparing students for commercial service.

The report's authors explicitly frame design within a marketplace context. Though they didn't coin the terms, it identifies the primary driver of trends as the transformation from an industrial to a knowledge economy. Alongside select academics from high profile programs, the report's contributors are weighted toward practitioners in conspicuous new economy businesses and consultancies: Pinterest, Google, IDEO. No social commentators or critics of design's neo-liberal basis were consulted.

"Ethical and humanistic values" are of concern only if there is consistency between a business' messages and its "products, services, and/or social behavior." It is then advised that college students be directed to "Evaluate design solutions in terms of their social, cultural, technological, economic, and environmental impact." That the report was generated by a professional organization ensures its perspective will be on the business of design. Still, *Design Futures* is an articulate advocate for the necessity that design education moves beyond the "industrial-age, message-centered perspectives on the fundamental principles of design." This is a more inviting environment to craft a relevant, critical, even radical design pedagogy. But even in this new context, attaining radicality in design pedagogy remains the same. It's still about confronting two nested dogmas of design: definition by (and servility to) the marketplace and the primacy of formal expression.

(B)

A challenge is then simple in concept, but potentially dangerous in practice. Students reflexively rebel against instruction that deviates from the popular norm of design as eye-catching sales tool . Not that this view has wide sanction among faculty. Presenting design as something one might study just for edification, like philosophy, is likely the most disruptive idea a teacher could ask students to entertain.

Generalizing design education is problematical as there is a variety of programs, and a sliding scale of emphases. As when examining professional design practice, focus is usually on the elite and exemplars. The vast middle is glossed over. Programs regarded as progressive may downplay their practice-orientation. Their difference is in offering promises of a higher positioning in the hierarchy of design activity. And the importance of formal achievement remains paramount.

Proof is found in job descriptions for open faculty positions. No matter how concept or theory intensive, programs require candidates to submit portfolios of their own work, and often, student work. A truly activist action, before even crafting a pedagogy, would be to scrap this obligation altogether. Is being a radical maker necessary to be a radical thinker or educator about design?

In practical terms, samples of student work are unlikely to be representative, simply statistically. Applicants will only showcase their best. Also, the lessons of other teachers will be integrated. If a professor's influence is pronounced, or there's evidence of limited formal deviance between students (the work all looks similar), it should be cause for concern.

Instilling a "house style" in an academic setting or enforcing adherence to a teacher's æsthetic betrays students in seeking an individual voice in or exacting investigation of their discipline. This aspect of education isn't what's usually addressed when the topic is pedagogy. Emphasis is typically on overarching philosophies and abstract assignments. But much happens around education that's more influential, creating or stifling opportunities to change the status quo.

(C)

Another radical action would be a dedicated, wide-reaching effort to educate educators in educating. The open secret of academia overall, not simply in arts and design, is how a terminal degree is the license to teach in higher education. Teaching isn't regarded as a separate skill or discipline. Only from K–12 is study of and practice in teaching mandated. Everybody's learning on the job, with variable focus (for many artists, it's an inconvenience to get a "teaching gig.") A classroom management course might pay more dividends than advanced typography.

I've benefitted from this situation. Advocating for a change could reasonably bring an accusation of trying to pull up a ladder behind me. Actually, my entire career is self-taught in graphic design, teaching, and writing. Reflexively, I want to champion self-actualization. But I recognize that it's the students that will suffer through our haphazard teaching-learning curves. (And I should credit here the valuable mentoring and counsel I've received throughout my academic career.)

(D)

Another circumstance that makes me question the value of untrained teaching, is uncomfortably close to the hoary "school of hard knocks" standard that's still claimed throughout design. The best practitioners are *de facto* considered the best teachers. "Street smarts" are thought to trump organized, systematized education. Having run a design business, no matter how small or short-lived, is regarded as superior standing to instruct in design. The irony is the professional justification for the process. A methodology that is alien to professional workplaces is utilized in practicality's name.

Fortunately, this is an extreme end of the design education axis. Though virulent, and untethered to the advocates' age, it's increasingly relegated to its natural habitat, the "portfolio schools." Still, repetitious formal drilling is the norm throughout programs, diluted somewhat with haltingly titrated critical content.

Even if focused on business applications, design education sacrifices both its authority and relevance by becoming "less academic." Business schools themselves are failing in their societal role through narrow, bottom-line instruction. In Duff McDonald's book *The Golden Passport* (2017), which studies contemporary business schools, the author notes that "Business educators have abandoned their academic role, which, aside from educating future generations, is to generate the possibility of critique and train students into doing it themselves."

The result is a cadre of virtue-signaling "shareholder capitalists" pursuing corporate interests at odds with their personally espoused values. Design echoes this bifurcation, maintaining its servile status toward business as its defining characteristic and primary purpose. If students

question this relationship, design teachers can be quick to disabuse them. Students rarely do, citing the need to "put food on the table," as if starvation was the only option.

Faculty were indoctrinated with this rhetoric during their instruction, when it was even less likely to be questioned. Their identity and relevance are based on claiming to best prepare students to serve a client's business interests. It's not as if an alternative is tested and found wanting; it's that there's no being outside the commercial imperative of design. It's that or the void.

(F)

In a 2018 interview on the Jarrett Fuller "Scratching the Surface" podcast, Elliott Earls, artist in residence of the Cranbrook 2D program, identified how the formal fundaments of design doesn't require the entirety of a curriculum to impart. "If you compress all your curriculum core graphic design courses down, you could learn all the foundational components of graphic design in about six months. The issues are so much deeper than that." Beyond the introductory courses, time isn't occupied exploring alternatives but applying those basic formal concepts to a variety of formats: posters, packaging, brochures, branding, video, web sites, apps. Emphasis is on house styles and identities: conformity. "Originality" occurs within a narrow context, a slight variation on an established theme.

However, we don't know what might come of truly crafting a pedagogy of individuality and exploration. If regarded as design instrumentalists, students are overwhelmingly being prepared to act as accompanists, not soloists or composers. Or, for that matter, inspired collaborators. Our historic and current instruction is formulating adept fakery. Design education has largely engaged in devising graphic "fake books" for practitioners, mentally and physically. In music, accompanists compile or refer to 'fake books' to guide them through unfamiliar tunes. In the absence of rehearsal time, these lead sheets provide the melody and basic chords so performers can convincingly play back up. A surface awareness provides a convincing background.

Design isn't practiced as immediately as a concert but is always to a deadline and often functions without the designer having fluency in the

subject. Research — the rehearsal — is usually shopping online for visual "inspiration": the Pinterest-ization of the field. The resulting product faithfully fits into the accepted genre and reigning style. Close enough for jazz and design.

Though on a sliding scale, design academia is coming to terms with the cultural and political complexity of design. A slow build toward a library of true books, ones that address these realities, will enhance progress. As Earls expresses, the issues run even deeper than that. While form- and practice-based texts on design proliferate, there are steps like Elizabeth Resnick's *Developing Citizen Designers* (2016), that deemphasize form- for difference-making. Its prescriptions may hew closely to the format of conventional design texts but pushes against and away from the characteristic topics and purposes for design.

(1)

A virtue of the *Design Futures* report is that it doesn't provide sample projects or program outlines. Teachers and programs are made aware of the trends, and then left to craft their own new, individual responses in curricula. This is a major break with the determination and homogenization that has long dominated design individually and discipline-wide. Instead of spreading uniformity, design education can become collaborative and generative.

Design Futures cites a critique of industrial era design by architect Alistair Parvin, as "something done to and for people, not with or by people." The same can be said of design education's application. Education also has a necessity to engage with rather than dictate to students and society.

This implicitly threatens the immediate authority and, more profoundly, the overall identity of many design academics. Abandoning the master/pupil model of learning that dominates U.S. industrial era teaching will leave instructors bereft of means and method.

A response is for teachers to work alongside students, to learn not only from but with them. Professors can perform the individual assignments they devise at the same time and be a group member in collaborations. This radically changes the nature of the classroom experience.

Meaning might prevail over mastery.

Paulo Freire's *Pedagogy of the Oppressed* is a foundational text in this regard and would be doubly explosive in a design education context. Clients are posed as the designer's oppressor in common design profession contexts but not the system in which they exist. A designer's typical formulation of "communication" seems paltry and frivolous in comparison to Freire's meaning, though they may seem *simpatico*: "Yet only through communication can human life hold meaning. The teacher's thinking is authenticated only by the authenticity of the students' thinking. The teacher cannot think for her students, nor can she impose her thought on them. Authentic thinking, thinking that is concerned about *reality*, does not take place in ivory tower isolation, but only in communication. If it is true that thought has meaning only when generated by action upon the world, the subordination of students to teachers becomes impossible."

This is only part of the equation. Assignments must reflect changed social and cultural circumstances. A continued diet of mock brochures, logos, splash pages, and packaging ossifies pedagogy. Syllabi should be less fixed than fluid. Projects should be, by turns, open-ended, where the expression is determined by the intention, and "real." As much as possible, projects should realize actual action in the world, as the organization Designers Without Borders does, rather than spawn endless faux objects.

To a large degree, design is predictable. Surprise has been limited to the formal wrapping and that response has shrunk significantly. Moving away from industrial era artifacts and instruction could enter us into a worthwhile realm of speculation. What design will be and how it will be taught will be truly theoretical. Uncertainty, however, is a tough sell to faculty, students, administrators, and accreditors.

Not to mention design readers and writers. *Design Futures* claims that our dynamic contemporary condition calls for an embrace of the ephemeral as an endpoint, overturning the longstanding striving for the timeless: "The end goal of design is 'good enough for now.'"

If this also applies to articles about design, I'm already there.

fuck all

The solution most commonly offered for improving or expanding writing about graphic design is to recruit more practitioners to the task. Or, to lure now inactive ones back. Unsurprisingly, it's almost exclusively _other_ designers that propose these remedies. Discussion quickly turns to methods to inject more money into writing, to offset the comparitively robust pay that comes from doing design. As a writer myself, I can't argue against that potential. But as a reader, offering higher fees for the same unreliable product isn't an advance.

To varying degrees, the writings of practitioners or those who rose up through the profession are always compromised. Directly or indirectly, these writers bolster their professional status and prospects in their texts. Why shouldn't they? Arguing a strongly held opinion is the hallmark of all good critical writers. That opinion _should_ align with a designer's business interests. However, a simple disclaimer must accompany practitioners' writing: _Warning: may contain ulterior or mixed motives._ This is a significant issue in design writing, where practice-related and practice-centric writers predominate.

Catalog essays for the exhibition _Graphic Design: Now in Production (GDNiP)_ highlight the problems with practice-related writers. Of immediate concern is their prevalence in the complement of essayists. Then there is the uncritical acceptance of propositions that speak more about the

writers' professional aspirations than the ostensible subject.

For profession-based writers, professional practice and "graphic design," are synonymous. Client-based commercial work is asserted as the graphic designer's sole legitimate expression. "We speak through our assignment," writes designer/educator Michael Rock in "Fuck Content," a 2005 article revised for the *GDNiP* catalog (and included in the design studio 2x4's recent book *Multiple Signatures*). This short essay is intended to be the definitive statement on the essential nature of graphic design. To that end, Rock pronounced a resolution of the "content" vs. "form" dichotomy. Form-making — graphic treatment — is declared as design's true content. "Just as every film is about filmmaking," Rock says, "Our content is, perpetually, Design itself."

Rock's stated purpose for the article is to counter a widespread misreading of "The Designer as Author," his oft-cited 1996 *Eye* essay surveying the phenomenon of "graphic authorship." To his dismay, designers considered the article an affirmation of the idea Rock set out to debunk. "Fuck Content" is the rebuke. According to the *GDNiP's* co-curator Ellen Lupton, Rock "admonished designers to focus on how things look and how they communicate, not what the message is." All that matters is *how* you do design formally.

Though cleverly argued, "Fuck Content" merely restates design's traditional, Modernist rationale. As he asks in the essay, so what else is new? In an ironic twist reinforcing the essay's throwback nature, Rock invokes Paul Rand to strengthen his case: "There is no such thing as bad content, only bad form."

Rock further channels Rand by remaking design history in his own image: "If you look at the span of graphic design, you discover, not a history of content but a history of form." Here, Rock's reading is accurate, in that the design profession and its chroniclers have emphasized and prized formal achievement. It also ranks as a truism: is there a formless design? A contentless one? Rock's perspective churns all design artifacts into conceptual slurry, roiling all distinguishing intentions into a blurry mass of form.

Rock's reductive view is absurd, particularly considering Modern

design's genesis. Of the few practitioners he cites — Rand, Zwart, Cassandra (sic), Matter, Crouwel — none count amongst design's polemical progenitors of form. Rock proposes that the German designer Jan Tschichold's impassioned, political text in *Die Neue Typographie* (1928) had no more significance than copy for the Nike Sportswear Fall Retail Campaign. However, the bracing innovation of Tschichold's form is inseparable from the urgency and import of his words. For many other designers of Tschichold's time and others before and since, design is a medium to ideals beyond itself. Especially beyond consumer culture.

The covert agenda in "Fuck Content" is to reinforce the status quo of design as service industry and the established hierarchy of practitioners. At the apex are moneyed culture and its servants. Overall, the *Graphic Design: Now in Production* catalog gives no love for graphic authorship, with the design writers Steven Heller and Ellen Lupton heaping scorn upon the poor concept, Lupton slapping it down in her two essays "The Designer as Producer" and "Reading and Writing." Why is graphic authorship so reviled and marked for elimination?

While problematic as a concept, graphic authorship implicitly (and dangerously) questions the purposes that design talent is put to, and the terms under which we appraise it. Eradicate content as an evaluative factor, whether self-generated or for non-commercial purposes, and we default to abstract graphic treatments possible only under the patronage of affluent clients.

Products of graphic authorship are also alarmingly compelling. In "Design Entrepreneur 3.0," (2011) Steven Heller back-handedly acknowledges the power of graphic authorship, attempting to siphon off its appeal to fuel his own synthetic movement. The number and variety of productions featured in "The Designer as Author" undermined Rock's contentions, speaking more persuasively than his recondite scolds.

The "insecurity" derided as motivating force behind graphic authors appears to afflict the most daring and accomplished contemporary and pastc designers and compels singularly inspiring and imaginative works. The standards of traditional, form-centric, client-based design are challenged and swept away. Designers may see this not as a bug but a feature.

Retrograde commentators regard graphic authorship as just another excess of the 1990s to be rolled back. To practice-centric critics, the nineties are what the sixties represent to conservative politicians. Both eras are regarded as times of indulgence, ugliness and chaos, where upstarts challenged their betters, and establishment verities were rejected. Critics railing against graphic authorship echoes right-wingers mocking the "permissive culture" fostered under liberalism.

Self-determined works are by definition more egalitarian than client-based design. Commercial design work is possibly as open since it's available to anyone for purchase. If you can afford it. However, Michael Rock isn't professionally invested in such work. And "Fuck Content" points toward a restricted design practice, not a populist one.

Rock discloses his thinking in an e-mail exchange reprinted in Frida Jeppsson's *In Case of Design — Inject Critical Thinking* (2010), which published an earlier version of "Fuck Content." In it, Rock dismisses "99.99%" of design as simply "an index of the culture that produced it." The remaining 0.01% "is the part that really bears up to close looking." A reasonable assumption is that Rock considers his work among that select one-hundredth of a percent. Once again, he harkens to design's past. An ability to stand apart from culture was another Modern conceit.

What is ultimately telling is that detractors of graphic authorship never claim that its works are incapable of the design paradigm Rock spells out in "Fuck Content": "... to speak through *treatment*, via a whole range of rhetorical devices — from the written to the visual to the operational — in order to make those proclamations as poignant as possible .... " Arguably, a graphically authored work has *more* potential to attain the ideals Rock proposes for design. Except it was not produced to a client's order, making it of *de facto* lesser status. The objection is about *propriety*, not quality.

A further statement from Rock's article is inarguable: "The choice of projects in each designer's œuvre lays out a map of interests and proclivities. And the way those projects are parsed out, disassembled and organized, and rendered may reveal a philosophy, an æsthetic position, an argument and a critique." A survey of the Michael Rock/2x4 œuvre maps an obsession with elite consumption, buttressed by abstruse theory.

Graphic design is fetishized, in keeping with the fetishized goods it frames. As Rock sets no boundaries as to the methods or ends to which design may utilize its potential to make, in the words of "Fuck Content," "proclamations as poignant as possible," we must assume that there are none.

With articles like "Fuck Content," the author Rock provides valuable intellectual cover for the elite class of designers and their clientele. His sincerity is evident as he proselytizes for an expansive and empowering role for graphic design. That it can only be realized by substantial capital is, for him, happenstance and irrelevant. It's about *form* not personal aspiration.

While he goes further than any other designer in rationalizing an exclusive construction of design, Rock still refrains from declaring any individual motivation beyond exemplary formal achievement and communicative efficacy.

Historically, renowned designers are always presented, and present themselves, as acting out of abstract principles. Their creative idealism transcends mundane careering to operate on a rarified plane of practice. In the foreword to Steven Heller's 1999 *Paul Rand* monograph, Swiss designer Armin Hoffman states "Paul Rand worked tirelessly with his students on the renovation and invigoration of our sign-world." For famed designer George Lois, he was the "heroic Paul Rand," whose "major concern was to strive for cause and effect in the creation of his work, and with tireless and selfless effort, teach write and inspire younger generations to march to his beat."

To biographer Kerry William Purcell, International Style icon Josef Müller-Brockmann had "... a near-religious longing to give one's self over to a greater truth." And never one to assume a low hyperbolic orbit, in the revised edition of *The End of Print*, commentator Tom Wyatt declared of David Carson, "The commitment was to original expression, ceaseless exploration, an unending quest to originate and assimilate, and to change what you were doing if you recognized it was looking rule-bound."

Amongst these aspirants, Stefan Sagmeister is decidedly self-effacing in his famed "Things to Do Before I Die," list. It starts straightforwardly enough — "Open and run a design studio in New York" — but still manages to end on an ardent note, "Touch someone's heart with graphic design."

It isn't acknowledged that designers might want to enjoy an exclusive lifestyle. To be like or rub elbows with their celebrity/thought leaders/industry titan clients. Or that it might influence their value system.

Having attributed graphic authorship to envy and a striving for status, might we also credit Michael Rock with the same causation? Yes, designers aspire to power, social position, and cachet. But they also hope, by declaring themselves a kind of "graphic auteur" to garner respect and stout fees. Rock isn't alone in having parlayed a reputation as a deep design thinker into an enviable career crafting (for instance) Kanye West-branded immersive theater experiences in Qatar. These are opportunities for power, position, and cachet that is risible to expect from graphic authorship.

For prominent designers, the reality of their relationship with elite consumption can be an uncomfortable state of affairs. Most espouse classless, left wing political attitudes. The conflict between championing an egalitarian access to exceptional design and the substantial capital required for realizing it has bedeviled idealistic designers going back to the British designer William Morris. The economics seem inflexible, pushing practitioners unremittingly into the arms of moneyed culture.

Resignedly, designers will sometimes tender explanations that they must "rob Peter to pay Paul." But the said theft isn't an imperative, it's a choice. As attractive as Paul's wares may be, the necessity to rob Peter to acquire them should give pause. It's not inherently wrong to desire fine objects, live and work in New York, travel and lecture widely, hang with Kimye's people. The problem is transmuting the desire for a lifestyle into a design theory.

That designers have an appetite for graphic treatment is obvious. What the response to "The Designer as Author" revealed was a hunger for meaning and self-determination. A choice of how to perform graphic design and have it judged on its merits.

"Fuck Content" is nihilism posing as revelation. Commercial work isn't at risk of being supplanted as graphic design's primary manifestation. If you find that practice, or its alternative, embarrassing and unfulfilling, then don't do it. But also refrain from tearing down everything in fear of having your position usurped.

Like it or not, our design, and our perception of it, says something about us. Design isn't a glossy and empty abstraction of itself. It's by and for people. Our content is, perpetually, ourselves.

I believe in design

In each of the communities I've lived I've encountered one of these trucks. It's always a white van, hand-inscribed by paint or permanent marker. The declaimed texts are a variety of Biblical verses and religious admonitions. From this base model, the individual owners accessorize. For instance, the van I knew in Massachusetts had a set of small crosses rising from the roof. The owner was a carpenter by trade, the construction doubly serving as advertisement. In Chesapeake, Virginia, where I now live, some of the texts are lettered on florescent colored paper. They're bright and sprightly accents to the bi-chromatic declarations.

The intention of the owners is for me to take notice, and I do. However, the next step should be for me to contemplate religious faith. And once again, I do. But in the context of design. For me, these vehicles are one manifestation an ongoing concern: the relationship of graphic design and faith.

It's because of my devotion to graphic design that I've always enjoyed encountering these vehicles. They've also been a constant of sorts as I've bounced around the country. Each is a refreshing, individualized visual delight roaming the streets. Just a bit of typographic whimsy amongst a flat-hued and airbrush-detailed monotony of cars. They're folk art on wheels!

Actually reading the texts can sometimes put a bit of a damper on

the gratification. Declarations of your potential (or inevitable) damnation can weigh on the mind, no matter the state of one's conscience or current karmic burden. It's a weighty message being delivered, and the deliverer isn't into mincing words or fussy formal demonstration.

As genre artifacts, these vans are rather muted. None display the special eccentricity or wild invention of a Howard Finster. However, such appraisal seems silly under the circumstances. Even though there exists a considerable financial market for "naïve/folk/outsider/visionary art" that makes such distinctions.

If I were to consign this van's graphic staging to a particular design genre, it would be "information design." Though it's liable to provoke a doctrinaire adherent of the school to choke in disbelief, the van has most in common with the Swiss International Style. In his eccentric way, the van owner is being direct and neutral in his presentation. The crude hand lettering is his Helvetica. Æsthetics of the kind scorned by Josef Müller-Brockmann aren't in play here. The Word is everything. However, the Holy Grid isn't intuitive and probably too fussy for this artist. You just do it and there it is.

But this isn't another claim that designers should appreciate the graphic naïve. For those who'd regard these vans or any application of such "design" as an eyesore, I'm not here to argue otherwise. Unless you're stuck behind or beside one in a traffic jam, you can let it roll out of sight and mind.

Also unseen and unconsidered is faith as a positively represented impetus and subject matter in contemporarily art and design. Historically, faith played a predominant role in art. More than simply being well documented in art history, you could say religious art *is* art history.

As design has been shaped by art history, religious art provided aspects that graphic design has incorporated. Emblems make their way to logos. Branding can be seen in the representations of religious figures. Historians know a figure to be a particular saint due to standardized features and attributes. What Peter actually looked like was unknown to artists. They accessed, and reinforced, the brand.

The favored position of faith in art has decayed to relegation as

antagonist. Organized religion has brought a lot on itself. An artistic apology for clerical child abusers is not a winning artistic statement. If you wish to examine the sophisticated realm of art, you will leave behind any positive depiction of faith. Artists will rightly point out that their criticisms are of *organized* religion. It's the hypocritical adherents and their oppressive systems that are lampooned and vilified, not the underlying message. Still, there is no overt promotion of or support for that message to be found in contemporary art. Only in the "naïve" ghetto will you find succor. For the art world, adherence to faith is the evidence that the artist is an "outsider."

Between the naïve and the sophisticated is academia, where the conversion often takes place. In the classroom, the expression of religious belief in design is something I've always encountered. As a teacher, I'm regularly presented student work with explicit religious content. In addition, many students cite their faith as inspiration and motivation for their designing.

I know that my evangelical students are representative of a significant demographic in the professional graphic design community. The statistics on belief in the population of the United States, for example, tells us it's not a minority position in this country. A 2007 "U.S. Religious Landscape Survey" by the Pew Forum on Religion & Public Life found that slightly more than 16% or respondents identified themselves as "unaffiliated" to any religion. Of the more than 78% of adults identifying as Christian, over 26% of those were members of evangelical churches.

Though I'm more worldly-minded, my experience critiquing religious content in student work has gone without contention or awkwardness. Students have questioned my ability to evaluate their work at times but never due to my personal spirituality or lack thereof. That I simply possess a contrary taste is far and away the leading complaint. If anything, I've been regarded as a fellow congregant as I've addressed their content with the same verve I do all material.

With eight years of nun-directed Catholic grammar school in my past, I'm quite conversant with the themes of Christianity, so I have a leg up there. However, I'm just as ready to take on design work based in other faiths and welcome the experience for my own education. If I've

articulated a common critique with devout design it's that a student's work isn't passionate enough. That appraisal pretty much goes across the board for student and professional work. Most graphic design suffers from an impersonality and detachment that resists audience interaction. For religious work, such an approach is distressingly mortal (bring back the Latin Mass!).

Passion is a common buzzword in creative circumstances. It also has a very profound meaning when associated with Christian faith. It's another abstraction with a disputable means of depiction. A literal illustration of passion was simply done when representational art was the norm. Just picture some aspect of Christ's pre-crucifixion ordeal. Infusing the art making process with passion, and coming to agreement that it could be distilled from the product, was and remains sticky.

The suitable method of depicting religious themes was a matter of contention when religious art was *the* art. Work that may now seem to be the epitome of the genre was deeply questioned at the time. The idealized and eroticized figures introduced by Michelangelo led to criticism within the Catholic Church. Too much extraneous drama ... and nudity. The rise of "Baroque" era painters such as Caravaggio has been theorized as the result of this internal dispute, predating the pressure from the Protestant Reformation.

My critique of students' faith-based design as lacking in passion is shorthand. What I'm attempting to convey, and often explicitly spell out, is that they've adopted tropes from mainstream graphic design. For instance, the cross is deployed as just another logo: slap one on and you're automatically evoking Christ.

That it's desirable for Christianity, or any faith, to be marketed as you would any commercial product seems problematic. However, the selling of faith is firmly established. Televangelists have long trumpeted the contention that were Christ amongst us today, he would utilize the methods they employ. From such variances schisms are made.

When discussing how to represent faith and its fervor with students, I always have in mind an artifact I received during my undergraduate years in art school. A woman proselytizing on the street gifted it to me for simply conversing with her. At the time, I was admittedly insincere about the

encounter. I wasn't open-minded: liable to reverse my lapsed Catholicism. But I was admiring of people who were so moved by faith that they publicly witnessed it.

The woman presented me a small book that I've kept to this day, *The Greatest Is Love: St. Paul's Wonderful Words About Faith, Hope and Love*, a Hallmark Editions publication from 1971. It pairs Paul's words from the second edition of New English Bible with illustrations by favored Hallmark artist Lois Jackson. The pictures are pastorals, depicting blond-haired, blue-eyed Caucasian children existing within an idealized, *Little House on the Prairie* rendering of pioneering times. They are descendants of Holly Hobbie, contemporaries of Other Hallmark favorite Betsey Clark, and precursor to "Precious Moments," vigorously sweetened sentiments of love and friendship.

St. Paul's adult declarations on love and faith are regularly out of phase with the sentimentalized childhood pictures. Only the simplest ("Love is patient," "Love will never come to an end") comport well. Some juxtapositions, however, are distinctly jarring. One spread offers a version of 1 Corinthians 13:3: "I may dole out all I possess, or even give my body to be burnt, but if I have no love, I am none the better."

The book logically renders the first line *I may dole out all I possess*, portraying it as a childhood swap of baubles. Things get complicated when continuing on to the words *or even give my body to be burnt*. That speaks of a faith so profound as to willingly accept martyrdom. Immolation is obviously a subject at odds with the illustrator's style.

Though other pairings are near as discordant, it's this one spread that makes the book meaningful to me. Actually, there's another essential element: that the book was presented to me under those circumstances. Design artifacts often derive their significance from associations with people and events. Designers are powerless to prevent or compel these connotations, particularly on a personal level. My experience acquiring the book has allowed it to survive in my collection for nearly 30 years.

The gift immediately felt at odds with the woman's demeanor. She was near to my age, partially the reason I stopped to converse with her. Her affect made her seem more sophisticated than the book she proffered.

But there's no accounting for taste, starting with mine. And perhaps it's a rationalization that I consider it likely that it wasn't so much for the imagery as the text that she distributed the book. Still again, it's just as possibly a shrewd marketing move on her part. Few of the people she approached and were able to converse with would be art students like me.

Yet few art students were and are like me. Looking back on my fellow art students, we were a diverse lot. The stereotypical art student was only one type available. Many would identify easily with *The Greatest Is Love* while a equal number would immediately reject any manifestation of religious faith.

The same can be said of my students now. I would present the Hallmark interpretation as an extreme that a majority of students similarly found incongruous. Yet the lesson had application, though the graphic approaches they employed were more contemporary and representative of sophisticated styles. Was it an improvement that instead of a Hallmark card, faith is represented in the mode of a gig poster or a rave? Or any trendy consumer item?

Many of the students were members of more youthful congregations: both in the average age of members and the founding time of the church. The graphic upgrades resulted in the win-win of contemporizing the image of the churches and gratifying the designer's own formal proclivities.

As graphic design often does, the 2D stylings echoed the architecture. Neoteric churches often were wrapped in fresh construction, not altogether different from modish retailers. Mega-churches' graphics and structures harkened to big box stores. With storefront churches abounding in our area — retrofitting all manner of gas stations, restaurants, offices, shops, and markets — I imagined, only somewhat facetiously, graphics that would overwrite or play off those of the original occupants.

My hope to witness the transformation of local Stop N Go convenience stores into a chain of God N Go's is admittedly less than reverent. That could also be thought of adapting, say, a white van to transmit scripture. My local Bible van is a storefront church on wheels. The Good Bookmobile.

The fate of faith-oriented design amongst former students is

something I continue to track informally, largely through social media. Having made no kind of precursor study or research, I can't say if there are more devout designers in this generation of students.

The same might be said of investigating the influence of sexual orientation upon and within design. Certainly bringing plain ol' sex into the debate (i.e. is there a feminine design?) will reliably roil the design community. If there isn't a distinctive formality to faith-based design, what's to talk about?

Just as there seems a more vocal left-leaning population of designers, is it that the secularists hold sway here too? Is there an underground of "devout" designers? Or are there no discussions because there's really nothing much to say? Does calling it out do the subject and the affected designers a disservice?

Historically, graphic design has found plenty of room for the ineffable in its theories. Not to demean either religious belief or Modernist principles but many of the historic and contemporary rationales for graphic design activity have been based more in faith than evidence. Gestalt principles are still unencumbered by objective verification, to name just one. Graphic design's traditional emphasis on rationality and neutrality immediately seems to herald a conflict with a sensibility highlighting transcendence. Rationalism has resided in cooperation faith for centuries, despite events in the recent past.

Secularism predominates in the contemporary graphic design commentariat, as does political liberalism. The central irony has been how religiously design's "rational" program has been adhered to. Evidence for universal languages of form and most other fundamental declarations were, and remain, in short supply. The vehemence exhibited by modernist-era designers when culture rolled on was akin to a Pope's response to apostasy.

Maximizing "communication" has been the central tenet of design. But if it matters exactly *what* is to be communicated, it's left unsaid. The success of transmission reifies the *process*, not the processed. Only the most extreme and universally reviled message meets with unwavering approbation (i.e. Nazi imagery).

No inverse positive, affirmative ideology enjoys the same attention from prominent design commentators. The cross, star/crescent, or Star of David haven't been obsessed over as has the swastika. Outside of the fringe and flirtations, the Nazi-appropriated mark is unlikely to regain prominence. The religious symbols have complicated existences. Within them strong positive and negative connotations are entwined. Exploring them would require a subtlety and sensitivity beyond the reach of typical design analysts. Ironically, trashing the swastika is the safe choice.

From the evidence, graphic design is most comfortable with commercial messages. The dollar sign or euro symbol may rarely manifest in graphic design yet is a tacit watermark of the practice. Having constructed itself as a profession, this is entirely in keeping. The church and the marketplace are one. But can graphic design be, and mean, more?

I continue to wonder about the absence of public discussion about faith upon creativity, though no more or less than any other intangible but heartfelt influence. Never mind about touching hearts with graphic design, what about *souls*? Is anyone making the attempt?

Most of the faithful design I see from students is meant for the believers. Yes, preaching to the converted. Context-less declarations of belief in a poster are their evangelizing. Witnessing one's faith publicly is, in itself, still a bold move. And active proselytizing is, for most, uncouth. But, in itself, the public declaration is insufficient: it must be accompanied with living by example. Words, however they are dressed up, either in magniloquent oration or resplendent typefaces, are insufficient. An extra-design circumstance — how one *acts* upon the words — is crucial in demonstrating one's faith.

As with passion, "faith" has a secondary, related meaning. It is the simpler one, of simply having trust. Trust can be seen as the ultimate goal of any design. The designer seeks to instill a message with authenticity and credibility. As with all abstractions, trust is a state that's subjective, dynamic, and impervious to a standardized formal expression.

Generating trust through form is possible but eludes teaching in formal terms. Such as hewing to asymmetric layouts. Trust transcends form. Or, trust is as trust does. From my own experience, the work that I have

created solely for myself is the work that makes the strongest connection with others. When I've deliberately and determinately turned inward, it's inevitable that audiences are drawn to follow.

This is obviously at odds with mainstream graphic design dogma, and fundamental Modernist principles. The singular is to be eschewed. The personal is not universal. The same can be said about the basic tenants of religious faith. Individual interpretation and elaboration is the definition of heresy. Followers aren't supposed to be inventors. In the design as faith context, "conforming" takes on additional, almost punning meaning.

But it's my own contra-rational belief that people pick up on the candor, commitment, and charity implicit in such work. Further, that it's this intently personal investment, rather than the purported rational/objective principles, that energized the audience.

Even Moderist heroes are acknowledging the personal role in their work. In a Design Observer post on the 2011 exhibition *Wim Crouwel: A Graphic Odyssey*, Rick Poynor noted, "Crouwel himself accepted long ago that his work is far more personal than he once claimed." "Far from suppressing his own creative personality in the way he advised, Crouwel was expressing it to the full. It just happens that this personality was inclined towards reduction and minimalism."

Interestingly, Poynor also turns to religious belief as simile for designers' personal creative philosophies, dubbing them "necessary fictions." A designer has to believe or audiences won't. The universal is personal.

However, a devout belief won't guarantee the greatest number of adherents. But those you touch will possess a higher devotion. You just do what's right, not what's convenient, or acceptable.

Debating the Bible van's formal merits is irrelevant. However, its design, by every measure, is authentic. I trust its essential message but choose to express it differently in my life.

When the van pulled in a few houses down, I walked over and asked the driver if I might document it. As I photographed its hood, I suggested he write his message backwards so as to read right in rear view mirrors. At first, he was mystified by my advice, until I referred to ambulances. He allowed that it was a good idea. And so design is revealed.

This is the cover page for the second section in this book, titled "Interlude with Designers." This chapter contains studies of contemporary and historical figures in design: Barney Bubbles, Jacqueline Casey, Vaughan Oliver, Stefan Sagmeister, Martin Venezky, Mark Andresen, and Andrew Breitenberg. In the course of these essays, the work of Paula Scher and others are also given significant consideration. "Beauty/entropy," was commissioned to accompany the exhibition «Vaughan Oliver: Walking Backwards» at Leslie University, August 2017. "Salvager" was commissioned as the forward for the monograph «Stefan Sagmeister» published by Ginza Graphic Gallery (ggg) Books, 2005. "The difference engineer" originally appeared as "Martin Venezky's beautiful melancholy" on Design Observer, August 2005. "Pesky illustrator" first appeared in «Eye» magazine #67, 2008; "Conjure man" was the initial submitted version. "Word!" was published in «Selah Index», Parallel Books, 2014. "Four sides of Barney Bubbles," "From Abacus to Zeus," and "The graphic designer and her presence," were posted at the Ephemeral States blog.

4 *B.B.*

Face one: Offset identities

*All it is is rock and roll but it's no big shakes. But at the same time I
think commercial design is the highest art form.*

*When I went to art school, we were trained to be designers — if you
could draw you became an illustrator; if you could just about draw, you
became a designer; if you were just hopeless they would put you into
exhibition display.*

— Barney Bubbles, *The Face*, November 1981

There's an astonishing quote residing on page 136 of Paul Gorman's
monograph *Reasons to Be Cheerful: The Life and Work of Barney Bubbles*.
Only graphic designers can fully appreciate it. It's in a brief anecdote that
succinctly summarizes why the man born Colin Fulcher is the graphic
designer *sui generis*. Non-designers reading the sentence would likely skim
right over it, unaware of its import.

The subject is the proposed title for musician Elvis Costello's third
album. The speaker is Costello's long-time manager and label honcho Jake
Riviera, once known as Andrew Jakeman. Bubbles had already designed
Costello's first two albums, as part of his role as lead designer at Stiff and
then Radar Records. "Originally Elvis wanted to call it *Emotional Fascism*

but Barney was totally against that, so it became *Armed Forces*."

By this time in the book, Gorman has provided numerous examples of notoriously strong-willed reps and artists contentedly deferring to Bubbles' judgment. That this instance stars the acid-tongued and head-strong former Declan MacManus is of no special import. (The degree of Bubbles' disfavor, however, intensifies between editions of Gorman's book. The first quotes Riviera that "Barney just didn't like it").

Costello himself relates a different, briefer account in his memoir, *Unfaithful Music and Disappearing Ink*, one that doesn't necessarily contradict Riviera's telling. "Accepting that no radio station would play a record called *Emotional Fascism*, the album was eventually titled *Armed Forces*," writes Costello. While Bubbles isn't explicitly given agency for the change (nor is anyone), the designer is immediately invoked in the next sentence: "It came wrapped in a folding envelope of Barney Bubbles' pop art design."

A simple swap of common for proper nouns illustrates what makes Riviera's statement so astounding: "Originally the client wanted to call it *X* but the designer was totally against that, so it became *Y*." That sentence, especially among designers, is unheard of.

Usually, designers take what they get. At best, they might boast of swaying the client to a particular approach for the art. Even among designers famed for their association with particular labels, such as Reid Miles and Blue Note, Vaughan Oliver at 4AD, or Barbara Wojirsch of ECM, this type of influence is unprecedented. And for designers overall? That's crazy talk.

In his book, Gorman's fuzzy on exactly why Bubbles enjoys such favor. Multiple individuals who worked with the designer testify to his "genius." It's the last statement in the book, provided by Nick Lowe on why there's a book in the first place: "Barney was the closest we'll ever get to genius, we've got no choice."

The constituents of Bubbles' virtuosity, however, aren't really articulated. This is unfortunately common with the majority of designer profiles. The subject's superiority is regarded as self-evident. *Just look at the work*. As rewarding as that is, the visual aspect is only one aspect of his facility. That Bubbles was provided unparalleled authority and latitude is established.

However, what's more significant and profound is what Bubbles *did* with his favor.

In terms of skill, he was virtuosic at everything he took on. Short of photography, he handled every possible aspect of realizing a graphic design work. His illustrative proficiency in pen was matched by his painting, equaled by his collage. His typography was unerring and exacting in contemporary and historic styles, plus displaying a range of arresting emotions and evocations.

But it was in his conceptualizing, its acuity and comprehensiveness, that he remains unparalleled. In many instances, Bubbles went places with his work that designers — and definitely clients — wouldn't think to go. Most wouldn't recognize Bubbles' endpoint as a potential destination. All the while, he was adhering to and espousing the fundamental, mundane commercial imperatives of graphic design and advertising. But rather than following the orthodox, predetermined route to a result, he truly started from zero, remaking design as he went.

Barney was a riddler wrapped in a mystery inside an enigma slipped within a foot square cardboard folder. That's the perception at the tone-arm's-length distance between an LP sleeve designer and the record-buying audience. Though Bubbles had the freest of hands over content, he declined to draw attention to his role by setting it in type. Even though he sported an alias, Barney Bubbles was prolific while regularly eschewing a design credit. To this day, making a full inventory of his work is an ongoing venture.

It wasn't, however, a striving for anonymity. It was a selective withholding that drew attention to itself. Bubbles toyed with ideas of identity and identification throughout his work. In this, Bubbles was fully invested, as he was in all pursuits. His design, his art, had no conceptual boundary. The design credit and lack thereof was an element of the design concept. That concept, and his art, extended outward and was ultimately his life.

As if one *nom de design* wasn't enough, Bubbles inserted an additional layer of offset identity by employing an assortment of fanciful pseudonyms — "Big Jobs, Inc., Grove Lane, Sal Forlenza, Jacuzzi Stallion, Dag, Heeps Willard" — or cryptic designations as identifiers: his VAT — tax

identification — number on Costello's *Get Happy!!* His mask donned masks; Bubbles existed as a Constructivist-decorated nesting doll.

The absent acknowledgements was another throwback move, much like the period styles and references Bubbles transmuted for his layouts. It was only in the late 60s, a few years before he began doing sleeve work, that it became customary for designers to be provided a credit. Skipping it was simply consistent on sleeves that graphically evoked the previous era.

By using alternate aliases, Bubbles showed his game wasn't anonymity but evasiveness. Ironically, a further proof can be found in his use of "Barney Bubbles" in design credits. Prior to his joining the Stiff circus in 1977, spotting a variation of "Sleeve design: Barney Bubbles" wasn't uncommon. While unusual in his graphics, he was conventional in noting his agency.

Personally and professionally, the punk era marked a transition for Bubbles. He pared down both his personal appearance and graphic approach. Gone was the beard, long hair and wardrobe of his hippy days. And his design, says Gorman: "brutal cropping, stark isolation of images, gritty photo-play."

However, while the "Barney Bubbles" moniker spanned these periods as his preferred personal identity, its removal from the album credits was simply conceptual due diligence. Gorman quotes Stiff staffer Suzanne Spiro: "As much as I got to know him, I never knew his real name and in a way I think it's a shame it's been revealed. If you asked him he would just shrug his shoulders and giggle."

Even then, it was a porous barrier. Work outside the Stiff/Radar/F-Beat network might note: "Sleeve design: Barney Bubbles" (Clover, *Unavailable*, Polygram, 1977) or "Sleeve design and artwork: Barney Bubbles" (Dr. Feelgood, *A Case of the Shakes*, United Artists, 1980). Still, releases with Bubbles' design such as Depeche Mode's debut *Speak and Spell* (Mute, 1981), and The Psychedelic Furs *Forever Now* (CBS, 1982) only acknowledge their photographers.

When asked how he regarded his role in his lone published interview (*The Face*, November 1981) and why he shunned a credit, Bubbles' answer would have made any old school Modernist design pro proud: "I feel really

strongly about what I do, that it is for other people, that's why I don't really like crediting myself on people's albums — like you've got a Nick Lowe album, it's NICK LOWE's album not a Barney Bubbles album!"

Practically, being dodgy about his credits had a deleterious impact on Bubbles' professional career. As noted above, bands outside of his home base sought him out. This extended to superstar territory: in 1978, The Who's management invited him to propose a design for *Who Are You*. (Bubbles' concept of spelling the title out in power cables was rejected but adapted for the photo that was eventually used.) However, according to Paul Gorman, Bubbles shopped his portfolio in 1982 "to some of the bigger music labels, only to hear his unsigned work had already been claimed by others."

It may have been a pragmatic response for Bubbles to award himself a credit on Wang Chung's *Points on a Curve* in 1983. The major-label job for Geffen Records was gained through the recommendation of photographer Brian Griffin and provided Bubbles a higher profile. Conceptual games be damned, he needed the work.

Gorman documents other brushes with high-profile music-industry clients, showing Bubbles had visibility and credibility in the field. Aborted and unrealized projects go with the territory. Gorman also cites unnamed sources as speculating that Bubbles' naming elusivity was a tactic to avoid tax problems. If so, it was inconsistent. And ineffective.

That Bubbles' was engaged in a comprehensive gaming of identity is affirmed by his extension of the play into the graphics. In at least two prominent instances, Bubbles inserted fanciful self-portraits onto album covers. Right away, this is the ultimate audacity for a designer.

The first example, considered a definite representation of his profile, is on *Armed Forces*. This is the record that Bubbles demanded and got a title change. He can be found in the abstract shapes to the left of the yellow paint splattered title "Elvis Costello and the Attractions Armed Forces."

In its original U.K. incarnation, this graphic is within the package, after unfolding the back flaps. The designer is literally behind the scenes on the album, embodied at the center of a mélange of high and low historical graphic styles. In a delightful irony, Columbia, Costello's U.S. label at the

time, evidently finding the U.K. cover unacceptable (a deliberately-kitsch commissioned painting of stampeding elephants adorned with discreet typography) made the inner splatter graphic the front image. Having rejected the designer's preferred layout as probably as too British and obscure with tiny type, the company punished Bubbles by putting his grinning face on its cover.

For the second (though Paul Gorman hedges that the image is possibly lead singer Lee Brilleaux) it would be in keeping if Barney Bubbles' profile was again dead center on the illustrative cover of Dr. Feelgood's 1982 album *Fast Women & Slow Horses* (Chiswick). Seeing stars after an implied punch from a buxom, boxing-gloved mare, a man's face emerges from the top of a large black ampersand. If it's Bubbles, he is again one with the artwork. He is (the) design. Another potentially sly reference is that as a designer, his role is an "&" to the musicians.

In adopting a creative guise, one evidently identical with his everyday semblance, he was in league with the musicians for whom he designed. Many adopted or were given stage names, especially at Stiff. Bubbles' was back-stage named. Even if using their natal names, artists craft professional personas. These are carefully managed and strategically deployed. However genuine and real that singer seems, it's a performance. Sincerity is how convincingly you repeatedly enact intimacy with an audience.

Bubbles' deep interest in the avant-garde art from the beginning of the 20th century also suggests a purpose. In her introduction of the catalog for National Gallery of Art's 2006 exhibition *Dada: Zurich, Berlin, Hannover, Cologne, New York, Paris*, Leah Dickerman, Associate Curator of Modern and Contemporary Art at the National Gallery, writes, "Artists within the movement gave birth to a striking number of alter egos, which served as parodic, at times debased, inversions of a rational and authoritative masculinity." Dickerman points to Duchamp's "Rrose Sélavy" as the ultimate reversal with the artist changing sex.

Bubbles never ventured into this realm of invention; his pseudonyms were all masculine or ambiguous. His life/design still adeptly illustrated how identity is mutable. Individuality is a postmodern playground, not a fixed state. He did this through the panoply of bespoke logos he generated

for Stiff, F-Beat and himself. Bubbles formed an identity that was composed of its antithesis: flux. He grasped intuitively the elements that make up graphic identity and handled them effortlessly. Along the way, he effectively branded musicians and labels.

Face two: Match prints

> I love rock and roll … I can't get enough of it! But I'm really sad the way it's gone. I find all the young designers … and I've talked to a lot of them … they think they're doing Art, and they talk about record covers as Art. They do one sleeve and they are already talking about what they are going to do for the next album cover. All that to me is highly suspect because you've got to wait, hear the music and meet the guys, and they tell you what they want and then it's up to you to deliver that.
> — Barney Bubbles, *The Face*, November 1981

> I had begun to find it increasingly difficult to control the quality of my work and to develop as a designer unless I was working on a pro bono basis or for a minimal fee for a design organization or design-industry client. This was depressing because I believed that the whole point of graphic design was to bring intelligence, wit, and a higher level of æsthetics to everyday products, the articles of mass culture. I did not want to be an ivory tower designer; I had little interest in theoretical exploration. My goals were to design things that would get made, to elevate popular taste through practice, and to make graphic design breakthroughs on real projects.
> — Paula Scher, *Make It Bigger*

> What is certain is that Bubbles maintained a powerful working momentum in the circumstances — drunken visits from The Damned, Wreckless Eric and others, Riviera and Robinson roaring into telephones and the odd cider bottle flying across the office. Only once did he find the lively atmosphere intolerable. An over-refreshed executive — it may have been Robinson — failed to hit the target in the lavatory on the floor

above Bubbles' desk, and ruined artwork with splashes that rained down from the loose floorboards overhead. "Barney was absolutely hopping mad," says Glen Colson ... "He came out screaming and shouting about that, and quite right too. But it was very funny."
      — Paul Gorman, *Reasons to Be Cheerful: The Life and Work of Barney Bubbles*

Barney Bubbles was a unique design talent in a discipline offering an array of singular practitioners. Placing him in context and characterizing his particular aptitude can be challenging. His specific practices weren't exclusive. He worked on design of music industry artifacts, in illustration, painting, video, furniture. In this variety, he was representative of the classic Modern design sensibility of total design.

Coming of age in the early 1960s, Bubbles was representative of his generation in many of his pursuits and attitudes. He moved from the standard agency practice to design for and about the rising youth culture (translation: he became a hippy). Popular culture — music — was supplanting corporate identity as the young designer's muse and preferred client.

Focusing in on Bubbles' particular obsessions and a serendipitous conjunction reveals his affinity with a contemporary designer who shares a similar career path and sensibility. Not only does this comparison offer insight into both designers' activity, it outlines wider import in how modern design tenets will diverge in application based on biography and geography.

If not overall, among American designers current Pentagram partner Paula Scher is Bubbles' closest counterpart. Immediately, there's a fundamental difference between the two: fame. Both do have one monograph apiece, though Bubbles' is posthumous. Scher is an established, internationally-renown and extensively discussed (though hardly examined critically) figure in design. Though steadily gaining in recognition, Bubbles remains a discovery and reclamation project. During his career, he could only dream of a visibility that readily came for Scher. Some can be attributed to his idiosyncratic design agenda. More to the limited regard afforded at the time to sleeve designers in the broader field.

Bubbles designed for a variety of labels but worked primarily for

small independents like Stiff Records and its offshoots. By contrast, Scher earned visibility while working exclusively for a major in her album design career. Their respective careers cross at Scher's employer, Columbia Records, the U.S. licensee of Elvis Costello and Nick Lowe albums.

In salient aspects, Bubbles and Scher coincide. Both made their names in record album design in the 70s, their activity roughly contemporaneous. Where Scher went directly from art school into the CBS Records advertising and promotion department, Bubbles began his design career in agencies and freelance a decade earlier, with occasional (and award-winning) forays into poster design for musical events. Overall, their career paths were roughly inverted.

Bubbles' first LP design was in 1969 (Quintessence's *In Blissful Company*, Island); Scher began designing albums in 1973 at Atlantic Records, moving to Columbia in 1974 until her departure nine years later. Bubbles, tragically, committed suicide in 1984.

Most significantly, they shared fundamental creative influences and strategies. Each began their album design career emphasizing illustration. Bubbles was his own artist, while it was an opportunity for Scher to commission her preferred illustrators. Her concepts were fairly straightforward and "illustrative," with a Big Idea verbal/visual twist, prevalent still in professional design. Heatwave's *Too Hot to Handle* (1977) features a Robert Grossman image of a giant Epic Records album melting on a scorching sidewalk; *Yardbirds Favorites* (1977) has a David Wilcox rendering of assorted birds on the front lawn of a suburban American home.

Due to servicing clients like Hawkwind and its offshoots, Bubbles' illustrations could be more outré and reflective of the hippy lifestyle. Still, they were descriptive and products of the same general method. A sleeve such as Kursaal Flyers' *Chocs Away!* (UK Records, 1975) with a melting chocolate airplane soaring into the sun fits easily alongside Scher's projects.

Some Bubbles and Scher works appear that they might be in dialog across time. The cover of *My Aim Is True* and its Keith Morris photos seem to envisage Scher's mid-1990s Public Theatre poster series. Both display black and white photographed figures silhouetted against bright flat colors.

Costello, however, wasn't dancing. He was being choreographed by Bubbles who stood behind the photographer, according to Paul Gorman, "throwing moves and poses behind the camera to inspire and animate the singer."

Both displayed a fascination with and virtuosity at reworking historical and vernacular styles. While they grounded their work in their respective country's graphic heritage, they readily and adeptly incorporated expressions beyond their indigenous borders.

Scher has consistently employed distinctly American type styles dating from the early years of the 20th century. Employing aspects of American Modern design was a hallmark of counter-cultural/contra-European Modern expressions championed in the 1960s. Push Pin Studios is the most notable example and influence cited by Scher. Her early work regularly employed Cheltenham as serif, Franklin and Trade Gothics for sans, slab serifs, or utilized typography derived from wood type.

Bubbles also drew upon American influences, though from later in the century, eventually favoring an active Reid Milestyled letterplay that expanded to conjure the pre-Beatles 50s and early 60s era of rock and roll. Otherwise, his type choices largely reflected his training at his first design job under Michael Tucker: "Very Swiss; very hard; unjustified; very grey." However, as did Jan Tschichold, Bubbles leavened his copy with standards like Plantin and Garamond.

A disparity is that Scher will regularly pursue a wholly typographic approach. Though no less expert and inventive with type, examples of a Bubbles type-only treatment are rare, such as the concrete poetry-inspired *Xitintoday* (Nik Turner's Sphynx; Charisma, 1978).

Bubbles and Scher's confluence is at early European Modernism, particularly Russian Constructivism. The coloration and structure of Scher's famed Columbia "Best of Jazz" promotion poster is the most renowned exponent of this influence, though eclectically fused with her favored wood type styles.

Bubbles referenced El Lissitzky's "PROUN" paintings to churn out a sleeve overnight for Ian Dury's 1978 Stiff single, "Hit Me With Your

Rhythm Stick." The Bubbles blender mixed in stamp kit typography and origami.

With the sleeve of *Armed Forces* (Radar, 1978), Bubbles manufactured a supercollider of high and low art allusions that condensed all his obsessions in one place. Scher has no comparable multiplex masterwork but, as with the "Best of Jazz" poster, produced tour de forces that drew upon single or fused references.

Foremost is her 1984 identity for Capitol subsidiary label Manhattan Records. Wisely steering her client away from representations of buildings, she intuited a flexible and practical identity based upon Piet Mondrian's painting *Broadway Boogie Woogie* (1942–43). The artwork is composed of the familiar De Stijl primary colored squares but reduced in scale and lacking the framing black grid. According to the Museum of Modern Art gallery label, "These atomized bands of stuttering chromatic pulses, interrupted by light gray, create paths across the canvas suggesting the city's grid, the movement of traffic, and blinking electric lights, as well as the rhythms of jazz."

Among the brew of art samples Bubbles splashed on the inside of *Armed Forces* is a segment of the classic Mondrian composition. Scher focused entirely on a later manifestation of the approach. Her identity reverberates visually and conceptually across multiple levels. Dovetailing together is a visual reference of music that also symbolizes the streets of New York.

While the formal aspects of Constructivism were a mutual, predominant attraction, for Scher the choice was always "pragmatic." The "vaguely constructivist look" of the "Best of Jazz" poster happened because she was "rediscovering El Lissitzky and Aleksander Rodchenko at that time." She was (and is), however, far from apolitical, evidenced by examples of opinionated work on a range of topical issues throughout her career.

Bubbles engaged the political ideals on another, personal level. On his self-titled blog, artist and Bubbles schoolmate David Wills writes: "The great Russian artist El Lissitski (sic) was a big influence on Barney's work. ... Barney later called El "a hack" — but as I said, I suspect that was because El later buckled under Jo Stalin and became another Social Realist doing

what he was told, something Barney always fought against with all his might."

Another shared feature is the use and treatment of information design and data visualization. Both conspicuously utilize charts and graphs set to serio-comic ends. The two designers have it both ways: the "neutral" design form conveying both rhetoric and fact. Absurdity, rather than clarity, is foremost in the content of the graphics and the decision to use the form. They become profoundly apt in exposing their often-farcical topics. The cool detachment heightens the irrationality.

With Bubbles, it's another episode of drawing attention to and disrupting the tropes of graphic design. He exposes the ploys while indulging in them. This may derive from a vacillating view of the value of graphic design. Layered on top of this is his similarly conflicted view of popular music. Bubbles highlights both the romance and reality of the rock and roll life for performer and audience. His devotion to the ideal of the music goes hand in hand with disclosing its disposable artifice. Graphic design is correspondingly ephemeral and profound.

In his interview for *The Face* in 1983, Bubbles stated, "I find it's a big racket. I think everybody should own up, first of all that they're doing it for the money and the art definitely comes second. All it is is rock and roll and it's no big shakes. But at the same time I think commercial design is the highest art form."

The two sides of the inner sleeve of Nick Lowe's first solo album, *Jesus of Cool* (Radar, 1978), expose these conflicts. One side offers a graph of "The Artiste At Work," over a monotone image of meshing machine gears. The horizontal scale details a chronological listing of Lowe's output as band member, producer, and solo performer. The left hand vertical legend captions a steadily rising numbered scale: "Creative productivity output extrapolated from estimated work hours against an inverse ratio of critical acclaim."

This is countered by the right hand caption for a sharply downward trending segmented line: "Actual analysis of product showing negative sales potential allied to public avoidance factor." The satirical take on the

lingo of A&R men echo the narratives of album tracks like opener "Music for Money" and "Shake and Pop."

On the reverse side, a photo of a gymnast, frozen mid-leap, head circled, is labeled "The Artiste At Play." The completion of the work/play adage is the closet to sense the graphic makes, with its image a dubious representation of the "artiste" and the activity an improbable leisure pursuit for a refurbished pub rocker.

The inner sleeve of Johnny Moped's *Cycledelic* (Chiswick, 1978) hews closest to the Modern intention of the information graphic form. Here he adopts the format of Peter Frame's "Rock Family Trees" to detail the band's lineage. However, though the graphic plays it straight (earning praise from Frame for improving on his concept) Bubbles sees fit to disturbingly set it over a photo of troops arrayed at a Nazi rally.

Other incidences result from an uncomplicated design ideation but with Bubbles' inventiveness shaping the result. Following its technological source, Bubbles devised a graph graphic for the logo and label of Radar Records. Eschewing the obvious sound waves, he creates a 'scope displaying signal pulses that spell out "radar."

The graphics of the inner sleeve of Elvis Costello's fourth album *Get Happy!!* (F-Beat, 1980) offer no edifying data. On the front, three ellipses represent "Big Man," "Tall Man," and "Extra Wide Short Man" with type scaled and weighted according to the description. The portrayal resembles a children's book page, or a basic expressive typography demo. Tying into the album's title, the obverse offers the "Happy Man," intersecting ellipses arrayed in an "atom" shape.

Incidences of infographics tail off in Bubbles' later years. The entirety of the front cover of Wang Chung's *Points On A Curve* (Geffen, 1982) is given over to a graph in a rare example of literality (save for the enigmatic Brian Griffin cover photo). And for the back of Billy Bragg's *Life's A Riot With Spy vs. Spy* (Utility, 1982), Bubbles anthropomorphizes a graph that updates a World War II propaganda poster: "Beware the Squander Bug" (which on the record's label, is captioned "A Ration of Passion.")

Where Bubbles made information graphics an occasional element in his sleeves, Scher's applications emerged after her album career. (Her

current cartographic paintings extend this interest into another medium.) Even if absurd in content, her use is strategic, never wandering into the surrealism of Bubbles' specimens. Her focus and wit are keenly fixed.

An early effort is the cover of the 1985 *Print* magazine parody issue: "The Complete Genealogy of Graphic Design." More Monty Python than Phil Meggs, the chart rambles through a bizarre cataloging of historical figures, most unconnected to the field. Arrows and dashed, solid, or squiggly lines suggest connections or couplings between unlikely figures: Herbert Bayer and Queen Elizabeth II seem to gotten busy (or something). If there's a commentary on graphic design history, it's decidedly elusive: "The whole insane chart moved through history until it ultimately arrived at Milton Glaser."

In *Make it Bigger*, Scher makes diagrams a central element of the text. She provides them throughout in a serial explication of her central thesis that "judgments made about graphic design ... often have little to do with the effectiveness of a given design in the marketplace and more to do with how human beings naturally behave in complicated hierarchical social situations."

At first, the diagrams are functional tinged with humor: illustrating the approval processes at her workplaces, or contrasting "power" and "peon" office set ups. She then proceeds into more subjective and astringent presentations such as "Diagram of a Meeting" and "Personality Types in Combination."

Unlike Bubbles, Scher isn't struggling with or exploiting any contradictory impulses in her design. Ambiguity is the enemy of effective design. With her no-nonsense manner, Scher debunks any romanticism in the creative process. Much of the book's text describes how worthy design is prevented: conditions related to the thesis above. Eluding them is the key, either through haste (rush jobs that short circuit the process) or indulgent clients (jazzers, mostly).

"Bob James was my first ideal client," writes Scher of the musician and founder of Tappan Zee Records, "His was the only approval necessary ... " Bubbles couldn't agree more: "It's just fun working with Jake (Riviera), we'd just walk around the block — 'cause he was so busy — it would all be done

in five minutes. I could actually do what I wanted to do without being told off by the record companies that say: 'Fantastic, but don't you think ... ?' and then they fuck it up!"

Arguably, Bubbles was allowed greater creative latitude in his situations. Major labels are risk- and cost-averse while the upstarts trade on the novelty of exotic packaging. Even as the company of Alex Steinweiss, who pioneered the idea of album cover graphics, Columbia was staid and corporate.

Bubbles' inventions were regularly bowdlerized or replaced in the U.S. as occasionally the musical contents of the albums were. That Columbia was the U.S. distributor of a number of Bubbles-designed albums amply demonstrates the reality. If Scher had any awareness of Barney Bubbles, he would have served as a cautionary tale.

Scher's is dead on in her analysis that the true determinants of design results are interpersonal dynamics and individual personality. Pushing distinctive design through the Columbia bureaucracy was likely a chore. However, she extrapolates this to all labels and fails to turn her jaded eye on herself.

Understandably, she attributes herself only the purest motives: "Money was irrelevant. It was more important to make uncompromised work." There's no reason to doubt her. But other motives go unspoken that play into her experience. One is plainly stated at the outset of her book: "Designers want to make things, or make things up, and have those things that they've made up seen, used, and appreciated by lots of people."

Scher omits an important diagram that would complete her presentation. It should describe the inverse relationship between "uncompromised" and "lots." In choosing to work for Columbia, she made a priority of the latter, depressing the likelihood of the former. Other labels, even other majors, offered greater creative freedom. Warner Bros.' catalog was home to a variety of offbeat and artistic sleeves. Even Atlantic, the label she left for Columbia, issued sleeves that boasted "intelligence, wit, and a higher level of æsthetics." But, in another unstated but crucial factor of the equation, they might not be of Scher's æsthetic.

Other indices on the missing diagram probably should include

geographical preferences. Working for Warners would likely require Scher living in L.A., which may be akin to a matter/anti-matter collision. And, though she excoriates it, a taste for corporate life. Stuffy as it may be, the corporate workspace was comparably sedate and neat. Scher may wryly depict the "peon" office she sought to escape. But as described by Gorman, Bubbles literally labored in a "pee on" space.

Life is a series of trade-offs or compromises. Scher's determination to defy this actuality is her defining trait. But where her otherwise refreshingly sober view of design activity lapses into fantasy is neglecting to account for this reality: choices must be made. Everything Scher says about the stultifying nature of corporate design is irrefutable. But the ultimate barrier isn't the system, it's her choice, the designer's, of where to labor.

Bubbles likely recognized the trade-off and struggled with it. The Wang Chung commission got him a visible (hit single) major label job. But *Points On the Curve* ranks as one of the least interesting works in his œuvre. While still avoiding the default cliché of sleeves with the de rigueur band portrait relegated to the back, it's a disappointing effort. But when he makes something distinctive for a major — like The Psychedelic Furs' *Forever Now* (CBS, 1982) — he sees it replaced with a New Wave cliché in the States.

Logo design is another difference between the two. Logos seemed to flow effortlessly out of Bubbles, all equally ingenious, no matter how spontaneous ("I phoned him and said, 'I want a logo. It's got to be black and white and square,' Dury told Will Birch. 'Then I heard somebody in his office say, 'Wow' and he said, 'I've done it!'")

He also deliberately fashioned more marks than he needed to — and probably was paid for. For both Stiff and F-Beat, he bespoke an array of marks that suggest a restless imagination or an abhorrence of design doctrine. However, they were masterful components of the labels' brands and players in the larger identity game Bubbles was playing.

Scher is brief and self-effacing on the subject of logos: "I appreciated clever marks that had strong, simple, positive and negative shapes ... but was never capable of designing them." She states her preference for typography-based marks, such as the Manhattan Records logo. And

though she discusses her Tappan Zee Records identity, its logo is neither reproduced nor mentioned. If it was Scher's creation, it contradicts her evaluation of her facility with form.

If Bubbles has an iconic cover image, one that transcends its specific usage, it may be Elvis Costello's second album *This Years Model* (Radar, 1978). Costello's confrontational, table-turning stance became a symbol of the post-punk era, which preserved the provocation of punk while broadening its sonic palette.

At its core, the image is a direct conception of the record's title and its source songs, a contraction of "This Year's Girl," and the "she's last year's model" lyric from "(I Don't Want To Go To) Chelsea." Putting the artist on the cover is the no-brainer design strategy. Bubbles complicates the reading by extending Costello's aggressive, anti-rock star poses from *My Aim Is True*. The U.S. version goes all-in in defying expectation, with the artist largely obscured, crouched behind the camera, peering over it at the viewer.

Scher's most recognized cover is one she regards mordantly: the mega-selling eponymous first album of the group Boston (Epic, 1975). Its appearance in *Make It Bigger* has the flavor of a musician dutifully but reluctantly performing a throwaway track that became a novelty hit. Scher gamely relates the gestation of the Roger Huyssen cover painting, perplexed at its ultimate ascendance to iconic status.

Of both the music and sleeve, Scher is dismissive: "Musically *Boston* is not a great album. "More than a Feeling" is decidedly mediocre, and so is everything about the album package, but it struck a chord with sixteen year-old boys and their girlfriends in 1976."

Even were I not of that specific age group at the time, Scher's trivializing of an audience sounds snobbish. And commercially antagonistic. Aren't sixteen year old boys and their girlfriends deserving of attention? More importantly, isn't that a substantive chunk of the popular music market?

Scher is too savvy to not recognize "the strange chemistry and karma of hit music. Hits don't really have anything to do with qualitative decision-making or careful planning. Genius or originality don't guarantee hits; you

can't even rely on predictable, salable mediocrity. Hits are happenings in a particular period of time that manages to capture the imagination of a large but specific audience in a specific and personal way that defies all logical explanation."

The lesson to and frustration for the graphic designer is that you can replace "hits" with "great graphic design" and it's just as accurate.

For that 16 year old me (and now, actually), *Boston* was an amusing trifle that I felt warmth for because of its hometown origin. And though musically it was the antithesis of the punk and new wave I was bonding with, it was a scrappy anti-corporate move. The record was a basement-made, against-the-odds triumph of Tom Scholz, a moon-lighting Polaroid engineer. That is so rock and roll. The sleeve was silly but what do you want?

By all measures, Scher *nailed it* with *Boston* as she did with no other sleeve. Her account of the hushed awe that greets her introduction as its designer verifies its power. The sticking point is that in her greatest success as a cover designer, Scher was simply a facilitator of the client's "idiotic" idea. *And the client was right*. That is *not* supposed to happen. I can only imagine Scher thinking, *If only that blockbuster had my design instead of that "stupidity."*

Barney Bubbles, who mined kitsch without irony, would be at peace with such a notion. A fleet of city spaceships smashing planets would be another day at the office for the guy that illuminated his own zany *Space Ritua*l. He got it: "All it is is rock and roll and it's no big shakes." Rather than dropping the quality of sleeves with this attitude, he elevated it.

The Bubbles/Scher Venn diagram intersects at Elvis Costello. Two cross over artifacts show the designers' affinities and departures: the 1980 U.S. compilation album *Taking Liberties*, and a *Trust* promotion poster.

Taking Liberties was a compilation of tracks that hadn't seen release in the U.S.: either U.K. single A and B sides, or album tracks deemed "too British" by Columbia and removed or substituted. Its release came on the heels of *Get Happy!!* and sought to capitalize on the proliferating import market. In a clever reference, its title comes from a lyric on the included

song "Crawling to the U.S.A," which satires American cultural domination.

Compilations represented a rare opportunity for Scher: "Repackages were generally nonpolitical album covers," she writes in *Make it Bigger*, "antidotes" to the wrangling that occurs over new releases: bones thrown to persecuted designers.

Beyond her position as art director, it's unknown how involved Scher was with the design. The densely set Franklin Gothic text is a Scher hallmark, along with its unfussy layout. Rather than commission an illustration or craft a total departure, the covers seems a concerted attempt to relate to some of Costello's previous releases. A 1979 Brian Griffin photograph of Costello in L.A. (which also yielded images that adorned *Armed Forces* and its attendant *Live at Hollywood High* EP) wraps around to the back of the sleeve. The picture has been inverted so Costello reaches to the left to grasp the noodly line spelling out the title.

In upper left-hand corner of the cover, the artist's name is spelled out all caps in a super bold sans serif face. The scale of the type and its tri-coloration are nods toward prevalent new wave stylings. Overall, the sleeve is tasteful, functional, and ordinary.

The lone gesture to the conceptual play of Bubbles' sleeves is the disc label. Adapting a design from the 1920s, the word "Columbia" is replaced on one side with "Costello." Though Bubbles regularly invoked and evoked period design styles, the impact here is blunted by the age of the sample. It predates the musical eras Costello channels in his music. Later designs would have been both conceptually and graphically more representative and interesting.

But the genuine Bubblesian meta-move doesn't come from the designers or is part of the album package. For the print ads, the text "And the corporation logo is flashing on and off in the sky" is placed underneath the legal text at the bottom. The line is from "Night Rally," a song excised from *This Years Model* and included on *Taking Liberties*. Was someone in PR hip to Barney?

The more prominent and telling intersection is a poster for Costello's 1981 F-Beat album *Trust*. Scher features this work in her book, the result of successfully lobbying for oversized posters. It's an instance where *she*

wants to make it bigger.

Source material and time are scant for the project. The Brits only provide a "grim" Photostat of an image intended to be the "back cover" (it's actually the front). Scher remains incurious about the source of the image. No credit or attribution is provided. It's a still from a Bubbles-directed video for album track "New Lace Sleeves," with a closeup of Costello's head and shoulders. Head tipped downward, Costello stares up over his horn rims. For the album's cover, Bubbles cropped the image and placed a handwritten title in the upper right hand corner. It's the shadow of Costello's specs on his face that grabs Scher's attention.

To mask the poor quality of the image, she pumps up the scale and the hue saturation. Perhaps as an unconscious gesture to the (musical) New Wave style of acid bright colors (Scher avers she can't provide a specific rationale for the choice), she fills the lenses of Costello's glasses with solid hues of red and blue. The portrait is bracketed top and bottom with the text TRUST ELVIS in the manner of a campaign poster. "Costello on Columbia" sprouts from the musician's left ear. All type is in Scher's preferred call-back slab serifs with the ear-emergent text set akin to a broadside.

Scher's proof for the poster's success is its subsequent widespread in-house theft when delivered fresh off the press. The volume of larceny executed by record company employees could be considered a measure of validation (where's the diagram for that?) but is hardly authoritative.

And fetching high prices as a collectable is similarly problematic. If sticky-fingered Columbia cogs snapped up the majority, scarcity could be the driving force. These rationales also don't affirm of Scher's original argument for the oversized poster: that shops would clear space for such a product. Did they? Maybe none were left.

As a Costello fan at the time, I was aware of the poster and didn't care for it. It possessed none of the smart, feisty energy of the music or graphics of the U.K. releases. Its coloration seemed affected, a cynical designer's sop to New Wave fashion. The typography was incongruously "American" and "soft." It felt more suitable for label-mate Billy Joel.

Altogether, it made a dynamic performer bland and routine. Then

again, maybe my desire was sated because I possessed an *Armed Forces* promotion poster, gifted by the owner of my local record store.

I agree with Scher that the poster is "well designed." Considering the standards of her work, that's hardly a concession, more a recognition of the obvious. Today, it's desirable to me, but because of its provenance. The poster is the same but I've changed; it's acquired new meaning. But while I admire it, I don't love it like practically anything Bubbles might have done.

Reflexively, I try to attribute this to something in the design and not in me. As always, I blame Modernism. Its intellectual framework still suffuses our minds and insists everything resides in the object. But sometimes that object stars metropolis-bearing guitar spacecraft and everything goes haywire.

Looking into the designer only gets us so far and isn't definitive. Bubbles loved rock and roll, a capricious but potentially indulgent client. His designs aspired to rock and roll in form: resonant, indulgent, transgressive … and merchandise. Scher preferred jazz and other less commercial musics. The artists were less image-conscious and open to illustration. They got out of a designer's way. Rock was messy.

For Scher, sleeves were just another "everyday product" to bring a "higher level of æsthetics to." Bubbles also endeavored for the latter but the former would be a gross simplification. He had abandoned the everyday product to embrace, for him, a higher plane of product. Albums had a special meaning for him.

It's a truism that a designer's personal engagement with the subject can result in better design. Bubbles obviously was more invested in rock and roll than Scher. I can't track her personal taste at all from *Make It Bigger*. But any attribution of that as a deciding factor is belied by all of Scher's consummate work for a variety of other cultural clients. All seem to have as much of her attention as any other.

And while the music didn't mean as much to her as it did Bubbles who played in bands and issued his own album, album covers did. Intriguingly, Scher cites three successive Beatles albums — *Revolver*, *Sgt. Pepper*, *The Beatles* — as emblematizing all design: "Everything everyone

ever needed to know about graphic design was in those three album covers." As exquisite as her taste is, it's ironic that none are the work of a graphic designer.

Two are famously by contemporary British fine artists. Peter Blake and Jann Haworth for *Sgt. Pepper*, Richard Hamilton for "The White Album," and long-time band friend, artist and bass player Klaus Voorman illustrated the front cover of *Revolver*. None follow the deliberate design process Scher adheres to.

(Though "The White Album" arguably might to a degree. Hamilton's proposal for the stark white cover was in deliberate contrast to the florid psychedelic fashion of the day. A strategic design move displaying an awareness of the marketplace.)

Even if the concept/sketch/execution stages were followed, the decision to turn to fine artists and not graphic designers set them apart from the norm.

In his process and product, Bubbles seems closer to the spirit of these iconic sleeves. His works could be startling blends of unexpected imagery and eccentric interpretations of commercial imperatives. The variable covers of *My Aim Is True* and *Do It Yourself* were Bubbles own skewed updates of the editioned "White Album."

Scher's covers are textbook examples of contemporary professional graphic design process at its best. Every step is exacting and the result highly polished and fluent. In her employ of top illustrators and photographers, Scher's sleeves were like the many popular records they housed, featuring top session players recorded in the best studios. Results were consistent and flawless.

For some, this was something to rail at: "... all those other faceless LPs involving this floating crap game of technically impeccable hacks," spat Lester Bangs in 1975. This attitude provoked another music, and another design, that valued spirit over proficiency. Or, more accurately, fostered a different definition of skill.

Scher was, and remains, an exemplary practitioner of the established conception of design. Bubbles expanded that model in every direction.

They each served their clients well. And the audience? As John Lydon chanted, "This is what you want, this is what you get."

Despite abundant and exemplary work in the area, Scher isn't usually included in the roll call of major cover designers, not the way Bubbles is. The reason may be that it was a short prologue to a long and distinguished design career. She quit Columbia and seldom returned to the form.

Considering the wonders to come later, this stands a major what if. Sleeves designed by the creator of the Public Theatre posters or Ballet Tech would have been epic. However, reading Scher herself, they may not have been possible within the contexts she chose to work. Leaving album design apparently was required for Scher to fully realize her design vision.

Though Bubbles anticipated his departure from album design in his later years and expanding into new areas, it wasn't by choice. He expressed regret about being supplanted by younger practitioners. "They're so creative — the kids that do the sleeves — it makes me feel so staid and boring, and I think: I've got to get out, it's time for me to go."

This is another facet of attitude: Bubbles was reflecting his client industry, not his profession. Rock and roll was a young person's game. At 39, he was a dinosaur. This could only be exacerbated going through the crucible of punk and it's past-rejecting ethos. Only through ferocious talent had he escaped scorn for his hippy origins.

Bubbles' potential beyond record covers will be the most profound *what if*. On his own, the early death makes the heart ache for what was never realized. For me, Paula Scher's masterpieces come after the cover career, in a steady upward trajectory of achievement. Many can't be predicted from what came before, which is only testament to her talent. Bubbles, despite his apprehension, showed no sign of his talent slacking. Comparing Bubbles and Scher heightened my appreciation of both. And sharped my sense of loss. Damn you, bless you both.

Face three: Bubbles' pop

One chord is fine. Two chords are pushing it. Three chords and you're into jazz.
— Lou Reed

For Barney Bubbles, ersatz is as real as false gets.

Due to his myriad puzzles and conundrums, it's tempting to look for a skeleton key to Bubbles among his diverse productions. Is there a deciphering work? There are masterpieces such as *Armed Forces* that showcase most aspects of his design imagination. And for that sleeve, he even placed a self-portrait inside center.

The written record is slim where he speaks directly about his work. And when questioned, he manages to be simultaneously forthcoming and evasive. Most artists profess to speak through their work and Bubbles labored to leave us little else.

However, we have a vinyl record to listen to. The best candidate for the definitive Barney Bubbles work would seem to be his own and lone album *Ersatz*, released in 1982 under the moniker The Imperial Pompadours. Issued on an F-Beat one-offshoot imprint also called Pompadour Records, *Ersatz* inverted a concession made to select performers.

Labels frequently pander to their superstars by allowing them to create their own cover designs, regardless of their objective skill at design or illustration. (*You* tell Bob Dylan how ghastly that painting is, Mr. A&R Man.) Flipping the script enters the realm of the commercial unnatural for a major label.

Such eccentricities were a regular feature of Bubbles' chief champion and sponsor, Jake Riviera. Issuing an album by the label's primary sleeve designer, even pseudonymously, is a prototypical perverse move. For instance, in 1980, Stiff Records issued the one-off joke album *The Wit and Wisdom of Ronald Reagan*. A shadow release attributed to Magic Records ("If it's a success it must be Magic!"), the LP sported grooved but silent tracks.

Bubbles' record should be filed with the 1982 promotion-only F-Beat LP, *The Art of Roger Bechirian, Vol. 1*. That album was a compendium of songs shepherded to disc by the ubiquitous engineer/producer (there was no volume two). It also featured an Alex Steinweiss homage sleeve design by Bubbles.

In his introduction to *Reasons to be Cheerful*, Billy Bragg says how Barney Bubbles seemed like another member of the band. However, as

simpatico and necessary as Bubbles may have been to those musicians, he was never regularly afforded such credit. Still, non-instrumentalists occasionally received equal billing alongside players. Bernie Taupin got props from Elton John and Procol Harum's Keith Reid was listed as band member.

Bubbles' circumstance has similarity with another non-performing figure, Peter Sinfield. For his "words and illumination" — lyrics and stage lighting — Sinfield was accorded full member status beginning on King Crimson's 1969 premier album *In the Court of the Crimson King* (E.G.) (which, coincidentally, music critic Robert Christgau dubbed "ersatz shit.")

As that group dissolved and reconfigured over their first four LPs, his role expanded to co-producer and noodling with a synthesizer off stage. When Sinfield was ultimately on the outs, he released his one and only album *Still* in 1973, on Emerson, Lake and Palmer's Manticore label. Lake was another original member of King Crimson, and the record had contributions from other former and current personnel.

Bubbles' closest and longest relationship with a band and its off-shoots was with Hawkwind. Influential as he was, the group never included Bubbles in their ranks. He is only one of six names listed on the sleeve of *X in Search of Space* under "optics/semantics," which echoes Sinfield's acknowledgement. Though arguably more distant from the action than Sinfield, Bubbles' band buds supported his own venture into recording.

Ersatz is a concept album, though not in the usual rock music sense. There isn't an ostensible narrative running through and connecting the separate songs. Instead, *Ersatz* manifests themes of eccentricity, obsession and substitution graphically and sonically. Layered on top is a fixation on World War II, an experience that though not lived, permeated the consciousness of Britons of Bubbles' (born in 1942) generation.

"Ersatz" is a German term meaning "substitute." Inherent in the word is the suggestion of wartime products. In the face of deprivation or scarcity, alternatives were fashioned. Coffee is brewed out of roasted acorns, tea from catnip. The connotation is of inferiority: bad goods.

Apropos for a sleeve designer, *Ersatz* is an album primarily of "covers," songs first performed by others. In a way, the album is, in its construction, a précis of Bubbles' music-related career. With 13 tracks, the first side

echoes the punk/post-punk style, which specialized in large groups of snappy, short songs.

Recent precedent existed from 1978 with Wire's 21-track debut *Pink Flag* (Harvest) or the 1980 Bubbles-designed *Get Happy!!* which sported 20 total tracks, ten to a side. The *Ersatz* verso presents a single, side-spanning track, reminiscent of a extended Hawkwind space epic.

The album's first side of cover tunes fulfills the replacement aspect of the title, declaring its own product to be a poor alternative. The songs are misfits to begin with, culled from the fringes of rock and roll's early days. They're affectionate piss-takes on novelties that were fairly alimentary to begin with.

Provenance isn't a concern: three of the tracks are credited to "(Unknown)." The most notable of the songs are still obscurities, known for being re-recorded by prominent bands. "Brand New Cadillac," appeared three years earlier on The Clash's third LP *London Calling* (CBS). In 1981, the Cars demo-ed a version of The Nightcrawlers' 1967 minor U.S. hit "Little Black Egg."

Among other topics, tunes extoll standard rock and roll subjects like Chinese food ("Moo Goo Gai Pan") and mustaches ("Fu Manchu"), space probes ("I Took a Trip on a Gemini Spacecraft"), psychedelic drugs ("I Want to Come Back from the World of LSD"), and ... fungus ("There's a Fungus Among Us"). Many of the originating bands hail from the States, home of millions of garages and attendant rock aspirants. Though numbered as discreet tracks, the songs blend and bleed into each other.

Bubbles wasn't coy about his intentions with the record. According to Paul Gorman, he declared to a friend that the music was "inspired rubbish, loud and in extremely bad taste." There's plenty of operative bands that flaunt that attitude, but anyone hoping for an anglo-Cramps is setting their expectations far too high. Bubbles scribbled out some rough outlines and let his collaborators fill them in. A full-fledged framework would be too confining. Lurching outside the sketchy borders was encouraged.

Though steeped in his humor, *Ersatz* isn't a novelty album, as it contains performed and/or assembled compositions. While the performances and "arrangements" fall decidedly on the anarchistic end of the scale, it

isn't due to a lack of ability on the performers' part. Bubbles deliberately mixed sawdust into his musical bread.

The record was assembled from sessions Bubbles had occasionally directed and participated in with sympathetic musicians, primarily Inner City Unit, ex-Hawkwind saxophonist Nik Turner's band. The performers' proficiency, however, was deliberately hampered by Bubbles' method. Musicians were given lyric sheets and a single listen to a tape of the songs they were to play.

Bubbles also performed for the record and was a competent musician in his own right. Recalling their mutual Twickenham College of Technology days, former Small Faces keyboardist Ian McLagan said Bubbles "was a huge fan of Big Bill Broonzy and could play pretty good gut-string guitar in that folk blues style."

The first side of *Ersatz* features songs with basic guitar/bass/drums rock accompaniment on each track with coloring provided by sax, piano, and organ. Performances are sloppy, by turns hung loose or studiously exaggerated. Every instrument will occasionally stray from regular order, becoming assertive or wandering off on its own. Drums follow a steady rock or tribal beat. The bass keeps to its lane, usually in sync. Vocals are spoken, shouted or comically-voiced.

Sometimes the vocals and instruments will be adorned with echo, evoking 50s era rock and horror movies. Inserted among the clamor are ersatz instruments: shattering glass, power tools, and bashing on a tractor-trailer. Crude sampling also plays a role, with fragments of Wagner spliced into the raucous second side.

Though Bubbles plangently proclaimed a trashy æsthetic, some other purpose seems at work with the willful amateurism and noise-mongering. An antecedent may be the Portsmouth Sinfonia, a British classical music ensemble that spanned the 1970s. It welcomed any comers, combining the trained, though on unfamiliar instruments, with rank amateurs. Though their performances were cause for hilarity, the intent wasn't humor or to mock the music. Participants were directed to perform to the best of their abilities.

Founded by experimental composer Gavin Bryars, the orchestra

was a high concept take on music and mastery. Fittingly, the famously untrained Brian Eno joined the ensemble on clarinet, produced their first two albums, and featured them on his *Taking Tiger Mountain (By Strategy)* (E.G.) track "Put a Straw Under Baby." Along with his avowed autodidaction in music, Eno often imposed physical and conceptual constraints on studio musicians that interrupted their prowess. His Oblique Strategies were employed in service of fresh attitudes toward music, to foster novelty and sass.

Bubbles' concept was lower but conveys a deconstructive reverence for the genre. He designed for and identified with the punk and new wavers. Overall, Bubbles had empathy with the misfits, his attitude being (according to Jake Riviera, speaking of Barney's work for Johnny Moped), "Bring me your dented and out of shape." Moped and his ilk represented a return to rock and roll's rough and ready Teddy pre-Beatles roots. Fervor and fun were critical components; mæstros could fuck off. It was deadly serious ("We mean it maaaan!") and flippant ("And we don't care!") all in the same band.

It could be that Bubbles decided to take this sensibility to its illogical conclusions. He's showing the youngsters how it's done. Or just getting in on the fun. Where early rock and roll was rudimentary by nascence, stripping songs down to their bones was a widespread new wave stratagem.

A frequent aspect of punk and post-punk covers of classics hits was toying with tempos. Rhythms were regularly sped up to a breakneck pace, slowed to a plod, or tooled to a robotic pulse. In increasing melodicism, there's Devo's version of the Rolling Stones' "(I Can't Get No) Satisfaction," (Bubbles designed the Stiff EP containing the song), Magazine's refrigerated Sly Stone "Thank You (Fallentin Me Be Mice Elf Agin)," and the Eno-directed Talking Heads slow burn version of Al Green's "Take Me to the River." The songs were veneration and negation in stereo, revealing the artifice of music as pop product and prayer.

Bubbles slightly extended the axis of anti-mastery that punk reanimated, nearer to the desired absurdity. To elude any semblance of commercial viability, he would have to drop below new, lessened standards. In 1979, David Cunningham's DIY project The Flying Lizards had

scored hits with their tinker-toy takes on "Summertime Blues" and "Money (That's What I Want)." *Ersatz* resembles a rough, joking demo of either, or the product of a poor mix.

In looking for antecedents to Bubbles' endeavor, a possible influence or confluence may be with an American group with lower-fi, hippier, and deeper roots. That connection combines *Ersatz*'s two sides and engages the records' covers.

Side two of Bubbles' record is comprised entirely of the audio collage "Insolence Across the Nation," and credited to Imperial Pompadours. Like its first side songs, "Insolence" is sparse; at its busiest it will have competing stereo separated voices over music and sound effects. The effort is less "Revolution 9" than a recording of an absurdist drama.

Bubbles friend and *Ersatz* performer Nik Turner explained to Paul Gorman that "Barney said he wanted to do something about the life of Hitler ... I selected quotations from *Mein Kampf*, Mad King Ludwig and Wagner and also from the women in all their lives, and then recorded random visitors to my flat reciting them."

With its Wagnerian bluster and Fuehrer proclamations, "Insolence" abandons all subtlety, abjuring metaphor for blunt force audio trauma. To quote occasional client Dave Edmonds, it's as subtle as a flying mallet. The sleeve listing for the track indicates it was "recorded LIVE at Krankschäft Kabaret." Krankschäft was a name subsequently used by a backing band for sometimes Hawkwind singer and lyricist and *Ersatz* vocalist Robert Calvert.

The side fades in on a distant jazzy saxophone-led instrumental that dips under narration. The first voice suggests a fairy or folk tale is about the start. The *Mein Kampf* quotations kick in around the 10-minute mark, arriving with a jolt and growing increasingly vile. Speakers frequently adopt pompous or cartoonish villainous tones, often undercut by sniggering and snide responses. After a crescendo, the Wagner slowly fades out as the track began.

Invoking Nazi Germany in a rock and roll context was neither unique or original with *Ersatz*. Nor was presenting fractured takes on pop songs. San Francisco-based avant-gardists The Residents went there years

earlier with their 1976 second album *The Third Reich 'n Roll* (Ralph). That LP mashed together skewed versions of singles and commercials over two side-long pastiches called "Swastikas on Parade" and "Hitler was a Vegetarian."

Third Reich is entirely comprised of merged mutant versions of 60's and 70's popular music (rock, funk, soul, folk) ranging from Count Five's "Psychotic Reaction" to America's "Horse with No Name." While the former is more in line with Bubbles' obscure tastes, the majority of the 29 songs are classic Top 40 hits, though frequently unrecognizable. Songs can overlap completely, or have components interjected into others. Where Bubbles listed the individual tracks, on its release The Residents left listeners to discern what ingredients made up their sonic stew.

Ersatz and *The Third Reich 'n Roll* are twinned inversions of each other on the Nazi aspect. Bubbles loudly places his Hitler content only in the tracks. His sleeve gives no indication of what's to come. Meanwhile, The Residents' grooves are devoid of any such references. But the album title and cover imagery prominently invoke the Nazi past. Swastikas abound on the cover, which features a Hitlerized Dick (*American Bandstand*) Clark.

Commercialization is a career-long subject for The Residents and pop music is a target rich environment for satire. But invoking Nazis blows away any nuance, resulting in camp. Bubbles is as unfocused conceptually with an offering that aspires to be "something about the life of Hitler." "Insolence" easily clears that low hurdle. It's an open question if it's anything more.

These were the early Margaret Thatcher years, which galvanized many musical protests. The right wing prime minister's nationalist, capitalist triumphalism outraged progressives of all stripes. Comparisons to Nazism and fascist states flowed freely. She was supported enough to serve eleven years as PM, and widely reviled. Either side could be tarred as insolent in their stance.

The parallels between the two albums suggest an awareness. Bubbles travelled to San Francisco in 1978, but there's no record he had any exposure there or subsequently to the Residents. But their arch humor seems just his style.

Bubbles could also be tweaking the fashion choices of certain musicians of the day. Some punk and post-punk acts flirted with Nazi symbols and imagery in ways that weren't apparently ironic or condemnatory. The Sex Pistols wrote "Belsen Was a Gas" — performed last at their final show in San Francisco. Naïveté and cheap outrage were criticisms leveled at musicians wrapping themselves in Nazi iconography. Bubbles could be making a blunt retort and providing a schooling in the actuality.

While disconcerting acoustically and in subject matter, "Insolence" is only half the record. Graphically, Bubbles emphasizes the album's wider sensibility of evoking the past. The sleeve design has a rough equivalence to the music. Both are unstable and convention-challenging.

But on the surface, music and design are opposed — another Bubbles contradiction. The package is simple, direct, restrained: a conventionally professional product. Variances are conceptual and considered.

An unruly, David Carson-like expression would be a reasonable expectation for the formal representation of the rowdy *Ersatz* content. Capability or appreciation for such a manifestation isn't an issue. Bubbles' portfolio amply demonstrates he could successfully adopt an anarchic, immediate styling if desired. The entire folding outer wrapper of his masterpiece *Armed Forces* is a study of coordinated commotion.

A major difference is that Bubbles is solely responsible for the graphic performance. In the design studio, he was an off-the-cuff genius. He excelled under the tightest deadlines and budgets, crappy quarters, and reduced means. Barney made great design out of literal garbage. On their own, the sound studio games, if transferred wouldn't bring the same crude result. Graphic dissonance in the *Ersatz* sleeve had to be subtler.

What aren't distinct, planned Bubbles quirks are ambiguous, attributable to pragmatic economic decisions or stylistic twists. For instance, though a full-fledged 33 RPM album, Bubbles housed the disc in a flat sleeve meant for 12-inch singles. This confuses expectation of what the nature of the record is.

In keeping with its throwback rock and roll, the package design is back to basics. Absent are extravagances such as die cutting for *X in Search of Space* or *Armed Forces*, photography, or even color. The only printing ink

employed is black, with selective screening to produce a grey tone. Just as might be seen on albums pre-*Sgt. Pepper* era LPs, the front cover featuring an image and the reverse consisting entirely of text: the track titles and credits.

Characteristically, Barney puts his portrait on *other* people's records, not his. According to Paul Gorman, the cover illustration is a freakish "Elvis Presley in the woodcut style of Flemish expressionist artist Frans Masereel." The brushed ink and cut-paper King sports an enormously elevated coif that bleeds off the top of the sleeve. The pompadour reinforces the throwback aspect, amplifying a 1950's era hairstyle.

Bubbles turned to this particular manner of illustration for a number of albums during this time, notably for a portrait of Billy Bragg and for his *Brewing Up with Billy Bragg* (Go! Discs) and for Inner City Unit's *Punkadelic* (Flicknife). A full-color example can be found with the flautist figure on *Imperial Bedroom* (F-Beat).

The album title is placed contra-commercially in the lower left-hand corner, as if spoken by the Elvis figure. Its playful setting is a frequent flourish from Bubbles' benign typographic trick bag. The "ER" is dropped out of "IMPERIAL" to complete "ERSATZ." It also forms by subtraction "The IMP" — a little devil. (Jake Riviera and Elvis Costello's post-F-Beat label was named Demon Records.) All text is reversed out, save for "SATZ," which is screened to grey. "IMPERIAL" and "ERSATZ" are capitalized. Is Bubbles announcing he's (the) Mock King?

"PLAY IT LOUD YOU TURKEYNECKS" dominates the back cover in large caps, filling roughly ⅔ of the vertical space (the cover figure definitely fits the description in its neck). The words are lifted from the album's kick off track, "The Crusher." "LOUD" is the sole text screened grey and placed behind the black text. Each letter earns its own underline to doubly emphasize the command. Minimal legal text (catalog number, label, artist name and album title) run down the upper right edge of this text.

All the text set on the back-cover text is force justified and styled contemporarily, rendered more expressively than the practical layouts of the 50's and 60's. That expressiveness manifests solely in scale and capitalization. The track listing runs the all caps titles together in a force-justified

block. The face is a Grotesque, similar is style to that found on the reverse of early Beatles albums (though not exclusively theirs).

The lone graphic is one of Bubbles' custom sigils: a stylized screw penetrating a thick black horizontal rule emblazoned with "ROCKDRILL". The "D" of this word is on the screw's point. This graphic appears anthropomorphized (as with "Timmy the Talking Toolbox" on the cover of Ian Dury's *Do It Yourself*) with a "face": opposed mirror-image open single quotes over a square/period "mouth." The trio can also read as "ego."

It's in the track listing that Bubbles visually echoes the music's instability. He does this primarily blundering around with titles across the package. The names of songs vary between sleeve and label, sometimes abridged, sometimes not, to no discernable reason. It may just be in service of typefitting, always a challenge with justified settings.

"Fu Manchu" on the cover is "Don't Fool with Fu Manchu" on the label, "I Want to Come Back from the World of LSD" is abbreviated to "I Want to Come Back from LSD." Other titles differ in tense: on the sleeve "There's a Fungus Among Us," on the label the fungus has moved on. And some are combos: "Gemini Spacecraft" expands to "I Took a Trip on a Gemini Space*ship*." (And rhymes!)

Apart from the dropped title text, Bubbles indulges in minimal type trickery, mostly in point sizes and capitalization. He does horizontally flip the "K" concluding "Back" in "I Want to Come Back from LSD." While often fanciful, Bubbles' typography was always judiciously deployed, never overpowering layouts.

As with the music, why be a stickler? Scratch out a clumsy guitar solo, scribble down titles on scrap paper. On the radio or in concert, they don't always announce the song titles, or mess them up. Who cares? What matters is how they *sound*, bro. Which is better after a few brews, honestly. These guys might consider rehearsing sometimes before hitting the stage. So "Light Show" (a wink about his alias and early career?) and that LSD song are flipped on the cover. It's straightened out on the label. Are you hear to rock or proofread?

The package comes with a plain inner sleeve but includes a bespoke record label extending the cover design theme. Labels have black text on

a solid white background. The face used throughout is an all caps bold condensed Univers, a regular BB choice for this usage. It's also used for a simple wordmark that features one of his shared character type treatments that forms "POMPADOURECORDS."

Screened to grey behind this vertically-reading text is another illustrated figure. This line drawn creature is what? A monkey? One song is "See You Soon Baboon." Or maybe a lizard? It boasts a curled tail and wears another wacky 'do. The simianewt is open-mouthed as if singing or shouting, arms raised with pointed index fingers as if dancing or proclaiming. It looks askance at us with a solid black pupil.

The design of *Ersatz* is a characteristically self-effacing gesture for Barney Bubbles. His name and his voice isn't on it. In what may be a nod to his musical co-conspirators, the package has similitude with Inner City Unit's first LP, *Passout* (Riddle Records, 1980). Rather than devise a grandiose or unique cover, it fits in with his overall direction in sleeve design at the time. He didn't place himself above or apart from his clients.

Bubbles' training was Modernist and he was an articulate student of design history. The total designer spread his sensibility into all creative forms. With *Ersatz*, Bubbles could now claim music with art, design, furniture, and video. A record was inevitable.

Across all his work, in all media, is the elevation of the mundane, a collapsing of low and high cultures, historical forms reimagined and re-contextualized, the integration of found materials, humor, adventure ... and games. He worked fast, made do, and reveled in and revealed with it. Accident was embraced and incorporated. Tangents were followed. Answers and identity withheld.

Ersatz isn't the key or the masterpiece but a synopsis of Bubbles' design, the order and the anarchy. In the end, listening to *Ersatz* isn't as satisfying or elevating as experiencing his other media, especially the design. After many listenings, it's growing on me, slowly revealing not secrets but the consistent question of his work.

Is this a real record? Isn't it just a one-off vanity project, a goof, for patrons that specialized in these kinds of things? Real in art usually means *more*. Is that a real measure of something's truth? That you're able to

repeat yourself? (What about say something once, why say it again?)

We'll never know if there was an intended follow up. Are there more songs in the can? It's not like your typical band's first release, and *Ersatz* contains all the best songs from their stage repertoire.

Everything about the record says one and done. *Ersatz* may exist just to exist. To be a real record, it had to have sounds on it, so Barney made some, having the most fun he could. It's the purest expression of his work as there was zero pressure to make a hit. Don't care for it? Hey, the record's title announces there's better elsewhere.

Barney Bubbles' work always seems to prompt the question, is he (for) real? The fucked-up quality of this record begs cult status: a feature for him, not a bug. The anonymity and pseudonyms, though, undermines his career. Does he really exist? And the graphic games, puzzles, secret meanings, variations. All commercial poison.

Bubbles never resolves the essential conflict of making a living doing something you love. There's a real romanticism to this willful contrariness and obscurity, in the work and the person. He just can't help himself. Bubbles should have been famous and may get there yet. But alive, he was having none of it. Only he could make an anti-vanity project.

Ersatz is real, it just isn't *right*. *Ersatz* is both. So, if you're in the market for Barney Bubbles, dis-order now! Ask for him by names. Accept all substitutes.

> No one I know, including myself, has listened to it all the way through. It is not meant to be.
> — Lou Reed, original liner notes to *Metal Machine Music (The Amine βRing)* (RCA, 1975)

Face four: BB King!

If Barney Bubbles was punctuation, he'd be an interrobang. He seemed incapable of the straightforward, singular expression. Everything divulged layers. His work and practice were a gestalt of contradictions and oppositions. Unpacked, it opened like a graphic Big Bang. Even a personal scribble from Bubbles exhibits minutiæ that provoke a close reading. Why would it be any different from the rest of his œuvre ?

In his forward for Paul Gorman's *Reasons to Be Cheerful*, designer Malcolm Garrett describes a message left for him by Bubbles, which included a rare self-portrait. "I SEE A VISION," it read, "I SEE A 'MODERN' WORLD." The text precedes then trails after the sketchy figure, crossing at chest level. It ducks under the upraised left arm, floating over the extended right. Even for a handwritten note, there's typographic play: "WORLD" bends slightly, distinct from the rest of the text, the W hovering sideways above the O. "I SEE" repeats. Is it a stutter? Change of mind mid-thought?

The Bubbles caricature is moving away from the viewer, arms spread wide, fingers splayed. He might be maintaining balance as he confidently strides, left foot forward, right angled back, across an invisible tightrope or baseline. He could also be closing in to embrace someone off stage. Or be strutting. Or dancing.

There's his signature *schnoz*, punctuated with a triangle and circle to form (according to Garrett) "Bauhaus nostrils." Bubbles may not be *seeing* a "modern" world but smelling it, and savoring the bouquet. His mouth is described with pointed, puckered lips that betray no particular emotion or action. He could be silent, speaking, or singing.

The character is dressed in a geometric shirt or sweater, adorned with Charlie Brown-like zig zags at the elbows. Double-lined angles meet in the center of his back. Below, a curve of buttock is described to suggest snug-fitting trousers. Though likely dashed off, he still captures the detail of fabric bunched behind the bent right kneecap.

Bubbles deftly crafted an irreverent and expressive image of himself. Certain details stand out for their incongruency, complicating the reading. Springing from the top of his head, there's what appears to be an unruly tuft of hair. He neglects to differentiate a shoe for the figure's right foot as he does for the left.

With Bubbles, the game is always afoot, so intention and accident vie for cause. Usually, defects are revealed as effects. Bubbles' work wasn't so much *designed* as *plotted*, like a novel. The larger the seeming flaw, the more purposeful he was: the "misprinting" of the *This Years Model* sleeve or the built in the scuff marks on *Get Happy!!*

Constantly manipulating aspects of identity, his penned persona is

leading a double life. That spiky skull sprout isn't just a coif, it's a gimcrack crown. And that undivided ankle shows him to be wearing a costume, that of a jester. Yet again, Barney Bubbles has purposefully blended high and low, this time with him in the starring role. He's his subject and Lord. The Fool King, or King Fool.

I see a "design" world conjured and ruled by Bubbles, the jester sovereign. He needed to create so prolifically, compulsively, in order to people that world. Its inhabitants were anthropomorphized combs, matches, handprints, paint splatters, typography, geometry, studio detritus.

He was a rare designer whose entire output deserves delectation and preservation. Every ad, every sigil, every sleeve, every sticker. Gorman's monograph is a worthy document but doesn't map the entirety of Bubbles' domain.

He relentlessly churned out design artifacts: album packages, single bags, ads, buttons, stickers, posters, programs, and occasional books. Alongside these he crafted inventive videos, furniture, paintings, collages, sculpture. It was more than being prolific out of necessity, pushed by the breakneck pace of his primary clients. Its politics were a tad on the anarchistic side, though virulently antifascist.

Some designs were part of a wider system. A single sleeve might continue the layout aspects of the album it was drawn from, e.g. the single bag for "(I Don't Want to Go to) Chelsea" and *This Years Model* . But this was an exception in Bubbles' work. He seemed to regard it as slothful to extend an identity into other artifacts.

And within his album packages, there regularly were inner sleeves, bespoke labels (which could vary in design from one side to the other), postcards, posters, stickers. Many albums sported unique logos, or had the many variations for Stiff and F-Beat. Bubbles also had his hand in illustrations and lettering, frequently wielding brush or stamp kit to create text. He should have been paid by the piece.

Bubbles production of countless supplementary, extraneous material was a hallmark of his profligacy. Within them, he didn't simply rehash ideas, he developed themes across projects and media. Some sleeves contained more than one.

There was uncanny portrait Barney (*Cycledelic*, *This Years Model*, all Nick Lowe albums, *The Future Now*). Painterly Barney (which includes most early works, *Seconds of Pleasure*, *Imperial Bedroom*, *Compass Point*); domestic kitsch Barney (*Armed Forces* front cover, *Do It Yourself*, *Mad About the Wrong Boy*). Surreal saga Barney (*25 Years On*, *B Stiff*, *Frogs, Sprouts, Clogs and Krauts*, *Speak and Spell*). Quotable Barney (*Almost Blue*, *Life's a Riot with Spy vs. Spy*). Music vernacular Barney (*Get Happy!!*, *A Case of the Shakes*, *Music on Both Sides*). Meta Barney (*This Years Model*, *Do It Yourself*). Broadening out to his overall logo designs, one theme emerges, so much so that his logo work might best be described as regalia.

In his last years, Bubbles' design for music increasingly referred back to the pre-1960s era of small, independent record labels catering to jazz, blues, R&B, and early rock and roll. It was a time when myriad upstart companies opened all over the U.S. that catered to local artists deemed problematic by the majors. (England's smaller market was dominated more by their indigenous majors and so didn't see the same flowering of labels until the punk/new wave era).

Bubbles' designs mimicked the visual accents of these labels with often geometry-based graphics featuring demonstrative type in keeping with overall commercial packaging. Only occasionally did Bubbles pointedly quote a well-known indie source. Typographically mirroring the album *Midnight Blue* by Kenny Burrell (1963) on the famed independent jazz label Blue Note for Elvis Costello and the Attractions' *Almost Blue* (1981) was Bubbles indulging in a double graphic pun. (A more slavish imitation was issued a few years later with Joe Jackson's *Body and Soul* (1984) paying homage to 1957's *Sonny Rollins, Vol. 2*.) Reid Miles' expressive typography was a regular go-to template for numerous other sleeve designs.

Looking to the U.S. for popular music inspiration was an established sightline. Emerging from skiffle, British rock and roll owes its existence to American expressions. Even groups such as Fairport Convention, which drew from and electrified British folk songs, were inspired by the Byrds.

The dominant, declared evocation for British bands was blues and R&B. Groups like the Beatles and the Rolling Stones celebrated African-American artists (literally) ghettoized in the U.S. In their native country,

these performers could only be found on small labels often named Regal, Imperial, Duke and King. Chess Records (originally called Aristocrat), contained all of the nobility. A major among the minors, its roster included Chuck Berry, Bo Diddley, Howlin' Wolf and Muddy Waters. It was, of course, named after its founding brothers.

The U.S. embraced the symbolism of royalty to ennoble its musicians. Representational democracy is all that but being the *President* of Rock 'n' Roll doesn't confer much glory. Maybe a Sinatra can carry "Chairman of the Board" and make it work. *Senator* of the Blues? Please. Elvis was the King. Aretha Franklin the Queen of Soul. And so on to Prince.

In a small irony, when Stiff Records released *Mil Gracias A Todos Nuestros Amigos* by Tex-Mex master Joe "King" Carrasco and the Crowns (1980), it didn't come in a Bubbles sleeve, but was outsourced to Chris "C-More-Tone" Morton.

As Bubbles overall turned to referencing historic music graphics, regalia surfaced as a theme in his logo work. Alongside toggling between a couple of typography-based logos for F-Beat, Bubbles established a three-pointed crown as the sole object-based mark. Perversely, he didn't use it for the aptly-named *Imperial Bedroom* (1982) (or *IbMePdErRoloAmL*, as Bubbles would set it), his last produced sleeve design for Costello. This was likely due to the crown's appearance as logo on *Trust* (1980), two albums previously. By the time Costello got to *King of America*, Bubbles had abdicated from life.

Bubbles introduced a new theme with *Get Happy!!* It was inhabiting album design's past. Elvis Costello's 1980 release marked his definitive break from a "brittle" new wave sound to adopting an overt soul and R&B template. Bubbles echoed this in his throwback design which fused day-glo new wave colors with a high contrast Reid Miles type vibe. Bubbles physically reinforces the retro move with partial lamination and the faux scuff marks on the F-Beat version.

(Another dated reference is my suspicion that the sleeve may be a sham 3D image. According to Tom Pogson, his cover painting for *Armed Forces* was intended to be 3D. The idea may have slipped one release. The possibility is raised by the curious hues of the intersecting parallelograms

on front and back. Also, the mysterious "bug" placed in the top corners front and back of the sleeve has a prominent "3" in its center, overlapping three sets of hypnotic concentric circles. The shape at the base of the "3" resembles a cap "D" with a pointed tail. A test viewing with 3D glasses was unsatisfying.)

Bubbles was as versed and discerning about the history of album graphics as he was in art. In addition to Reid Miles, Bubbles channeled record design pioneer Alex Steinweiss. Mostly, he evinced the music graphics "vernacular" (scare quotes used as they were performed by trained but usually uncredited professionals) prior to the 1960s, when his deliberate anonymity was the professional standard.

This theme didn't dominate and was applied to other releases that invoked rock and country roots music. It generated a studied timelessness in Bubbles' sleeve work, different in nature with his other pastiche motifs. Evoking fine art and album graphics dislocated Bubbles' work from its specific date of manufacture.

The generalized reference to past album graphic styles replaced the overt quoting of high art sources. This is most evident in the transition from *Armed Forces* (actually, an amalgam of *all* of Bubbles' themes) to *Get Happy!!*

Overall, with the entirety of his work, Bubbles was composing his own undeclared visual *Lipstick Traces*, drawing connections as author Greil Marcus did between music, art and design across history. The resulting diagram was like a spirographed circle. Bubbles wasn't at the center, he was throughout.

That this theme came late and last in Bubbles' career gives it a special poignancy, though there's no evidence it held any for him. As noted, it was likely a pragmatic conceptual move, reinforcing and resonating with what was placed in the grooves. It was self-referential but reflexivity wasn't new for Bubbles. It was upon returning to sleeve design at Stiff that a self-consciousness entered his work. The process of design and its artificiality became a constant, overarching subject.

His self-consciousness also manifested in questioning his relevance as a sleeve designer. As early as 1981, in his lone printed interview, he

lamented being "staid and boring." "I've got to get out," he said, "It's time for me to go." Two years after the publication of that interview, Bubbles went.

I see a vision of a "post-modern" world where Barney Bubbles stuck it out longer. Maybe he'd still be with us even now, 76 years old, frail or hale. Following two designers he inspired, Peter Saville and Malcolm Garrett, he would have moved beyond full time sleeve design, and into other media.

But, like Saville with New Order, Bubbles would continue designing for musicians with who he had a special relationship. Hawkwind, naturally. He and Elvis Costello would get past the *Punch the Clock* rejection and continue their fruitful collaboration. Nick Lowe and Billy Bragg would also remain patrons. For them, Bubbles would even take on CD packaging, though he was indifferent to the format.

As his contemporaries Hipgnosis did, Bubbles would concentrate on video, overcoming his trepidation with the inability to manually edit and manipulate the medium. MTV and adventurous ad agencies provided him with a sufficient stream of clients seeking something surprising and cost effective.

He was even able to branch out into documentaries and features, appreciated for his eccentric but affectionate take on British culture, politics, and domestic decor. It amused him to be shown on the BBC, because now it was where you see BB. He was still cagy about his name, dubbing his production company Phulcher Philms.

He converted his *Elephant Dollars* film script ("a short film featuring rock'n'roll, but incorporating a love of trash movies, pulp sci-fi, bad true romance and the dumbest of humor. Its æsthetic is cheapness, surface flash and hipness") into a series that gained respectable notices, particularly when aired on the American PBS network.

Vinyl came back, after a fashion. Bubbles returned to album art to joyfully launch into designing a round of commemorative box sets resplendent with new artwork and lavish companion books. There were no design credits.

Eye magazine still published Julia Thrift's "In Search of Barney Bubbles" article in 1992. However, it came with a different slant and

ending. The designer was agreeable to being interviewed about his "sordid past" but remained evasive and dismissive about his work. "BB is King of the Bargain Bin!" he proclaimed.

Eventually, there was a documentary on Barney Bubbles, from a Phulcher Philms protege. Rumor was that Bubbles actually directed it himself. Though photos were shown of the young Barney, the filmmakers substituted other, associated figures speaking Bubbles' interview lines. These bogus Barneys were either silhouetted, sporting obviously fake noses, or were friendly stand-ins with prominent proboscises, like Billy Bragg and Pete Townshend. (To make up for the aborted *Who Are You* commission, the band hired Bubbles to package one of their myriad rarity collections.) Each received a caption identifying them by a Bubbles pseudonym.

The biopic's last scene featured Elvis Costello (identified on screen as "Declan McManus *et al.*") casually handling a copy of *My Aim Is True* as he relates the story of Bubbles directing him through the cover photo shoot. Hanging on the wall behind Costello is the canvas of *Snakecharmer & Reclining Octopus*, the "Sal Forlenza" painting used as the cover of *Imperial Bedroom*.

Concluding the tale, Costello stops speaking for a moment to actually focus on the album cover. "Barney did all these letters individually, you know," he then says, "the ones spelling out 'Elvis is King.' He may have spent more time on that than I spent on the music!" A beat. "That was Barney. *He* was King."

The picture suddenly jumps, as if the film has leapt from its sprocket holes. In faulty magic marker, a scrawled word is then jerkily inserted into the frame: *Fin*.

This essay draws details and quotes about Bubbles' life and work from Paul Gorman's book Reasons To Be Cheerful: The Life and Work of Barney Bubbles *(Adelita, 2010).*

The graphic designer and her presence

It's Jacqueline Casey's world, we're just living in a reflection of it.

In the early 1990s, before ever envisioning a career in design, I spent months facing a framed copy of Jacqueline Casey's 1985 poster *Russia, USA Peace*. It hung opposite my desk in the Massachusetts College of Art and Design Development office. Then I knew nothing about design's history or Casey's reputation. But the poster seemed to me ingenious and perfect. It was everything design was *supposed* to be.

The print came to the office via an exhibition of design alums I helped organize. At the opening reception, I chatted briefly with Jacqueline Casey. The show was my first exposure to her work and I expressed my appreciation to the frail, soft spoken woman. More than any other piece, or even her photo, when I look at *Russia, USA Peace*, I think of that short exchange of pleasantries. After all, she was in it, as was everyone on our planet.

The poster features a monochrome photo of Earth, shown in full in the upper right corner. Printed in a varnish, it floats in a black void that fills the poster's frame. At the base of the poster runs the letters RUSSIA, the *R* and concluding *A* extending off the trim edges. The characters alternate in a solid, vivid red and reversed out white, which form USA.

Casey created the work for the exhibition *Images for Survival* organized by the Japanese Shoshin Society. The collection marked the 40th anniversary of the atom bombing of Hiroshima. At the time, a nuclear

conflict between the two superpowers was the direst threat to humanity. Russia was then, technically, the USSR. Now, the poster seems prescient and timeless both in appearance and message.

In all of Casey's œuvre , this work may be most emblematic of her method. She was the foremost U.S. practitioner of the International Style and deserves inclusion among its exemplars anywhere. While Müller-Brockmann is the style's most renowned and doctrinaire practitioner, it was Casey that fully demonstrated its potential as an accessible design methodology. Müller-Brockmann may have generated the most music posters in the manner but it took Casey to make that style sing.

Casey represented an advance for the International Style separate from the "New Wave" represented by Wolfgang Weingart. (And it took another supremely talented American woman designer — April Greiman — to make *that* approach resound.) New Wave sought to bring down to Earth an airless typography ("do we live on the Moon?"). It didn't make it breathe so much as make it hyperventilate.

In her process and product, Casey bridged the Swiss and American Modern strains: a fusion of the best Müller-Brockmann (discipline and structure) and Paul Rand (personability and formal imagination) could offer. She was the fulfillment of Modern intent, methodical *and* human.

High Modernist design overall developed from a celebration of mechanization and systemization. Its foremost performers operated sleek, clock-work devices of representation. Casey became the ghost in that machine.

A comparison of *Der Film* and *Russia, USA Peace* is instructive. Both are signature works of the respective designers. The core aspect of each is a depiction of an effect of light: Casey using varnish, Müller-Brockmann an overlap that implies light projected through a transparency.

In this spot varnish, Casey engages the materiality of design, subtly. Müller-Brockmann is all about the ink that resides on the sheet's surface. Material effects and manipulation: stock, die cuts, emboss, seem almost vulgar in his context. Casey's usage is rare for her and typically restrained.

Staying true to the International Style's formal fundaments, Casey infused it with an open, flexible sensibility. Müller-Brockmann's design was

an austere intellectual exercise, a distillation to craft a formal representation of a message's "essence." He pared to the pure. His favorite of his works was the blank verso of the printed sheet — *this page ideally left blank.*

Müller-Brockmann was ultimately unable to transcend language and its subjective confines. So, ironically, words became the primary, often sole, constituent of his works. For Müller-Brockmann, language was text, another formal element to arrange, along with image — ideally, usually — geometry and color. Its role was limited to being positioned, scaled and read. That reading was singular and apparent.

With posters largely consigned to phenomena that could be reduced to names (activity, performer, venue) and dates, he self-selected the ideal forum for his essentialist art. The greatest challenge was overcoming the initial public reaction to his graphic austerity. Once normalized, the field was clear.

But it was Jacqueline Casey that fulfilled Müller-Brockmann's promise, to divine and impart essential messages. She was able to summarize complex and arcane subjects using a limited but endlessly adaptable palette of effects. Overall, she orchestrated a wider range of topics, imagery, color schemes, graphic elements and compositions. Casey was a maximalist of the minutest.

Her 1971 poster for the exhibition *Goya: The Disasters of War* is illustrative of her ability to realize a concise, evocative message. She condenses Goya's paintings to an expressive, active spatter. It's simple and readily recognizable, but also ambiguous, suggesting paint and blood equally. This is consistent with the many shapes that adorn Casey's posters, forms that often toggle between representation and abstraction. The "JC" of the poster for an exhibition of her work is a deliberate, telling manifestation of this treatment.

Most importantly, Casey utilized language as a resonant, variable communication medium, beyond simply being *text*. Language's manifold character wasn't to be transcended but exploited. Müller-Brockmann's design denied language's nature, Casey's embraced it. She would split words apart as if they were atoms, to reveal their component elements and spin off additional illumination. For instance, in addition to the nested RUSSIA/

USA display, OIL is accented within POLLUTION for another poster.

Variety in typeface was naturally found in heads and titles, though Helvetica still dominated. These texts could perform, reinforcing and representing the poster's topic. At times, her typography approached concrete poetry in forming patterns and exotic arrays. *Mediums of Language* is a natural showcase of this impulse, where the occasional tool of repetition and stacking signals language's structuring and multiplicity. Type becomes dimensional, a framework, multiplies, breaks apart.

Casey regularly has more body copy in her posters than found in Müller-Brockmann's. This is always set in a regular weight of Helvetica — exclusively set in ragged columns hung from their heads. Depending upon the overall layout, the columns may be horizontally spaced unevenly. Or, in *Intimate Architecture*, rotated 90 degrees to echo and extend the shape of the pleated dress hem.

On the boundary of text and pure form are characters constructed from basic shapes, such as the 'SIX' of *Six Artists*. Characters are forms in their own right, though more charged and defined than the primary shapes that populate Casey's posters.

Casey employed a wide range of imagery as a regular component of her posters. She was willing to employ representation while maintaining a connection with abstraction. As previously noted, her abstractions frequently straddle the borderline with representation (the "cups" of *Coffee Hour*). At the same time, her abstract forms play different roles across works depending upon context: here symbolic, there pure geometry, elsewhere metaphoric.

Casey was also working with subject matter that while more diverse than that addressed by Swiss Internationalists, was still limited to focuses conducive to the minimalist approach. MIT wasn't showcasing the broader hurly-burly of culture. The preponderance was art exhibitions, music performances and technology-related matters, where charts and graphs resided naturally. Though limited in topics, Casey wrung maximum meaning out of her reduced subjects and process.

Her achievement shouldn't be cast only in contrast to Josef Müller-Brockmann and the International Style. Her work deserves regard within

the entirety of design activity, historically and conceptually.

Though diffuse and amended, Modernist principles still permeate most of design practice. Many critical statements are often posed in relation or opposition to Modernism. Modern design still lives as design's default position.

In this context, Casey's work serves as an executive summary of our discipline, an ideal *fig.1* textbook illustration of design's most effective product. It's design not at its most minimal but its most succinct.

Beauty/entropy

All design discussions must take place in the context of Modernism. Particularly, the influence of the European strain, disseminated and adapted worldwide as the International Style. Like it or not, the terms of how design should be crafted and perceived were set by the myriad disciples of European Modernism.

Those terms are primarily formal, layered with the insistence of a self-effacing strategy on the designer's part . It's a role that's risible in theory and unworkable in practice. This has gifted us the paradoxical situation where work that exemplifies all that design should do — be compelling, edifying, and evocative — can be designated as aberrant.

To explain away this "deviant" work's import, it's often marginalized. The audience is deemed minimal, the purveyors ineffectual. These concerns form the backdrop against which Vaughan Oliver's work exists. It's all the things great design should be. Not just album art — the most influential medium for his generation of practitioners — but for design overall.

Though dominant, the European Modern version wasn't the only expression of being modern in design. Most prominently in the U.S., there was a declared modern instinct that stood separate from the utopian, avant-garde crusade. William Addison Dwiggins was its exemplary practitioner. This moderate, apolitical (but socially responsible) sensibility was also dedicated to engaging contemporary technology and concerns, but

without scorning history, or sentimentalizing it.

Vaughan Oliver is transcendent as a continuation of this generous modern impetus. At the same time, he's comfortable with selected formal elements of European Modernism. To term him postmodern, however, oversimplifies his status.

In the 1970s and 80s, designers such as Hipgnosis, Barney Bubbles and Peter Saville more readily exemplified the postmodern impulse and pushed design into complex, contemporary conceptual areas. Oliver consolidated these approaches and brought new challenges and possibilities.

The design collaborative Hipgnosis was a major driver moving album design away from descriptive representation. In practice, the sleeves were regarded as just another form of product packaging, and followed its pragmatic conventions.

Made up of former film students, Hipgnosis emphasized photography and used it to present elaborate, surreal dramas often having only tenuous or indirect connections to the music. The musicians themselves either were cast as actors in the designers' productions or relegated to the back and inserts of sleeves. If they appeared at all.

Barney Bubbles was a major influence on Peter Saville, and both self-consciously mined art and design history in their work. Both collaborated with photographers to generate imagery, establishing long-standing, productive working relationships with a few favored collaborators. Bubbles occasionally staged idiosyncratic scenarios that often included the musicians. Saville favored highly realistic photos employing experimental techniques to render objects and scenes.

The work of these designers would have been well-known to Oliver during his late-70s art education. In his book *Visceral Pleasures*, critic Rick Poynor noted that Factory Records band and Saville client Joy Division provided a "doomladen soundtrack," (p. 73) to Oliver's immediate after-school years, and that 4AD label founder Ivo Watts-Russell was "nervous of seeming to imitate" Factory design (p. 75).

Oliver blends aspects of these designers' approaches, but moves well beyond the descriptive and into the evocative and oblique. Imagery could be fully abstract, as with the imagery for David Sylvian and Robert Fripp's

The Road to Graceland. It could also be indeterminate, establishing moods through terse, ambiguous narratives, beginning with the first 23 Envelope sleeve, Modern English's *Mesh and Lace* (1981).

Though not as prominent or prevalent as in Bubbles' work, Oliver also indulges in conceptual play whereby the artificiality of the package and process of production is exposed and made an element of the design. He displayed this early, with the sleeve for *Colorbox* (1985), which consisted of a reproduced sheet of a Japanese printer's make-ready. His 1994 exhibition catalog/monograph *This Rimy River* places the printing process in the foreground, sporting registration and crop marks.

Oliver's work is esteemed for its typographic imagination. His compositions mix classic exactitude with contemporary invention. They often feature eccentric serif and script faces drawn from old type sample books. Sans serif typefaces such as Univers and Futura regularly appear. His choices, emphasizing established faces, will mix the older and contemporary types to achieve a balance that largely avoids having the design tied to its particular historic moment. As much as such a thing is possible, Oliver's work can seem to reside outside of time.

Falling somewhere between typography and photography are the calligraphic treatments of some designs. Oliver credits former assistant and partner Chris Bigg for introducing his "expressive calligraphy" to v23's designs in 1983. They were central elements of the covers of Heidi Berry's *Love* and the *Lilliput* promotion, and similar marks can be seen in the *Walking Backwards* exhibition identity by Studio Mothership. The marks are ostentatiously hand made but suggest without coalescing into words. Purely gestural, they function as abstract drawings.

Hand-lettering and illustration were commonplace in early 20th century, non–European Modern design. Oliver's frequent use of calligraphy echoes this, however he trends Modern in his consistent employ of photography . The inversion of representation and abstraction demonstrates how Oliver can be of and outside his time.

Decoration has been derided in design since Adolf Loos' infamous "Ornament and Crime," a foundation Modern text. Reacting to the florid excesses of Victorian design, any graphic element deemed extraneous was

to be purged. The overall "decorative" aspect of Oliver's work is measured; patterns are restrained, as are flourishes of all types, emerging naturally within compositions.

He also manipulates illusionism in his frequent use of three-dimensional models in his design. Modernist design declares its flatness.

Oliver almost exclusively trades in illusions of dimensionality. This diversion is most pronounced with dimensional typography, creating an involution of reality and artifice. In Vaughan Oliver's world, the surface is a series of progressive layers.

He is unmatched in identifying and coordinating a variety of distinctive image makers when orchestrating his works. He has worked with photographers Simon Larbalestier, Dominic Davies, Nigel Grierson, and Jim Friedman, and artists Marc Atkins and Shinro Ohtake. Beyond general descriptors such as being eccentric in subject matter or presentation, interest in abstraction and the mundane, no overall style can be assigned to these imagists. While certain themes and elements (as with his preferred typefaces) can be noted across his productions, Oliver has continually surprised in how he has expanded his palette. What at first strikes as uncharacteristically Vaughan Oliver, soon securely fits into his œuvre. His signature is difficult to distill but profound in effect.

His æsthetic choices are natural outgrowths of his early creative influences, such as photographer Joel-Peter Witkin, as well as a reflection of the varied music of the 4AD catalog. (Though, to Watt-Russell's chagrin, it is often characterized as ethereal and dream-like, despite the presence of prominent noise-makers like the Pixies). Before delving deeply into the particular designs, the sleeves immediately signaled that it contained nonpareil music. That the design offers depths to plumb is, in itself, significant.

Oliver's work goes further in establishing album covers as parallel artworks, inspired by but sometimes untethered to their patrons' immediate promotional concern. Those patrons are the musicians and the label, whose interests can diverge. Because sleeves are another form of product packaging, the notion seems absurd and self-indulgent on the designer's part. Designers themselves instinctively recoil (while envying) the prospect, compelled by the Modern self-effacing convention that undergirds

professional practice. However, there is ready and established precedence for such a situation.

Fittingly, the model comes from music, that of film soundtracks. Movie scores are composed explicitly to serve another artistic experience. It's accompaniment. But soundtracks are almost always available as discrete works (some musicians offer compendium albums of their varied soundtrack work, covering numerous films.) Many are highly prized in their own right, separate from and independent of their source.

It's problematic determining if and how a successful album can make its design iconic (and vice versa). Paula Scher's relationship with her iconic design of the first Boston LP is a complex case study in contradictory lessons. But it seems a truism that a striking sleeve should only enhance interest in the music.

How prominent a role the designer should play remains an area of tension between designer, commissioner, and audience. Modernist convention demands that the design and designer assume a supportive, secondary role. The designer is never the star of any show. In music: a graphic roadie. However, especially among its ardent proponents, such diffidence is paradoxical. Eminent design from Dwiggins to Müller-Brockmann to Vaughan Oliver isn't celebrated for being inconspicuous.

Though flexible in its manifestations, Oliver's design is consistently audacious. This prominence distressed some on the 4AD label (Poynor in *Visceral Pleasures*: "... 4AD bands have on occasion ... resented, or rejected outright, his highly recognizable graphic signature." p. 21). A bold, parallel art was felt to overshadow, and draw attention away from the musicians. It's at least a small irony that artists so dedicated to unique musical expressions are more comfortable with more conservative wrappings.

While Vaughan Oliver's work has been readily and widely praised for its visual splendor, insufficient attention has been given to his practical skills as a designer working in a competitive commercial realm. Ivo Watts-Russell has spoken on being educated early by Oliver on the necessity for and potential of a consistent unified design approach.

A fundamental grasp of branding and identity systems underlies Oliver's stunning graphics. He brought a dedication and energy to a

number of fringe acts on a small, fledgling label. Watts-Russell gave Oliver admirable leeway but only after the designer articulated his shrewd knowledge of marketing. The relationship between designer and label was symbiotic. If self-indulgent, it was a munificent selfishness. Oliver holistically unites the music and package.

Oliver had a more personal, knowing reading of people's association with design generally, and albums specifically. He recognized the gift aspect of a package, that a rich design can be interpreted as generosity toward the potential owner, imbuing it with a deeper, emotional significance. The album could be like a relic, a talisman.

This sense is inherent in Japanese culture but western, Modern thought abstracts and depersonalizes its audience. Packaging is a tool, a strategy, nothing more. It's inherently disposable, emotionally and physically. Oliver is the rare designer whose work speaks to people empathetically, as co-enthusiasts, not as consumers.

Most significantly, his work affirms how beauty — æsthetic adventure and indulgence — is, in itself, a concept. As noted, Oliver's work has substantial conceptual depth. However, though it is likely intuitive, there are few designers historically dedicated to fashioning such visually profound work.

The Modern movement (particularly in its avant garde avatar) introduced new notions of form, while ostensibly denying its primacy. Visual rhetoric — using form to persuade — was considered cheap, unserious, and a relic of history. But Oliver draws thoughtful, relevant beauty back into the conversation, unifying the pre-Modern and avant-garde.

There is precedence for this merging, right in the heart of the Modern movement. It's in the recently discovered, surreptitious artwork of women Bauhaus students. These pieces presciently fused personal biography and gender identity issues with the school's formal obsessions. Gertrud Arndt's photographic *Maskenselbstportraet* series or Marianne Brandt's collages and untitled self-portraits bear intriguing correspondences to Oliver's work.

Oliver defies design's central conceit: that it creates order out of chaos. The actuality is that all design substitutes a selected order for

another of perceived lesser value. The Modernist agenda is to eradicate everything previous and install a perfect, timeless replacement.

Oliver's work exposes this ruse and its arrogance. Nature quickly and relentlessly asserts itself, famously in the form of Modern architecture's leaky roofs. Oliver's designs are documents of a culture where opposing orders are in constant friction. It's all in the realization of and response to the actuality that things degrade and decay. Cracks appear, mold grows, shoots sprout. Either you decry, defy and constantly attempt to patch it up. Or accept and work with it.

His luscious graphics may suggest escapism, but in this, Vaughan Oliver is essentially a realist. His compositions and typography can be expressions of perfection: every element judiciously placed, structured seamlessly. Other times, it's as if the machinery, the industrial process has broken down, stuttered, or gone haywire. Oliver presents the world as it is, awakening us to the beauty in the entropy.

Salvager

This is a book of religious art.

No church commissioned any of the work but it's all devotional. As "graphic design," such a claim seems absurd, and Stefan Sagmeister likely regards it pretentious. Admittedly, I don't believe it either, anymore than I've believed any supposition I've made about anybody's work, including my own.

If this is dissembling, what does it say about much of design? You're holding a book packed with metaphor and attribution of aspect. I'm supposed to look at a houseplant and think German lighting conglomerate?

Design's also pragmatic and most at ease talking in worldy terms of customer fulfillment and budget endowments. However comfortable clients are negotiating with designers in practical terms, they want the designer's product (and hence, their own) to be adored, venerated. Make it sexy, make it holy.

Take Caravaggio's paintings. His religious scenes were pretexts for promoting clerical authority. They commissioned him after all, the media maven of the time. Does it drain the wonder from art to learn this fix is always in? What negates the ulterior motive? Time, subject matter, talent? Discuss.

Or, turn these pages and witness (cautionary?) tales celebrating the flesh and the profane. Observe mundane manifestations: nature itself and

everyday objects forming the designer's innermost thoughts ("And the rock cried out!"). See obsessions with perforation, the humors, luminosity, and the multiform state of all subjects and objects. Behold man as his own (en)graven image.

"Designer"? I'll offer a new title: *Salvager*.

Too rich for you? Come back tomorrow and I'll have another take. That's design, isn't it?

The difference engineer

Since its publication, Martin Venezky's *It is beautiful ... then gone* (Princeton Architectural Press) has met with scant (any?) critical review. With few surveys of this kind being published, every release seems worthy of examination. Significant questions are still being asked about the monograph's role in design and differing approaches to the form.

That *It is beautiful ... then gone* has kept below the radar is unfortunate but, in its own way, in keeping with Venezky's work. With its oblique origin (he proposed a book on his teaching), lack of hyperbole, and discreet scale, *It is beautiful ... then gone* seems to deliberately defray attention. In its non-intuitive way (for design), the book demonstrates why Venezky is a distinctive figure in the field. And it's not for the reasons you'd expect.

Venezky is recognized as a strikingly original formalist. He gained attention early, with a feature on his Cranbrook projects in *Eye* no. 10 (reproduced in *It is beautiful ... then gone*) and an image on its cover. For much of the 1990s, Venezky had a dream showcase: art directing the feature magazine *Speak*. He was also selected for the first National Design Triennial at the Cooper-Hewitt National Design Museum.

Popular and critical opinion focuses almost exclusively on the beauty of Venezky's work and his unique methods of generating it. Though not necessarily a Luddite, he eschews the digital for "design made difficult": time-consuming, handmade constructions in which found imagery plays

a prominent role. Efficiency is subordinated to efficacy. Opinion on the quality of Venezky's work isn't unanimous, though not rising to the point of controversy. (Are there any more formal outrages left?) He has been criticized for incomprehensible layouts (*Speak* editor Dan Rolleri admits that Venezky's distinctive style limited their ad sales), and the limited practicability of his processes and products.

Venezky's accomplishment is not so much in the innovation of his form, but its ability to summon a particular, subtle mood that is unique in design. The designer declares it plainly in his writing; Venezky is a literary designer, both in his underappreciated talent as a writer, and in his design sensibility. The title of his conversational introductory essay states it clearly: "Design and Melancholy." Is there any other designer with this perspective on their activity? To link these two things is professionally risky, but for Venezky, essential.

Venezky expresses design in terms of decay, memory, and " ... the shadowy world of before, the impending excitement of things on the verge, and the discarded world of after ... " This is lousy copy for a capability brochure. The title of this book itself is a statement of impermanence, evanescence, and loss. Design famously boasts of timelessness, order, and celebration.

Typically a promotional vehicle, graphic design trades in the positive. It is rarely reflective or ambiguous. If form is called upon to send a message, to generate a mood, it is decidedly upbeat. (Except in the realm of information design, where the message is: what's love got to do with it?) Even if not flaunting smiley faces, the common graphic design presents a "Have a Nice Day!" air. What distinguishes the exemplary practitioners is their willingness and ability to break that cheery façade. They dig deeper, mix it up, have shadings, play minor chords.

In its purposeful and fragmentary nature, Venezky's work evokes more deliberative moods. But it is never dispirited. It is affirming by compulsively collecting then remaking life's debris. Everything is of value, and utility. If the hallmark of art is making us rethink the commonplace, Venezky's work is made worthy by his transformations of the ordinary. It is a feat of observation, acquisition, and dedication. His results are dreamlike

in the way dreams stage their dramas on cheap sets. Your everyday digs stand in for Paris, or outer space.

While *IIBTG*'s contributing writers name-check prominent artists (Malevich, Léger, Calder) when discussing Venezky, they surprisingly overlook a more obvious relation: Joseph Cornell. This influential artist famously compiled and collaged. Cornell also did commissioned magazine and self-initiated design work, constructing his own melancholy world from salvaged scraps. Where Cornell employed images of Medici princes or Lauren Bacall, Venezky uses antiquated found photographs. It lends both artists an out-of-time aspect to their work that is mysterious and evocative.

Venezky's products are the antithesis of what's considered the finest proof of formal design success: "inevitability." Inevitability is a sign of conformity: that a popular Platonic ideal exists of what design should look like. The "inevitable" design channels that ideal. This is often advisable. Design often needs to acknowledge and meet expectations to create effective meaning. But, as an artifact of culture, design should also at least occasionally expanding it. By adding melancholy to design's sensibility, Venezky brings a maturity to the field, the possibility of conveying something deeper than synthetic cheer or disinterest.

As mentioned before, Venezky is a very literary designer. His typography reveres words; his stuttering repetition of characters savors the experience of characters. Violence isn't being done to language; it is being exercised, indulged. A careful consideration of his layouts shows an ultimate concern for readability, with classic typefaces in somewhat quirky, but regular settings. Variations on norms are measured and rarely inaccessible.

IIBTG' reminded me how unremarkable I usually found *Speak*'s covers. (I was a rare subscriber.) And this book's cover is similarly restrained. Compared to Venezky's stunning poster work, they're puzzling letdowns. But this is further evidence of his appreciation of the specific task at hand. He engages the entire article, not merely the flashy opening spread. The covers are of a piece with the whole issue, setting a low-key and intriguing tone.

IIBTG' still misses opportunities. Even if he considers his pre-Cranbrook work unrepresentative or embarrassing, it would be enlightening to see Venezky's design before the apotheosis. Was there no precursor? Did he undergo a wholesale transformation? And to mention but be given such a tiny sample of his *Spec* magazine project is frustrating. Where design monographs are usually too graphic design-centric in their estimation, *IIBTG'* gives no perspective on Venezky's place in the field. Two abstract essays from staffers at the same art museum is one too many (they also qualify as client testimonials).

The teaching material that initiated *It is beautiful ... then gone* here becomes an interesting but unrealized addendum. The student works are doodles without context. Unlike Venezky's explication of his studio collages, there's no explanation of whether or how the student imagery was used as more than abstract exercises. Form is never an end in itself for Venezky, but the school projects never go beyond form.

It is also unfortunate that Venezky didn't include his philosophy statement ("Design that wants what people want") from the website of this firm, Appetite Engineers. It is one of the most succinct, sensible, and inspiring statements on design that's been written. It would've been nice to have it on paper with the work.

But what is on the pages is welcome and enlightening. *It is beautiful ... then gone* isn't meant to be the definitive statement on Martin Venezky's design. Like the work it holds, the book's an attempt to convert the ephemeral to permanence, melancholy to delight. The possibility and the promise of making things into, and seeing things as, their opposites is the contrary intention of this book. It is beautiful ... and here.

Pesky Illustrator

Design needs a term equivalent to "multi-instrumentalist" in music. It's an awkward expression but descriptive of a demonstrable "cross-platform" ability. In addition to being a composer, modern recording technology allows musicians to become one-man bands. The skill in design is arguably broader: there's potential to author text, design type, make images, and pull it all together into a product.

Practicality makes this exhibition rare though examples of this multi-skilling go way back (16th century, Geoffrey Tory). But we still don't have a term. (Something perhaps like polyglot? Polygraph?) Usually, we choose the most prominent.

Illustrator-designer Mark Andresen is a long-time documenter of New Orleans, now exiled in Atlanta. He fled only an hour or two ahead of Hurricane Katrina, accompanied by his wife Paula and their cats. Among their few belongings was a box of notebooks Paula insisted on taking, and the computer hard-drive he grabbed. The hard-drive contained images of most of his work. But of the physical pieces, little more than a tenth was eventually saved from the subsequent storm damage and looting.

Andresen has strong opinions about art, design and politics. Especially about the practices of FEMA, the U.S.'s Federal Emergency Management Agency. And is unreserved when expressing them. Few discussions on the Speak Up design blog lack a *(continued on p. 144)*

Conjure man

The VouDou practice of conjuring is an evocative metaphor for illustration. A conjurer employs common, native materials to "evoke Spirits for practical ends." An illustrator crafts an image to summon awareness toward a worldly result. There's also the magical, unpredictable, and somewhat spooky aura that surrounds conjuring. It's otherworldly. And the most profound imagery is ultimately ineffable or affective beyond its constituent colors, forms, and materials.

This comparison is apt when applied to illustrator/graphic and type designer Mark Andresen, long-time New Orleans documenter, and now, exile. He fled an hour or two ahead of Hurricane Katrina, accompanied by his wife Paula and their cats. Among their few belongings were some notebooks Paula insisted on taking, and the computer hard-drive he grabbed. Nearly everything they left behind, including the bulk of his life's work, was ruined. The hard-drive contained images of most of his work. But of the physical pieces, little more than a tenth was eventually saved from the subsequent storm damage and looting.

Now situated in Atlanta, Georgia, he simultaneously downplays his personal account while doing all he can to invoke the memory his former, adopted home. He's determined not be defined solely by his personal tragedy, yet is resolute in keeping its spirit animate. Like a psychic medium, he's conflicted: charged with giving voice while (continued on p. 144)

Pesky illustrator

demonstrative post from "Pesky Illustrator." He's keeping at it, rambling, determined, selfless, and sardonic. *(continued on next page)*

Conjure man

uncomfortable being the focus of attention. At the same time, Andresen's voice is distinctive on its own.

That voice is a rough mix of channeled personalities. Andresen describes himself as a blend of Marcel Duchamp, the reincarnated White Russian spy Sidney Reilly (who's still grudged about his Bolshevik murderers), and Klattu, the Michael Rennie character from the sci-fi film *The Day the Earth Stood Still*: "I'm a bit alien to what passes for normal and I think my karmic task is to wake up planet Earth to change."

Andresen has strong opinions about art, design and politics. Especially the practices of FEMA, the U.S.'s Federal Emergency Management Agency. And is unreserved when expressing them. Few discussions on the Speak Up design blog lack a demonstrative post from "Pesky Illustrator." He's keeping at it, rambling, determined, selfless, and sardonic. *(continued on next page)*

The ideal of making something enduring and preserving the past was impressed upon Andresen early. He grew up in the New Jersey suburbs, where his parents were artists, but his father gave up art to work on the 1960s U.S. space program. His mother was an amateur Egyptologist, capable of writing hieroglyphics. On a trip to New York's Metropolitan Museum, one image captivated him: "I saw the hand of some ancient Egyptian artist in the moment of putting quill to papyrus ... it struck me what immortality is."

He studied art at the Pratt Institute in New York from 1967–1969, but dropped out before graduating, and hitchhiked across the country. Back in New York he began work at an ad agency, and in the mid-80s, moved to Atlanta, to work as a designer on *Atlanta* magazine. Andresen enjoyed the work, and was successful at it, though he seldom lasted long in a job.

He moved to New Orleans in 1987 when he was offered a job redesigning *New Orleans* magazine. Andresen found the city to be an endless, vivid source of imagery-the people, the culture, the architecture. A "place of carefree joy and mysterious pleasure." What isn't outwardly flamboyant can contain wonders: "the front door is nothing to speak of but it's lush on the inside."

His fascination with VouDou led him to be initiated into the religion. VouDou isn't a practice you can observe: you must be a "participant or nothing" to witness its activity. VouDou brought Andresen a new perspective on his creative activity. Illustration and VouDou are joined in "pulling out the hidden meanings of things." The true essence of VouDou is service to others, as image making is also a revelatory act for its audience.

Andresen's *New Orleans* job ended in a year, after a falling out with the editor, so he moved into freelance illustration, primarily for ad agencies. But Andresen's mercurial nature extends to his illustration and complicates matters. He found illustration representatives befuddled by his responsive, chameleon changes of media in his work. One-trick ponies are easier to place (and show). But Andresen's expressions go beyond pragmatically marketing himself. Ultimately, the demands of the project determine the illustration method.

When he was called on to create an image of the *17 Mardi Gras Indian*

Chiefs, Andresen turned for the first time to realism. He wanted a recogniz-able, group portrait. Four hundred hours of study of gouache technique resulted in the final work, reproduced in a now rare poster.

Illustrators are proficient in a variety of methods, and Andresen, like a good conjurer, is adept with what's on hand. He presses letterforms in the form of rub-downs into image service.

Andresen moves between illustration and design, sometimes com-bining the tasks on jobs, and regards himself as more the latter than the former. To any given project, his awareness of the entirety of the process brings ideas beyond the typical illustrator. He strives for literate graphics, responsive to the design situation and possessed of a depth of knowledge of the subject.

Some jobs have paid long-term dividends, such as his on-going rela-tionship with McIlhenny Tabasco Sauce. Andresen has crafted thousands of illustrations for the family-owned business over just a few years, from the de rigueur leprechauns for St. Patrick's Day ads to dancing Cajuns adorning Tokyo subway cars. Andresen's commissions from McIlhenny are now on hold, as the company recovers from being hit hard by both hur-ricanes Katrina and Rita.

In 2003, Andresen was contacted Monique McCall of the New Orleans mayor's office to remake his city's symbol. McCall, who handled graphics for the city, had begun restyling the iconic fleur-de-lis. Andresen investigated other symbols but was directed to return to McCall's original drawing. By hand, he redrew the symbol, providing a symmetry that was missing from previous incarnations. Andresen considers himself a "co-creator" with McCall of the resultant mark, as she established the "essence" of what emerged.

Still in use, the logo was used broadly, from stationery to choco-lates. This widespread treatment became another bittersweet aspect of Katrina. Normally, a designer would thrill to behold his logo on every city vehicle. But not if those vehicles ended up on your TV screen, awash in floodwaters.

Merely observing has never satisfied Andresen: he remains an informal, often mordant commentator on design blogs. He's likely to

weigh in on anything: sexism in the field ("Must seem irritating to competent women designers to always be excluded or patronized, except for the anointed few. If it's changed up in the star-celebrity designer Pentagramworld Pantheon someone tell me differently."), the vulgarity of popular culture ("There will never be another "Guernica" because that requires a consensus of decency and outrage. I think the absence of both is a sign of a death culture in progress"), and his choice to employ a pseudonym when posting comments ("I'm for anonymity whoever wants it. The reassurance of non-traceable identity in a world were real privacy issues are eroding seems like a subject worth studying. As Hakim Bey, author of "The Temporary Autonomous Zone" writes, in the future being anonymous will be a privilege.")

His visual punditry went public in the early 1990s when he sent *Emigre* editor Rudy VanderLans "funny faxes" — some of which ended up in its pages — that commented wryly on the magazine's obsessions. Such as Andresen's conceptual "My New Typeface." "The typeface consisted of only two characters," VanderLans recalled, "one had all vowels placed on top of each other with the instruction 'use for vowels.'" Consonants received a similar treatment. "This was during the days when we published a lot of experimental typefaces in *Emigre*. Mark has a way of bringing people down to earth. His tongue-in-cheek type submission made good fun of the absurdity of some of the so-called experimentation of the time."

One of these whimsical submissions became an actual typeface. For the text on an early 1980s music club poster, Andresen used fragments of Caslon swash italic press type. He repeated the process to expand on the few original letters. Zuzana Licko then tweaked Andresen's creation, establishing a baseline, while Andresen expanded it to a full character set. Emigre released the font, appropriately dubbed "Not Caslon," in 1995.

In the midst of a decade littered with extremist type fabrications, Not Caslon was a conspicuously sly creation. It transcended the timely and disposable faces that proliferated, being contemporary in conception and historic in reference. Not Caslon remains an eccentric and refreshingly unaffected typeface in name and form. Applications have ranged from Madonna and Lou Reed CD packages, to scarves, wine bottle labels, and

Cirque du Soleil.

Andresen showcases the entirety of his talents in a 2001 specimen booklet for the typeface. He wrote, designed and illustrated an episode when his VouDou godmother, Reverend Lorita Honeycutt Gamble ("not a cartoon ... a decent lady working spiritually") dispels a troublesome ghost, the former occupant of a coffin discovered buried in Andresen's front yard. Through the Reverend's ministrations (which include cigars, beans, rum and a rooster), the 200-year-old spirit is induced to return to his casket.

The sampler is just a taste of the visual flavours catalogued in Andresen's 2006 book, *New Orleans As It Was*. It's an elegy to the city that is comprised of work scavenged from saved notebooks and what survived in the storm. Andresen's original intent was to create a limited edition as a gift to people who had helped him after Katrina. Rudy VanderLans offered to help with the design, and suggested contacting Gingko Press for wider distribution. At his wife's urging, Andresen proposed the book. Gingko agreed and put the project on a fast track to release.

The publisher took the book as submitted. For Andresen, the process of organising the images was wrenching but therapeutic. To do the project helped him from "unravelling" in the year following the disaster. Portrayals of the after-Katrina destruction were set aside. The lone image related to the aftermath is on the book final page: a man, chest high in floodwater (fleur-de-lis symbol on his T-shirt), balancing a box containing a child on his head. The sketch is made on a Red Cross info sheet for evacuees.

Images of New Orleans' "fleeting moments" are interspaced with brief texts and captions by Andresen. He portrays musicians, preachers, chiefs, monuments, "absurdly comedic" structures, the "walking, talking surrealism of Mardi Gras." While he apologetically terms his words "purple prose," they are sentimental but never maudlin. "The population of this city always knew they shared the land with ghosts of the past. You can count among those spirits the pirate Jean Lafitte, Buddy Bolden and Louie Armstrong; the fancy ladies of Storyville; the countless drifters and adventurers who came down the Mississippi River looking for work or trouble; and the elegant Creole families who carved civilization out of the swampland; the French, Arcadians, Spanish, English, Germans, and later

the Irish and Sicilians. And, of course, the slaves and Free People of Color who brought their own Afro-Caribbean secrets to this wild place." When his relatives wonder why he didn't draw "nice things" instead of "hookers, old buildings and winos," Andresen dryly replies that "They stood still for me."

VanderLans designed an all type cover for the book that has it resemble a placard, or historic marker. It also suggests those New Orleans houses with plain doors Andresen cherished. VanderLans' own photographic explorations of Western landscapes make the book the product of two artists intimately engaged with place.

Katrina was a diving point for Andresen and the city, and ending that stretches on. He lives and works now in his wife's hometown of Atlanta, still a struggling "working stiff," who gives little thought to career building. Practically all the work he scrapes together comes, ironically, from New Orleans. Andresen remains a "sucker for pro bono." He teaches occasionally, stays connected to the designers' network. "Designers cluster," he says. Illustrators are lone wolves, who, more than designers, regard their peers as competition.

Andresen's house in Metairie section of New Orleans has since been repaired and sold. Work still comes from New Orleans but not enough to make a move back feasible. He doesn't foresee returning physically anytime soon. New Orleans is a "cubist city now," he says, "all angular and broken." For the 2007 design annual issue of *Print* magazine, Andresen wrote a short piece on illustrators from New Orleans, that typically directed attention away from himself, and contained far less of the story he could write.

"I'm still feeling dislocated. I am now a man caught between two cities: one I remember and one that survived." He's adamant that Katrina not dominate his life but sometimes he's breached by the anger and sorrow of the loss. The sorrow is for the city, and a way of life. Andresen isn't sentimental or despairing of the work that he had to dispose of after Katrina. "I can always draw again," he says. He knows too many people who suffered much greater losses.

Atlanta yields some subjects for his sketchbooks but nothing like New

Orleans: "water and trees," "outcroppings of weeds." There will be no more jubilant images of that city from Andresen. But there will be others. "I need more. I don't think of myself as only an illustrator but some broader, designer sense ... a conceptualist."

It is this broader sense that's Andresen's strength, and a rare example of his full potential and ability. As skilled and inventive as he is as an illustrator, it's almost a disappointment that he represents other people's words, and writes in blog posts. Andresen is a natural storyteller, possessed with a unique voice and the ability to wholly give the tale form, from the shape of the words' characters, to the accompanying images.

In this way, the Not Caslon type sampler stands as his most through and effecting work. An Andresen account of Katrina could be that tragedy's *In the Shadow of No Towers.* Presented with this proposal, Andresen demurs; he left and didn't experience the full calamity.

However, though he'll always, by choice, be associated with New Orleans, his stories could be about anything. The stories would likely be lush, discomforting and very real.

Word!

There are strange geometries in the township of Enkanini, South Africa. On their own, the simple diagonals aren't that odd. It's that they're painted in vivid hues on the sides of the township's homes. Those houses are clustered shacks, constructed from scavenged metal like unrolled food cans. The regularity of the lines and the simple presence of color are sharp contrasts amidst the makeshift structures and surrounding squalor. Ramshackle huts are transformed into flags of fortune for the area.

In addition to the geometry, there are also stenciled words and birds that also decorate the townships of Masiphumelele, Langa, and cross the border into Gambia. The spray painted words, mostly in English but occasionally the native xhosa spread across the exterior walls, and move out to public spaces like brick walls: "uthinxo luthando" (God is love), "hope," "my soul clings to you."

The stencils are handmade and carefully crafted. Their greatest curiosity may be that they carry a specific, identifiable typeface. For the type *connoisseur* (and few are to be found in the townships), it's Fred Smeijers' Arnhelm Bold, in a usage perhaps unimagined by its creator.

The artworks are the initiative of Andrew Breitenberg, under the moniker of "Selah," from a Hebrew term meaning "pause here, and reflect on that." They are components of a public art piece titled *These 3 Remain*, the most recent exponent of his ongoing personal mission in South Africa's

townships. That mission stems from his commitment to his Christian faith, expressed through an equal devotion to the power of design and art.

The influence of religion as motivation for and subject of art is well documented. In design, however, expressions are scarce, despite the prevalence of religious belief worldwide, often prominently declared. But the landscape of design has been determinately secular with rationalism as is cornerstone. Andrew Breitenberg's history and activity provides a rare glimpse of how the twin fervors of faith and design interact. From a wide perspective, the manifestations are unsurprising. Yet there are subtleties of interpretation deserving notice. Reduced to its simplest form, Breitenberg's life and work lies at the intersection of two books: the Bible and Norman Potter's *What is a Designer*.

Breitenberg's route to Capetown and engagement with design includes two significant, prior points: Swarthmore, Pennsylvania, and Amsterdam. It was during his undergraduate study at Swarthmore College, a renowned private liberal arts institution, that he first explored graphic design — as a cultural activity. His interest grew from contemplating the practice, form, and meaning of writing. Swarthmore's open and challenging intellectual environment allowed him wide latitude to survey "word work." A major question of those investigations was "why do things look this way?" The physical manifestation and implications of the word had to be confronted.

It was during this inquiry that a teacher suggested Breitenberg read Potter's book. In it, Breitenberg found his "second Bible," one that continues to define his purpose. "(Potter) teaches that a designer must act for the community — of and for the people and that design is a socially negotiated discipline; that it is relation-seeking. In that sense, I think graphic design is both the conversation I have with a single mother outside her mud hut, as well as the piece that we paint on it together."

The product of Breitenberg's studies was a thesis titled "Publication," that was staged as an installation. It addressed viewership, the objective and subjective aspects in the act of looking. For its presentation, Breitenberg envisioned a performance with the audience literally standing within the thesis, for a total immersion in the topic.

The text was printed out as large posters, "A0 sheets as if they were A4," and mounted in the College's gallery. The unprecedented presentation was funded by a special grant from Swarthmore's president. It led to Breitenberg 2001 awarding of a B.A. in Critical Visual Studies — a major of his own devising.

Having entered the orbit of graphic design, Breitenberg embraced the discipline as career after graduation. He moved to Manhattan, set up a freelance practice, and further immersed himself in graphic design's nascent critical literature. It was a classic learning on the job experience, centered on the recommendations and commissions of one client, Sarah Welch.

After a year in New York, he returned to his hometown of Virginia Beach in southern Virginia. However, the area provided limited opportunities for challenging graphic design work, especially of the kind that addressed Breitenberg's concerns. In 2005, he set off on a pilgrimage to the Netherlands, to investigate graduate study and the famed design culture. His expectation was to apply to the Werkplaats Typografie supervised by Karel Martens and Armand Mevis. Instead, he became one of the first students in the Editorial Design program at Graduate School for Art and Design, Utrecht.

It was during his graduate study that Breitenberg first addressed his concomitant concerns of faith and design. Where religious texts had once been at the forefront of formal beauty and innovation, their contemporary status was moribund and uninspiring. No greater disparity between the transcendence of a text and its physical manifestation was extant than in a contemporary Bible.

A peculiar challenge to faith seemed in play: maintaining one's veneration of the most exalted words when presented in the most insipid vessel. It was an oblique parallel to ongoing typographic arguments over the role of formal invention when setting texts. If any words should transcend its display, shouldn't it be the Word?

For Breitenberg, it was disheartening to browse the Religion shelves of a bookstore. The bland packaging hadn't abated with the public Christian foments in the United States. Perhaps it intensified. Just as

evangelicals declaimed from corrupt texts, the favored design was ordinary and trite.

Breitenberg devised a thesis project to reimagine Bible verses in an active typography that matched his conception of the word, to elevate its worldly presentation. Opinion on the proposal split the faculty and students. Some objected, finding it an unsuitable subject and insufficiently objective. A dissenting faculty member insisted that Breitenberg expand his focus, and realize verses from other religions. While open on general principles to such an undertaking, Breitenberg resisted the wholesale transformation of his intention. His desire was to illuminate his own faith, and to craft a personal design statement.

The dispute over the thesis proposal was an added tension within the nascent program. Dissatisfied with the overall direction, Breitenberg left the program after a year. He elected to remain in Amsterdam, founding the Office for Editorial Design with Harmine Louwé, one of the Graduate School tutors.

"As his teacher I had seen a lot of his writing and liked it," says Louwé, "When he decided to stay in the Netherlands we gave collaboration a try. Andrew would function as the writer and editor, while I took care of the design. We set up as a loose partnership, which we would bring to life whenever a certain job would call for it. We could function in advertising agencies but also work on cultural jobs or create business identities. It's a wonderful feeling when someone completely understands what you're trying to do visually and can add words that make it better. And the other way around when I could add more meaning to his words, because they really spoke to me."

They set off on a period of ideal commercial work, creatively and financially. Their projects included development work on Nike's "Just Do It" campaign relaunch for Europe, the Mid-East, and Africa, T-Mobile Environment design, and brand guidelines for Sony Global.

Though the aborted thesis project was behind him, Breitenberg hadn't abandoned the desire to align his creative work and his faith. The lucrative commercial work was no more a salve under the circumstances. Even with its advantageous circumstances. The next, and current step,

came about casually, though possibly inevitably.

Dutch friends introduced Breitenberg to visiting South Africans. Their voluble affability immediately appealed to the naturally gregarious Breitenberg. In response to an invitation to visit, Breitenberg spent five weeks in early 2007 travelling through the African country.

The trip was "not a vacation but preparation," says Breitenberg. The itinerary included areas not on the tourist itinerary: the townships. His hosts were excited to share the entirety of life in South Africa. Once exposed, Breitenberg found the country's culture more "home" than that of the Netherlands. Shortly upon his return to Europe, he was organizing a fall move south.

Initially, Breitenberg was associated with church groups and ministries working in townships around Cape Town, working on a variety of charitable and community projects ("caring for kids with HIV/AIDS, helping at orphanages, teaching English to domestic workers and laborers, feeding locals who go hungry, mentoring students"). As documentation of his activities and as fundraising devise, he began an ongoing series of "Field Reports" in collaboration with Louwé in Amsterdam.

The two devised the Reports' format, with Louwé designing the individual pieces from Breitenberg's writings and images. In response to her layouts, he would develop further content and adapt what has already been produced.

Breitenberg was also producing graphic design work for use in the townships. He described one such effort, a small-scale branding exercise, in his first Field Report: "We are teaching kids to read during an after-school program and they run evening programs as well. I am also working with the director to create a logo and materials to raise awareness. We must raise awareness in the township itself; the idea is to put a big logo on the side of the van so that when the kids see it coming they'll remember and run for the house of hope ...."

Reduced to its essence, this is a standard design brief, set to employ typical design strategies to arrive at usual ends. But as much as such a thing is possible, it's design activity coming closest to a pure expression of the "doing good" impulse at the center of design modernity. And

the stakes, arguably, are higher and more immediate. At the same time, Breitenberg was designing for a variety of cultural clients, nearly all pro bono.

In his various efforts, Breitenberg always sought out opportunities to create public artwork of some kind. Increasingly, the impulse took on its own life, becoming both representative and reality of his ideals. Through his charitable actions, he was acting upon God's Word: his faith's demand to act in this world to its betterment, to show compassion for humanity. It was a "writing" of the word upon the world. Now, he set out on an agenda to literally manifest that text.

Breitenberg's undertaking is equally motivated by art and the devotional. He confesses an uncertainty that the work deserves the status of art. He regards them as language works in the nature of those he admires by Paul Elliman and Jenny Holzer. A variety of stylizations are applied to the texts inscribed on all manner of surfaces. They are affirmations of art, the word, people and relationships. "I write on rusted, ruined machinery, burnt walls and discarded trash because I believe that God writes on us in the same way. ... And the third world Africa has taught me ... that literally any piece of abused, abandoned, worthless scrap, can be made beautiful with love and time."

The house-painting program came about with the permission of township leaders and the individual residents. Labor was often done in company with township children; less contributing constructive effort than a boisterous spirit to the proceedings. Response was immediate and gratifying, instilling a pride of place. However, the destitute circumstances of the inhabitants prompted an understandable confrontation. A young, Caucasian American is likely to have resources the natives don't. Breitenberg was approached by a local, "How much will you pay me to paint my shack?" Informed that it was solely a volunteer effort, he eagerly requested his home be decorated.

Breitenberg's effort is arguably only cosmetic and reinforces the commonplace critique of design as surface treatment. The decoration's contribution to the township is ineffable, though no less weighty for people possessing vital emotional lives. It signals an awareness that their

plight is recognized, and their desperate need for hope. Apartheid's legacy of poverty is deeply rooted and intractable. In the meantime, the reality is that surface dressing is substantive.

Progressing from the incidental and anonymous creations, Breitenberg adopted the Selah name to distinguish his deliberate street art of stenciling texts and images. The enterprise is his commitment to art and a further pledge of dialog with people of the townships: "The greatest part of doing street art is the conversations that unfold as the piece is painted. Words have power. When I write for people who live in shacks and orphanages and on the side of the road, we watch dignity grow into their lives as they smile, lift their heads and thereafter point at the small tin shack and say with pride 'that's my house.' And the stories that they tell us of their own lives — of the experiences they've lived through, the suffering and injustice — and in some cases, the beauty of recovery — all these stories are the true medium for the message. It's in their stories that these words are lived."

For Breitenberg, being human carries significant responsibilities, more so if you're a human designer. For instruction on those latter duties, he turns to his second Bible: "(Potter) teaches that a designer must act for the community — of and for the people and that design is a socially negotiated discipline; that it is relation-seeking. In that sense I think graphic design is both the *cohave* with a single mother outside her mud hut, as well as the piece that we paint on it together."

Breitenberg is now negotiating the art realm to achieve recognition for his creative work. He's exhibited in a number of curated Cape Town group exhibitions, showing drawings and photographs of site work. Breitenberg's primary challenge has been simply creating non-site-specific objects. To facilitate the work that exists and is to come, he's built a physical and virtual space that "also aims to create a good environment for discussion about the process and reasons for the artwork."

Breitenberg's work is a knowing graffiti, an action that unlike the prevalent street art, which proclaims individual aggrandizement, truly speaks to and for the community. In its stylization, the work might be dismissed as lacking a spontaneous expression. Graffiti, however, long ago

fell into rote gestures and was readily absorbed. Its status as "transgressive" is ripe for upgrade to transcendent.

In context of the recent design world fetish for socially active and altruistic design, Andrew Breitenberg took the extraordinary step of acting on his conviction. His is a deliberate, direct response through art and design. It's speaking for and to its audience. In the words of his artist statement, "My method reflects the values of the African communities in which the work takes place — the power of conversation, negotiation, listening, and community. The work is entirely collaborative by definition. It is discovered, not imposed."

This is the cover page for "Omnigraphy," the third and longest section in «Process Music». It offers a variety of critical studies of artifacts, examining specific works by design figures such as Elliott Earls, Paul Rand, William Addison Dwiggins, Josef-Müller Brockmann, Rudy VanderLans, Stefan Sagmeister, and musicians Van Dyke Parks and Cornershop. Artifacts that are considered include mass-market and progressive magazines, interactive multimedia works, designer monographs, design specimens, photography books, protest posters, and music albums. "The angel is my floating-point!" and "Fuel full pull poll pool cool cook book" appeared in «Emigre» magazine, issues 39 (1996) and 44 (1997) respectively. "U & M-B" was published in shorter form in the Reviews section of «Eye» 64 (2007). "A viewer's guide to periodic literature" appeared as "Seeing and reading" in «IDEA» 314 (2006). "File under nowhere" is from the Emigre "Various Types" catalog (2004). The critical book review "The good just is" was published under the book's title in the scholarly journal «Dialectic», volume 1, issue 2, fall 2017. "12 views of 120 posters" was commissioned as introduction to the catalog for «Graphic advocacy: international posters for the digital age 2001–2012» (2013). "Re: Song Cycle" was commissioned for the book «Palm Desert» (1999). Except for "Go now," which was written for this book, all other works appeared on the Ephemeral States blog.

The angel is my floating-point!

*To get nowhere you must traverse every known universe: you must be everywhere in order to be nowhere. To have disorder you must destroy **every** form of order. To go mad you must have a terrific accumulation of sanities.*

— Henry Miller

A Design Hystœrical

The object of these pages is to relate the story of a laser-piece. The CD-drive is sitting on the desk in front of me; it is cool now. I am putting this down to remember the experience, because I shall probably never review another like it.

Throwing Apples at the Sun is, so far, a unique artifact in design. Elliott Earls' self-initiated CD-ROM project significantly raises the temperature below simmering discussions about design authorship, commodification, and technology. Immediately, Earls deserves recognition for introducing a work that demands and is deserving of such consequence.

The scope of the work and the personal investment involved in producing it far outstrips the typical self-promotion pieces seen from designers. While Earls' prospects probably aren't as limited as Henry Miller's at the start of *Tropic of Cancer* ("I have no money, no resources, no hopes. I am the happiest man alive"), *Throwing Apples* is a professional gamble

marked by generosity and commitment.

Throwing Apples at the Sun challenges a broad range of conventions and skirts numerous precipice edges. Two issues of major concern are the relationships between art and design, and the potential of a nascent design criticism. Earls means for this work to have "residual meaning" within design, while substantially enlarging its vocabulary. The new words he's introducing are familiar terms within art. Critically, this work prompts detailed analysis and interpretation. It would be disingenuous to release such a product then insist, "if it looks good, it is good"[1] when the spotlight shines. I don't respect this critical challenge because the work is hyper-cerebral, complex, experimental, or non-commercial. It is due to Earls putting his ideas out there (primarily on these pages) and inviting response.

My first significant exposure to Elliott Earls' work was in *The Graphic Edge* (Booth-Clibborn, 2000) anthology, where Rick Poynor rated him four entries. Two were interesting-enough products of now-familiar Cranbrook assignments. The other two — posters called "Nude Language" and "My Head Hurts" — were peculiarly enigmatic (acknowledged by Poynor's placing them under his "Conceptual" and "Raw" headings). Formally, the two seemed more comfortable with the necessary and problematic reduction to image for book collections. No surprises here; posters come closest to the art model and dominate design representation.

Conceptually, though, the pieces suffered more than the other selections from being wrenched out of context. The ambiguity wasn't off-putting — just mildly puzzling. Did I have to be Cranbrook-aware to get this? Taken together with the "Man is my throat sore" image in *Emigre* 26, Earls was evidently a designer having physical reactions to intellectualizations — but responding in kind.

In short measure, Earls' typefaces and promotion posters started popping up like smash-hit-singles. The works were intriguing because of their mystery and strange-making of familiar forms. One typeface mutated Cyrillic characters into Roman: typing in tongues. Others looked as if they'd been left unused too long in the 'fridge and sprouted roots and shoots in the crisper. They were wittily organic in the digital environment — and slightly menacing. These fonts were growing — into what?

Then, somehow, I wound up on his mailing list, and a poster advertising *Throwing Apples* showed up at my former office. Here was the "album" that the postersingles were preceding. The promotion's sensibility was determinedly oblique. "Number 7 from Eight Studies for a Portrait of Henry Miller"? It was all attitude and allusion. No attempt was made to describe what the CD-ROM's experience was.

Prosump(tive)ump

Earls has provided a significant paper trail about his ideas. Though given the opportunity to discuss the work with him, I felt his writings provided adequate context. "WD-40," his contribution to *Emigre* 35, serves as a comprehensive preface to *Throwing Apples*. The statement is flat-out linear in comparison to his representatively garbled comments in the Seventeenth Annual 100 Show catalog.

The "Nude Language" poster becomes clearer as an initial expression of intent. Overlapping quotes from Jack Kerouac ("The Origins of Joy in Poetry") comment on the power inherent in language along with strategies to gain personal control. One quote could be a preface to the CD: "'Burroughs maintains that the only way to counter the playback techniques that are used by others (personally and politically) to control use, is through 'counterrecording' and 'playback,' a procedure of repetition, manipulation and purposeful distortion used as a tool of analysis and aggression."'

For Earls, design is a battleground of cultural self-expression. The designer must confront oppressive social forces to assert an individual, progressive voice. Commercial interests commodify revolt and usurp creative independence. The designer must adopt strategies to elude co-option and engage an audience. And s/he must show them a good time.

So, what can a poor designer boy do, 'cept package for a rock-n-roll band? From the writings of theorists and literary figures such as Alvin Toffler, Hal Foster, Italo Calvino, and others, Earls has modeled the "prosumptive designer." Existing between producer and consumer, the prosumptive designer is a self-initiated, risk-embracing, Renaissance figure. Computer hardware and software, from Quark XPress to Quicken, provides the tools to avoid dominance by the marketplace. Defamiliarization

or 'ostranenie' (strange-making) is utilized to highlight and transcend conventional readings of material. The prosumptive designer must be passionate, committed, and true to self while reaching out to other designers and non-designers alike.

Earls also says, I could be wrong about all this. Post-modernism[2] has left us authorless (no heroes) and unable to locate or maintain a radical impulse (no anti-heroes, either). The torrent of technology and theory is likely to swamp and short out our higher brain functions. And that may not be so bad. Perhaps an intellectual dyslexia is the only recourse to pastiche. Originality is the garbling of your sources. The inevitable becomes a strategy. Don't fight the current, get swept along in it. Dry land is a lie.

Pull Down the Menu, Upright the Table Lox Position

Earls has amply detailed the underlying motivations of his work. However, no manifesto accompanies *Throwing Apples*. While it is the product and representative vehicle of his ideas, the CD is no dry design exegesis. "... Finally, the greatest of God's laws, always entertain," he declares in "WD-40." Earls will be uncompromising in his building. But it's a funhouse/concert hall, not a lecture room. You can check your head, or bring it for some serious play.

Throwing Apples is a long, involuted visual and audio groove. Seduction, not dissection, is the order. Looped throughout is a phantom chorus of voices commenting, announcing, and instructing. Like the man said (I think it was Lester Bangs), rock lyrics ain't poetry. Neither is the textual material contained herein, though much is clever and evocative word play. A skewed stew of literary, religious, and cultural reference recombine into mock-profound pronouncements.

Visually, the piece is a banquet of Earls' unique graphic sensibility. "Ostranenie" is an overriding design aspect that he handles adroitly. Consistent throughout is a studied anti-mastery that makes natural the morphing fonts, scrawled illustrations, blurred and grainy images. QuickTime movies are home videos-in-overdrive of various travels: city cab rides, suburban streets, ruins. Dolls and plastic figures stand in for humans, box and dance. Crudely drawn machine parts merge with those of bodies. Kitsch, clippings, and ephemera become central characters. Active

and static images layer on top of one another, dissolving and revealing.

As with his fonts and posters, *Throwing Apples* abnormals the conventional. If a medium as new-fashioned as CD-ROM can be said to have customs. The program takes the form of a bizarre, mutant application within the desktop. Windows pop up within the display environment, a stylized palette appears dead center of the screen, and the top menu bar offers four specialized selections: "Grooves," "The Book of Kings," "Nudes," and "'Ostranenie.'"

The "MasterCylinder" is engaged upon start-up: a scrolling selection of five posters now made interactive. The posters are diagrams and blueprints of a culture collapsed in upon itself. Simultaneously high, low, and no-tech, they fuse obscure artifacts and recognizable icons into awkward but genuine schematics with personality. Binding the works together are Earls' classics-gone-to-seed fonts. Selecting aspects of the poster with a diagrammatic suit icon triggers QuickTime movies, sound effects, spoken-word pieces, and text windows. At times, activation points seem to follow an infinite progression through activated layers.

"The Book of Kings" moves through seven spreads of an old, discarded book, *Great Inventors and Their Inventions*. Most pages have been significantly intruded upon with sketches, scribblings, and photos. Others rest untouched, or bear the notes of the original owner. "Book of Kings" provides less evident layers and active areas than "MasterCylinder." Selecting images animate flashing texts and repetitive voices that expand upon the imagery.

Overall, the work is cleverly arranged. The operator (a new term is needed for those-who-play interactive CD-ROMs) can move through the work either through the different menu selections or the palette. Grooves correspond to MasterCylinder images and certain Book pages. The standard CD-ROM idea of a search/scroll is replaced with a reshuffling. While you are given options, navigation isn't the precise concept. The program's construction reinforces the theme of intellectual dyslexia. Fragments fail to coalesce to definite meanings, nor do they attempt to.

Success in this medium may be measured by the inadequacy of a linear narrative to describe the work. When performed correctly, the

project should demonstrate an alternative experience. *Throwing Apples* successfully exploits the potential of CD-ROMs and is natural to the medium. A minor caveat is that the posters perform a bit awkwardly in the compressed environment. It is impossible to see them whole except as "Overviews," which presents them at the scale of a book reproduction. However, their presentation as explorable environments re-imagines the function of a flat, designed surface. It also questions scale and proper viewing distance.

Dat's Entertainment!

The idea of a crude, mutant program is engaging and humorous. The customized control palette is a wonderful touch that I wish had been taken further. Earls plays off the default windows and type that comes with the Mac, setting his program against the operating system. (Selecting certain texts on the posters call up a message window with the same text, only in default type.) I would, however, enjoy seeing his fonts take complete control of all texts, and having him skew the rigid geometry of the window frames themselves. ("We control the horizontal, we control the vertical.")

Critiquing the music is a real taste-defining area. Conceptually, the grooves are an additional layer of activity, not quite soundtrack, not quite in sync. Stylistically, the tracks are a rap/rock fusion of Beat-box rhythms, sampling keyboards, and metallic guitar intrusions. The "presumptive designer" made me think of the legend "design will eat itself" which head-lined *Emigre*'s The Designers Republic issue (issue 29). This music has a reverb of Pop Will Eat Itself, also. The jukebox jury verdict is that Earls can play and stick some hooks. This is, I know, faint praise from a guy who can't even play air guitar convincingly.

The grooves stay organic in their rough-hewn, garage band demo sen-sibility. At other times, it seemed as if I was hearing a cover version of The Beatles' "Revolution 9." Earls refers often to outdated, pre-digital technol-ogy, particularly in "The Book of Kings" imagery. The opening seconds of surface noise, bluesy harmonica, and languid guitar compliments this characteristic. There is an expectation of wax cylinder recordings, popping Victrolas, tape hiss. More contrast between manual effects and synthetic sounds would be interesting. While I have no technical problem with his

electric playing, I'd urge Earls to unplug more often.

The raw character of the visuals is echoed in the audio tracks. The incessantly rapid videos and synthetic beats are occasionally off-putting. Earls is always shouting, putting on some accent, or electronically modulating his voice. It's soothing when he and Darlene Earls try some off-key harmonizing on the choruses of "Love Can Dig A Ditch, Love Can Build A Bridge" — after a staccato, top-of-the-lungs, ranting verse. The sound effects are crackles, feedback whines, crunching guitar chords, driving pulses. Except for, perhaps, "Oranges of Hieronymous Bosch," meditative isn't in the *Throwing Apples* vocabulary. This is in keeping with a work about dissonance, cognitive and otherwise. Though the soundtrack may not be to all tastes — the same can be said for the graphics — it's consistently disturbing and frequently catchy.

Pseudominous

Earls also supplies a punning, deadpan wit throughout. Clicking on a doll-head image calls up a text window: "this does nothing." The "Help" screen is terse: "It's pretty simple. Single click on objects in windows." Yeah, I wish. Selecting certain poster texts call up windows that repeat the same words or tosses in a question mark. You're on your own.

Overall, the text is a stream of punning, profane, and pseudo-profound gibberish. As such, the tangle of dyslexic phrases are hit-and-miss. The occasional gem — "She is indeed, both the tigress and Euphrates" — makes up for others' falling flat. Is the phrase Earls or Henry Miller? (Is it real or Memorex?) The point seems to be that it doesn't matter. The text is riffing. Earls constantly skirts the edge of monotony and annoyance as another cryptic phrase or snatch of blurry, high-speed video is activated. If you're hunting down meaning, it'll frustrate. To those accepting a cerebral seduction, it's eye and mind candy.

Synthetically produced misreadings, however, are highly unstable. They often come off as forced and self-conscious. Employing all these high culture references suggests a commentary on the material. Is the implication these particular ideas will seize up the cerebrum? That's what many traditionalist critics suggest. Everything circles back to itself or points to ersatz Henry Miller? Is it all just input, any literature will do?

All is grist for the mill. Many of the references in *Throwing Apples* are familiar pop culture/postmodern fixations. Astro Boy can't help but make me warm and nostalgic. It's likely that this is all an extended gag (joke and choke) on Cranbrook/avant-garde design fixations. As parody, its half-masticated and partially digested code codings hit the mark.

Ostranenie Angels

Earls cites a number of influences directly in his writing. Resonances of other artists are heard in *Throwing Apples*. Containing images and ideas going back some four years, the project suggests a monumental accretion or grand scheme. As such, the CD resembles a small-screen *United States I–IV*. For her epic performance work, Laurie Anderson gathered together a "... special blend of music, slides, films, lights, tapes ... hand-gestures ... and more ..."[3] to make a fragmented, multi-media narrative of our country. By turns wry, irritating, mesmerizing, hilarious, and tedious, Anderson fashioned a singularly amazing and moving performance piece.

Throwing Apples is similarly a catalog of effects. Some pieces recall Anderson strongly. "Oranges of Hieronymous Bosch" is reminiscent with its processed voice relating a profound/banal dream over a minimal instrumental track. Unlike Anderson, Earls' unprocessed or unaccented voice is rarely heard. While accomplishing the distancing, strange-making intent cheaply, this aspect is worth more treatment time. Many of the process sounds are standard distortions. The voice in "Oranges" is identical to Stephen Hawking's voder and it's difficult for me to break that association. Is this intentional?

United States relied upon its breadth of effects and non-stop blitz of stimuli for its impact. The media was message. Broken into its component parts, the work was a triumph of do-it-yourself, low-tech. The virtuosity was in Anderson's orchestration of the elements. Her wit, invention, and intelligence held it all together. *Throwing Apples* shares this. There are certain talents at which Earls excels, others where he holds his own. At its best, the resultant work questions the ideas of expertise and specialization.

"Book of Kings" is a interactive variation on Tom Phillips' long-running artist's book *A Humument*. This "treated Victorian Novel" is a déconstruction of a discarded 1892 novel purchased as both canvas and

content-provider. The artist draws new narratives from the original text by highlighting words between and across lines and painting over the remaining copy. Inspiration for the artwork grew out of an interview with William Burroughs and his "cut-up" technique.[4]

Earls' book shares this reference point with *A Humument* but is its own distinct work. *Great Inventors* was evidently selected as source book for more rhetorical purposes. It is backdrop and sub-text. Earls layers over the existing text rather than restructuring it. The book is a metaphor for his own invention (as the original text describes technological "first steps," so Earls' counters with an image of a child performing the same action), and a literal homage to those whose shoulders he stands upon. "Book of Kings" is the most direct narrative, a story of technological invention and inspiration.

William Burroughs provides a foothold for all these artists. Each is engaged in dislocating meaning with a sensibility summarized by Burroughs' quote: "language is a virus from outer space." Earls' intellectual dyslexia resembles Burroughs' cut-up technique, which is cited in "Nude Language." Earls' spin is slicing and dicing the cut-ups: most importantly, Henry Miller. For his inspiration, Earls' has swerved into literary territory and a generation of cultural renegades. Henry Miller is guiding angel for, in Earls' words, "...a well organized attempt to integrate life and art."

Paris or Prince Tops?

Miller is, on the surface, far from the template for a graphic designer. Get blind drunk, start a fight, screw in an alleyway, spew up in the street, stagger home and ... knock off an annual report? From conversations I've overheard at AIGA gatherings, this is what many (male) designers would have us believe is their usual working method. The toll it would take on their clothes alone suggests otherwise.[5]

Miller is symbolic as a romantic vision of the artist, lustily pursuing and copulating with the muse. A legion of frequently inarticulate, pure painters hard-core pore over his writing. For many, being an artist is living a certain lifestyle, not just making pieces. Unfettered by conventions, they are true artists, responsible only to the truth. But is uncompromising ego(t)ism a useful model? Is my life inartistic because I eschew alcoholic excess,

am faithful to my wife, and am willing to work in collaborations?

Considering its patron saint, *Throwing Apples* is rather discreet. There's two nude women on the CD case. One torso is prudently tucked under the flap. The male nudes are fig-leafed and masked by triggerable areas. (Two are also very time-conscious, wearing watches, unless this is a porn reference.) Henry Miller's view of women isn't the most enlightened. Neither are traditional fine art portrayals of the female form, which Earls references in the depersonalized, headless nude torso. While this isn't a CD-ROM Henry Miller reader, why isn't the scatology factor pushed? Would it be too raw and real?

If I was to ask Earls anything, it might be if any of this work was done when he was really fucked up. There's the appearance of rough-and-ready, unstylized slapdash in *Throwing Apples*. However, there's a greater distance between computer keyboard-to-CD-ROM than typewriter keyboard-to-book. Impulsiveness doesn't follow easily with computer technology.

Prince is also cited in "WD-40" as a multi-versed artist, representing music. Like many rock stars, he's venturing into interactivity. In a prosumptive move, he adopted that symbol-as-name, according to some reports, to break the dominion of his corporate record label. Pop music offers many noted multi-instrumentalists, from Paul McCartney to Dave "Foo Fighters" Grohl. Prince, however, matches Henry Miller in artistic sexual obsession. Amongst the determined one-man bands, Todd Rundgren strikes me as more suggestive of Earls. Rundgren was an early video pioneer, released an interactive music CD (song fragments you could shuffle into new compositions) as his last title, and has always been a master pop contrarian. If you buy this comparison, *Throwing Apples* is Earls' *A Wizard, A True Star*.[6]

He Piston Convention

Commodification preys on the mind of contemporary design practice. This dance-with-the-devil discussion is ever-present and perplexing in all creative activities. The issues involved are complicated and far from straightforward. Art, which plays to a narrower, privileged clientele, is far from pure. Design's current self-consciousness likely reflects

the unabashed commercial boosterism that has dominated the practice. Observing designers' responses to the marketplace reveals rationalization, invention and evasion.

Throwing Apples represents an effort to completely control the creation, manufacture, and distribution of a mass-produced work. Earls is only indirectly beholden to corporate interests through the manufacturers of the equipment.[7] "Prosumption" is meaningful if it leads to investigating and occupying the codes of commerce. *Throwing Apples* is provocative by making a narrative of itself as a commodity. Usually, the product is stood apart from the artwork, to not sully the æsthetic event. This distancing has become increasingly hypocritical and troublesome to maintain. The marketplace doesn't just lurk behind the art, it is encompassing. Artists and designers must deal with this reality to have relevance.

Another interesting example of commercial narratives is the changing nature of type promotions, which have become increasingly "creative." Type is no longer the building blocks of language, selected for purely for-mal reasons. Fonts are and have stories. The situation is more complicated than choosing a face because it signifies "cool" or "classic." Emigre pushes this, with the biographies that accompany many of their fonts. *Throwing Apples* is the most baroque construction yet invented to sell type.[7] Then again, the type could be selling the CD-ROM.

Throwing Apples may also be regarded as a prototype art kit. You buy the art: the CD, and get the makings of your own: the typeface. Artwork has always served as a generator of more art, though not as explicitly. The idea of commodity is twisted back on itself. The prosumptive designer, though, doesn't purchase fonts.

In The Rad Zone (React-or Going Critical)

Earls makes a number of radical and revolutionary claims for the prosumptive designer. His product is a persuasive argument for his ideas. There are, however, constraints to his ideal. Technology and talent will only do so much.

Throwing Apples couldn't exist without sophisticated hardware and software. The issue of access to all these technological products needs to be raised when the potential gets glorified. While everything Earls uses

is "off the shelf," those shelves aren't within everyone's reach. A select few have the technology necessary to make and experience his project. This situation is, sadly, old news, and has arisen with every new art/communication medium.

We're closer to pluralist access, but there's still a long ways to go. What happens to the poor prosumptive designer in the interim? It's futile and ridiculous to suspend production while everyone catches up. By that time, new technology will be introduced and we're back to square one. A world where everyone can manufacture their own CD-ROMs is a fascinating one to consider, but is not imminent. Proclaiming the prosumptive designer may be economically premature and creatively frustrating.

Is *Throwing Apples at the Sun* radical? Radicals are extremists. This CD will be anathema to traditional designers. It's even put off adventurous artists I've exposed to it. But traditionalists are an easy target. Earls has grabbed the author flag and sprinted far downfield. One team will cheer his progress, while another claims he's stepped out of bounds. Such a narrow field makes transgression less profound. We may also question striving to radicality for its own sake. The attempt invites confusing signifier with signified.

Throwing Apples continually undercuts itself with its dyslexic language and self-references. The undermining ceases when it comes to Earls being a designer and his products.[8] This is pragmatic. Unless he's funded, it's likely Earls needs people to buy his products. But making the leap into fiction may be the decisive radical act. I want to call in an order for a font and instead get one of those processed voices telling me: *this does nothing*. Or instead of Earls' current bio (which consists of his birth date and where he did his undergraduate and graduate studies) there's a story of how he lost his virginity.

Catching Hell From the Fathers

The conception of the prosumptive designer continues the traditional emphasis upon the designer as meaning provider and arbitrator. When all is selected and shutdown, how the work is interpreted is a mystery. What of the prosumptive audience? Who are they? From the evidence of *Throwing Apples*, they're designers. Earls' theorizing is a justification for

designers to clear a wider space for their activity. To be authors and artists. However, outside of design, no justification is needed. Given the opportunity, all types of people will get hold of the tools of production and create. Theory isn't required.

As Andrew Blauvelt noted in *Emigre* 38, asserting an auteur status for designers contradicts Barthes' assertion. For all the talk of post-modern author death, no one suggests killing him or herself professionally. Might a new anonymity actually be in order? (As opposed to the fictive, non-mediating, modernist figure.) Could this be the true insurgency? Instead of inflating your stature separate from the audience, you accept an indefinition. Join the culture! The audience has only the work and themselves.

Rather than reinforcing the all-in-one impulse, it may be subversive to encourage the collaborative. Change requires numbers. Group dynamics also bring their own æsthetic and pragmatic rewards. I admire Prince, but also R.E.M., who, like more and more bands, equally share songwriting credits. While Michael Stipe writes the lyrics and gets the attention, they all share in the real profits — and keep playing.

Apocalypservice (Riverrunon Sentence)

Cultivating creativity is a serious business and a devotional pursuit. Until we have the prosumptive audience, it doesn't really matter that one person accomplished *Throwing Apples at the Sun*. If it inspires someone to just design fonts, or make videos, or compose music, it's successful. Prosumption is back-story. Earls acknowledges this and has put the CD out on its own terms. Curious viewers should turn it on and enjoy an exceptionally lively experience.[9]

On the title window, a version number (1.0) is given for the program, indicating an intention to upgrade the work. This is another novel twist upon the traditional artistic process. Will Earls be growing or refining the piece? His recent "Venus Dioxide" font promotion poster could easily be incorporated. It is said of many artists that they actually labored on one career-encompassing work of numerous parts. Earls might be taking this literally. Paul Valery also said, "A work of art is never finished, it is abandoned." An artist should have abandon ....

Footnotes:

1 Not Elliott Earls. The author takes full and complete responsibility for this quote's appearance, and the consequences.

2 If this review were a CD-ROM, the sound of hundreds of designers groaning would be heard as your icon passed over this word.

3 Laurie Anderson, "Yankee See," ©1984 Difficult Music, *United States Live*, Warner Bros. Records.

4 Tom Phillips, *Works and Texts*, New York: Thames and Hudson, p. 255

5 With Vaughan Oliver, though, all bets are off.

6 Todd Rundgren, *A Wizard, A True Star*, Bearsville Records, 1973. For those unfamiliar with this obscure treat, it followed Rundgren's double-album pop masterpiece, *Something/Anything?* — which yielded the hits "Hello It's Me" and "I Saw the Light." Disenchanted with the ease of churning out hits — it took him only three weeks to record three sides of the LP while playing all the instruments — Rundgren struck out in a decidedly anti-commercial, eclectic direction for his next release. Wizard mixed his multi-instrumentalism with band support over one 56-minute (!) LP of nineteen tracks. Todd mixed stirring anthems ("Just One Victory"), moving cover tunes ("I'm So Proud"/"Ooh Baby Baby"/"La La Means I Love You"/"Cool Jerk"), synthesizer-driven instrumentals ("Flamingo"), punk fury ("Is It My Name?"), goofy studio pranks ("Dogfight Giggle"), and more into a glorious compost. To top it all off, the LP had great cover art (a die-cut-corner gatefold sleeve) and avant-garde literary credibility (a verse called "Star Fever" by then-unknown poet/record reviewer Patti Smith printed on a band-aid insert). Moral of this story: it's a compliment.

7 Coming in second would be Thirstype's "Kulture Kit," with its up-front agit-prop, abstract impressionistic catalog, and fantastical, illustrated postcards. An animated version of those images would be something to see.

8 For example, the credits on the CD case utilize his fonts but are classically set in centered and justified alignments.

9 And I should mention the beautiful package that holds the entire piece.

From abacus to Zeus

1: The occasion determines the type

It was Paul Rand's 100th birthday. I thought I should send a card and, finally, express my feelings about the famed designer. Really, if you're going to write about design, how can you not consider its most storied practitioner? Not to would just be bad form (ha ha). Sure, I cast him in cameo appearances for an article here and there. Often, I admit, in an unflattering light. It was time to give him his full due.

I intended something short and sweet but not sloppy. Something along the lines of "Hey! I get it! ♥KFG." It seemed appropriate under the circumstances, Rand not being much for sentimentality, despite all the ♥'s that dot his work. But soon I was scribbling thoughts all across the card's inside, down the back, and over the front, obliterating the picture, and the printed message. I ended with a cluttered, unstructured mess. Mr. Rand might regard it as a deliberate provocation, an in your face on his big day. Worse still, I ended up expressing my love for *someone else*.

2: The birth of a new package

On the occasion of Rand's centenary, Chronicle Books brought out a new edition of *Thoughts on Design*, the designer's first book. Here was the primary document of graphic design, available again in paperback and for your Kindle. I first wrote "modern graphic design" in that last sentence but

realized the modifier was unnecessary, redundant. By design's accounts, this is where it *all* began.

Though moderately priced, I wasn't tempted to pick up the new edition. That's because I'm fortunate to own a copy of the 1951 Wittenborn & Company second edition I purchased at a library remainder sale for $1 — a steal from its previous owner, who had to fork over $5, according to the penciled notation on the title page. Since this was billed as the return of the landmark tome, I could just consult my find to opine on the Master's masterwork.

I expeditiously navigated the book's 136 main text pages: 97 of them entirely composed of reproductions of Rand's work or containing no more than a paragraph of text, another 16 either totally blank or having just a caption for the facing page reproduction of a design piece. But I quickly became disoriented when I perused on-line commentaries on what I'd just encountered.

The first perplexing instance was reading Michael Bierut's introduction for the reprint, posted at Design Observer. The subtitle for the article on the site's home page immediately didn't jibe: "On Paul Rand's 96-page masterpiece." 96? What was he counting? Reading the article, I was confronted with other disparities.

"This, perhaps, has never been said better than in the book's most quoted passage," Bierut wrote, "the graceful free verse that begins Rand's essay 'The Beautiful and the Useful.' Graphic design, he says, no matter what else it achieves, 'is not good design if it is irrelevant.'"

I had just read the book and couldn't recall such a passage. And it wasn't as if the text was that long to slip my mind. You could possibly commit the entirety, captions included, to memory then recite it verbatim in short order. "Graceful free verse"? That described *nothing* in my copy, all straight prose paragraphs. Were we reading the same book?

It turned out we weren't. When I read the blurb on the Chronicle Books web page for the book, the discrepancy became clear: "One of the seminal texts of graphic design, Paul Rand's *Thoughts on Design* is now back in print for the first time since the 1970s. Writing at the height of his career, Rand articulated in his slender volume the pioneering vision that

all design should seamlessly integrate form and function. This facsimile edition preserves Rand's original 1947 essay with the adjustments he made to its text and imagery for a revised printing in 1970 and adds only an informative and inspiring new foreword by Pentagram partner Michael Bierut. As relevant today as it was when first published, this classic treatise is an indispensable addition to the library of every designer."

What is being advertised as "seminal" is actually *supplanted*. The 1970 version removed earlier examples of work, added new ones, and substantially reworked and abbreviated the text. For example, these are the words being quoted as opening the first essay:

"Graphic design —
which fulfills esthetic needs,
complies with the laws of form
and the exigencies of two-dimensional space;
which speaks in semiotics, sans-serifs,
and geometrics;
which abstracts, transforms, translates,
rotates, dilates, repeats, mirrors,
groups, and regroups —
is not good design
if it is irrelevant."

Rand actually began his first book this way: "To interpret the modern approach to visual communication as mere sensationalism is to misunderstand the very spirit of our time. In advertising, the contemporary approach to art is based on a simple concept, a concept of the advertisement as an organic and functional unit, each element of which is integrally related to the others, in harmony with the whole, and essential to the execution of the idea. From this standpoint, copy, art, and typography are indissoluble. Editorial layout, promotional matter, direct mail, packaging, book designing, and industrial design are governed by the same considerations: function ... form ... production process ... integrated product. Such an evolution logically precludes extraneous trimmings and 'streamlined' affectations."

Not so uplifting. What was terse to begin with becomes practically

telegraphic. "Adjustments" glosses over a substantial elision of the book's look and meaning. While not exactly misleading, the publisher's blurb and Bierut's introduction vault in their claims between decidedly different books. The 33-year-old Rand is given credit for what the 56-year-old wrote. In his new introduction, Bierut states that despite his age, the younger Rand "was ready" to compose his first book. His subsequent rewrites suggest otherwise.

Matters grew more complicated when I consulted my copy of what is said to be Rand's second book, 1985's *A Designer's Art*. This "revised and updated" volume incorporated and adapted much of *Thoughts on Design*'s content, with further rewriting, substitution, and addition of imagery. This book saw reprint by his estate in 2000 (the edition I happen to own) and is now, itself, out of print.

That *Thoughts on Design* has been technically unavailable for 44 years is then doubly immaterial. By its author's choice, Rand's original conception is long gone.

What was cast as an event really isn't one at all. The blurbs properly note that this new book is the 1970 version. However, they do so without noting how dramatically different it is from the first. And if, as claimed by its publisher and forward (then parroted by many design outlets),the book's message is "as relevant today as when first published," shouldn't we see and read precisely what *was* first published?

3: Why make changes?

Whatever one thinks of Paul Rand and his ideas, the book is a classic: a landmark artifact of graphic design history. I'm usually not much for *should*s, but it's a book that should stay available. Without an awareness of the concepts identified with Paul Rand, you can't understand much of graphic design activity globally over the past 80+ years, either production by Rand's disciples or his detractors. And I'd readily grant Rand and his estate purer motives than, say, David Carson's attempt to nullify critics by rushing out a revised *The End of Print* after only five years with fresh editorial dissembling.

In spirit, the *Thoughts* are the same. Rand abandons none of his core principles. This isn't a Tschichold-like renunciation. But in many details,

the doctrines are shaded and lessened. In the first of the three-paragraph preface to the 1970 third edition, Rand points out the changes: "In this edition of *Thoughts on Design*, the writer has made certain emendations. However, these do not materially alter his thoughts or intentions. It is for the purpose of clarifying some of the ideas and enriching the visual material that a portion of the text has been revised and a number of illustrations have been replaced." (The second paragraph becomes the core of the even shorter preface to *A Designer's Art*.)

More is going on than Rand honing his arguments and writing skills. His use of the term "emendation" displays an erudite self-deprecation. Supposedly, Rand was insecure about his writing ability throughout his life. But while he didn't perform a large-scale retreat from his essential positions between editions, corners are rounded off and edges trimmed.

Rand also simply needed to have the book live up to its title. A suitable name for the original would have been *Thoughts on Design of Advertisements (and Application to Select Book and Magazine Covers)*. It was a narrowly focused study that neglected a broad swath of commonplace design activity.

The 1970 edition expanded the circle of artifacts only slightly. The additions that likely necessitated the book's overhaul were corporate trademarks. In the years between editions, the logo became the locus of Rand's practice, renown, and theory. Corporate identity was key in every way. And nowhere to be found in *Thoughts on Design*.

This absence is a case for the creation of *A Designer's Art*. But why gut the first book in between? The omission of logo and corporate identity work created a yawning chasm in that first book, one that Rand elected to backfill. The 1970 edition papers over the gap: *See? I knew it all along*. Simply put, it's revisionist history. If anything, Rand was *behind* the curve in directly addressing the rise and eventual dominance of corporate identity in design activity. To be fair, he was busy *driving* the development in his own work.

To talk as if the reissue is the work of the young wunderkind is to misrepresent the reality. For instance, in *Fast Company*'s "5 Timeless Marketing Lessons for Today's Brands from Visionary Designer Paul

Rand," approvingly quotes the master "in his remarkably prescient 1947 book *Thoughts on Design* about the value of surprise in marketing": "For an advertisement to hold its own in the competitive race, the designer must steer clear of visual clichés by some unexpected interpretation of the commonplace."

The problem is, again, that Rand did *not* write that in 1947. Instead, he wrote this: "However, for the advertisement to 'hold its own' in a competitive race, it must be off the beaten path by some more interesting device: the abstract symbol."

These two statements are distinctly different. The original instruction calls for a specific formal device in any and all instances, regardless of subject or situation. The modifying directive "If this symbol is too obscure in itself, it should be balanced with universally recognized forms" is as demonstrative. And intellectually suspect.

Though common Modernist design dogma at the time (and still quite detectible today), a belief in the actuality of "universally recognized forms" has, to be charitable, not worn well. Tellingly, Rand saw fit to completely remove this chapter altogether; "Individuality and Abstract Forms" is retired for the new "Imagination and the Image."

The replacement text is less prophetic than anodyne. It took Paul Rand nearly four decades in the design profession to counsel against *cliché*? How influential was that 1947 book if it made this decree necessary? Meanwhile, the remedy ("some unexpected interpretation of the commonplace") could possibly be *less* specific but only with some effort.

However, as with many of Rand's pronouncements, his writing skill seems to be in making vague hand-waving *sound* authoritative. Overall, rather than giving assertive testimonies, Rand seems more to be struggling to find things to say. The obvious evidently ranks high. To deliver these basic instructions constitutes an unkind indictment of his profession. It's a wonder Rand is so revered by his fellow practitioners. No enemy has depicted designers as so clueless.

4: Terra nova

In assessing Paul Rand's seerage, we must recognize that neither the content nor the context for the 1970 book was the same as the 1947

original. The intervening 23 years, with Rand's accretion of accolades, the climb to exalted stature within his field, all played a substantial role in how that 1970 edition was received.

That the edition being considered is not the original doesn't automatically negate the claims. And it's just as possible that appreciation for the book's achievements might *increase* were we to evaluate that 1947 edition. But, on the whole, the design profession doesn't really care to know. 1947, 1970, 1985, 2014 ... what's the difference?

To argue that these variances are irrelevant is to assert that words don't matter, that specific meanings are unimportant. This goes against Rand's own clearly articulated belief. Why *make* these changes unless words, and meanings, *are* significant?

Of the qualities that Rand is honored for, high among them is precision. If it is to be said that he was "prescient," we must alter the start date on his clairvoyance by over two decades. We must also say that, in a number of subtle yet profound ways, he got it wrong. He also clung to problematic opinions throughout revisions.

For instance, in "The Symbol in Advertising," the crucifix is claimed to be "a perfect union of the aggressive male (vertical) and the passive horizontal (female). And it is not too far-fetched to infer that these formal relations have at least something to do with its enduring quality." The passage remains in the 2000 edition of *A Design's Art* and the current *Thoughts*.

Is it not too far-fetched to catch at least a whiff of misogyny here? Rand's reading of the crucifix is utterly cultural. It may also be a concept borrowed from Adolf Loos' influential 1908 essay "Ornament and Crime": "The first ornament that came into being, the cross, had an erotic origin. The first work of art, the first artistic action of the first artist daubing on the wall, was in order to rid himself of his natural excesses. A horizontal line: the reclining woman. A vertical line: the man who penetrates her. The man who created it felt the same urge as Beethoven, he experienced the same joy that Beethoven felt when he created the Ninth Symphony."

As a foundational document of Modern design thought, it's in keeping that Rand might incorporate a Loos reading of form, acknowledged

or not. It's an open question if Rand even knew Loos to be the source. But Rand wasn't reticent to footnote. Might it be that the full quote was deemed too risqué by a genteel practitioner?

(A further, peculiar aspect of the Loos reference is that there are at least *two* similar but different versions of the "Ornament and Crime" article in circulation in print and on-line. Most feature the crucifix reference, while others, notably the current book collection of Loos essays, do not.)*

Rand wandering into the "Oriental and Occidental thought" of the *Book of Changes* to provide corroboration can't salvage a maladroit rationale. Again, Rand seems to be casting about for "objective" reasons for what were intuitive choices. He's trying too hard.

It's readily acknowledged that advertising copy was the template for Rand's writing. Short and snappy, ad copy is all about assertion with minimal, if any, evidence. It trades on received wisdom, brooks no ambivalence nor admits to nuance. All of these are hallmarks of Rand's text. The copy within the ads he designed for Benzedrine Inhalers blends perfectly with the surrounding heady theory he produces. Product and process; it's all the same.

Another noteworthy aspect of the original *Thoughts* redacted in later editions is the citation of sales figures for advertising campaigns. In three instances (Dubonnet, Coronet, Air-Wick), Rand footnotes his text on specific projects to flourish hard, high numbers: "After the introduction of Dubonnet advertising in March, 1941, when manufacture of the product was started in the United States, sales increased more than 1000%. Yet the retail price of Dubonnet 'made in U.S.A.' was $1.49 against a previous import price of $1.59 ... a differential certainly not great enough to account for the tenfold advance in sales."

While taking care to dispense disclaimers that his design might be exclusively responsible for the sales increase ("It would be impossible, of course, to prove that this popularity is due entirely to Coronet advertising"), Rand's proffering of such statistics was plainly meant as affirmation of his craft's ability to boost bottom-lines. It also suggests we could read the book's cover as more than an engaging photogram pattern. Might it be a sly reference to calculating revenues?

Now, and for many years previously, such bold reference to *gelt* appears crass. It sets up an awkward straddle: design has to proclaim its practical, economic viability while eschewing quoting actual earnings. The door can be opened to a dangerous conclusion: the most effective design is that which sells the most.

This places too much power in the hands of the consumer, who has historically been portrayed by designers as, by turns, intuitively discriminating *and* damnably philistine. Design's policy is to move the goalposts. Precise evidence of sales of specific products is dropped for a corporation's overall prominence in its field (see: IBM).

Design continues to have an ambivalent, if not inconsistent, affiliation with evidence for its effective power. The uproar over AIGA's restructured "Justified" competitions is a case in point. The core scorn was for the requirement that applicants provide some objective measure of the design's success. For many practitioners, it's vulgar to tout a design's ROI ("Return on Investment") as an aspect of determining its quality.

It's to Rand's credit that he wasn't above hitting the spreadsheets to prove his dedication to advertising's *raison d'etre*: profit. "Accessible ... æsthetic development" is all well and good but not on the company's dime. Had Rand continued the practice, we might salute him as intellectually daring and progressive.

A few years ago, an art history panel at the College Art Association annual conference featured a unique and controversial paper. Instead of turning to critical opinion of the time, the researcher actually investigated gallery sales figures to determine what the influential art of a particular era actually was. What might seem commonsensical was, in this context, radical. Art's own connection to sales is no more pure or less tangled that that of design.

A service that *Thoughts on Design* provided was to emphatically situate graphic design activity in relation to fine art. All while performing a deft, if ultimately unsuccessful two-step that supplied design with its own discreet identity. Rand's intended end to consider graphic design in a contemporary art context was visionary. His route there is unconvincing. In terms of locating graphic design in culture, *Thoughts on Design* was a major

missed opportunity. Rand just didn't have the chops. This is *not* to say that Rand was at all unintelligent, just unversed in art discourse. An unfortunate legacy of the book is design's ongoing cramped and retrograde view of art, one that stifles any substantive discussion.

Were Rand truly aware of and comfortable with his times, he might have articulated a progressive, coherent position for himself and his activity. He could reasonably claim a status as the most influential artist of his day. Unfortunately, in his ruminations, Rand stays within the realm of an outmoded æsthetics, leaping over the immediate European Moderns to those of a recent, but superseded group.

Rand chooses a flavor of Modern more to his taste. By the calendar, Roger Fry's musings are nearly contemporaneous with Rand's activity. However, the people quoted are backwards looking. They describe art that, however meritorious, was no longer the leading cultural edge. Just as soon as graphic design establishes a Modern identity, it is shackled to the past.

Discussing the art portions of *Thoughts on Design* is arguably moot. Except for the most artistically naïve graphic designers, which actually encompasses the majority of practitioners, Rand's art philosophizing is considered pretty duff stuff. Those bits get skipped. However, his meditations continued throughout his writing career and were part and parcel of his total ethos. Cutting out the art aspects of *Thoughts* and focusing only on his direct design theorizing excises the book's heart.

Publication of *Thoughts on Design* fired a starter's pistol for a race between Rand's reputation and developments in art. Rand's stature easily outpaced the latter. His design fame quickly grew to proportions that made the accuracy or relevance of his theorizing beside the point. Rand created his own reality.

5: Terra incognito

By summoning only select critics to support his "functional-æsthetic perfection" Rand skirted the prominent art thinkers of the immediate day to find succor from early 20th century British critics such as Bloomsbury Group member Roger Fry that valued æsthetics and scorned social utility. Notable by their absence are any contemporary art critics of about the

time of the original book or later. In his thinking about art, Rand was particularly retro and Anglophilic his entire life, steering clear of our country's pioneering Modern art theorists. Foremost amongst them is Clement Greenberg, whose view of art was antithetical to Rand's ambitions.

Passages like this from the 1939 essay "Avant-Garde and Kitsch" wouldn't sit well: "A society, as it becomes less and less able, in the course of its development, to justify the inevitability of its particular forms, breaks up the accepted notions upon which artists and writers must depend in large part for communication with their audiences. It becomes difficult to assume anything. All the veritie involved by religion, authority, tradition, style, are thrown into question, and the writer or artist is no longer to estimate the response of his audience to the symbols and references with which he works."

Greenberg demolishes the idea of sureties and verities, while almost a decade later Rand proclaims them. Throughout his writing career, Rand posits a near-monolithic culture that could be entertained and commanded through the application of carefully crafted "symbols and references."

The capitalism system that nurtured Rand — with Rand reciprocating the love — was his vehicle for bettering society. For Greenberg, it's "in decline" and "finds whatever of quality it is still capable of producing becomes almost invariably a threat to its own existence ... Today we look to socialism simply for the preservation of whatever living culture we have right now."

Worse still is where Greenberg would place graphic design and advertising. It's the "kitsch" of the essay's title. "Where there is an avant-garde, generally we find a rearguard. True enough — simultaneously with the entrance of the avant-garde, a second cultural phenomenon appeared in the industrial West: that thing to which the Germans give the wonderful name of Kitsch: popular, commercial art and their chromotypes, magazine covers, illustrations, ads .... "

As you might expect, Greenberg doesn't have kind words for kitsch: "Kitsch is mechanical and operates by formulas. Kitsch is vicarious experience and faked sensations. Kitsch changes according to style, but remains always the same. Kitsch is the epitome of all that is spurious in the life of

our times. Kitsch pretends to demand nothing of its customers except their money — not even their time."

Rand could legitimately counter that he also rejects formula and stylistic volatility. If Rand's critical lights traded in an early Modern highbrow snobbery, Greenberg was exhibiting his own singular style of snooty with his remarks on designed artifacts.

Greenberg at least addresses what was in formation and, for good and ill, played a key role in forming. What would have made *Thoughts on Design* truly perceptive would have been to engage the avant-garde art of his day, and the thinking behind it. In many ways, the world in which Rand's work was experienced was more in line with the tastes of Roger Fry. Culture didn't change so abruptly.

But if *Thoughts on Design* fit the prevalent æsthetic context in which it appeared, said context was rapidly being ousted. I quote Greenberg not to certify his views. He's had a legion of legitimate opponents. It's to illustrate where progressive Modern thought traveled in art. But yet again, it may all be extraneous. In the end, it's unlikely that even Rand's preferred culture experts would embrace advertising.

6: A rough test of quality

This level of analysis may be heavy-handed. It's widely accepted that Rand's book are essentially portfolios, not objective explorations or expansions of ideas. They are polemics, repeatedly underscoring one word set large: *Modernism*.

If played properly, in its time and ours, repetition can be moving. Most artists delineate an æsthetic space and draw upon and over it for the entirety of their careers. This is merely to affirm what *Thoughts* is: a personal/professional validation. And what it isn't: an open investigation of creative possibilities.

Monograph or manifesto, to properly assess *Thoughts on Design* and its relevance, critics and commentators need to contemplate the original artifact within its historical moment. It's more than a scholarly interest. Creators can't be trusted to interpret and preserve their own visions, or to understand the implications that "emendations" can have on their art and image.

While Rand pointed out his textual modifications and the substitutions of images in his 1970 edition, he made no mention of his layout changes. Apart from the cover image, the later book sports an entirely different look. His desire to rework his words, an area not to his expertise, is reasonable. Design is another matter. Substantial revisions here should garner attention.

With Paul Rand, even minor formal moves are significant. For him to embark on a wholescale reimaging of a book is conspicuous. For it to go unmentioned by the designer, and unnoticed by its audience, is noteworthy at least. Even if benign, the scale of this particular change begs explanation.

Rand didn't consider his creations inviolate. He reportedly offered to tweak his iconic UPS logo and resolve a formal irregularity at his own expense. If there's an aspect to the redesign that smells suspicious, it's that the design audience pays it no mind.

Though the abacus photogram remains as the book's cover graphic, a typeface substitution is evident that carries over to the interior pages on the revised editions. The original titling Futura Bold font is swapped out for Rand's beloved Bodoni ("an example of a basic design that never goes out of style and a reminder of Dewey's 'a work of art is recreated every time it is esthetically experienced'"). The terminal colon after "Thoughts on Design" is also excised.

The original interior layout is an airy, straightforward asymmetric presentation with touches of Rand "sparkle" to enliven the structure. Generous margins surround ragged-right blocks of Baskerville, which dresses all interior text, save for the book title on the title page. An eccentric setting choice is to disdain hyphenation, leading to some gawky line-ends. Still, it's a less egregious typographic flaw than the double spaces after punctuation (!) found in his typography a year previous for *Modern Art in Advertising*.

Footnotes are set at the bottom of text columns, with captions usually aligning to the left edge of images or occasionally floating independently, if not placed on a facing, otherwise blank page. Images of Rand's design work and the main text largely occupy separate pages.

However, in chapter 4, "Versatility of the Symbol," he places a perfume bottle tight to the base of the text block to the right, energizing that page's layout.

Another arrangement that could count as fanciful is the title page. A thin-ruled flag-like frame of six sections holds the majority of text, set opposite the book title.

All told, the original book has 159 numbered pages, plus ten Roman-numbered introductory pages. Another feature that did not survive emendation is French and Spanish translations of the text, set in the back of the book (save for the introductory material) in two narrow justified columns of smaller type.

The entirety of this scheme is junked in favor of a layout that graces all successive Rand pamphlets and books. The "Transitional" Baskerville is, perhaps, deemed (literally) insufficiently Modern. It's replaced with the favored Bodoni, whose high contrast makes it a dubious text face, though classic in appearance.

While the body copy remains in ragged right settings, the point size jumps to an over-standard scale. The look is reminiscent of Large Print editions or a children's book. Combining the latter with the pedantic tone of much of the text conveys a patronizing air to the affair.

The text columns now reach to the top of pages, filling more of the vertical space. The narrower left measure opposite the main text columns now contain chapter heads and footnotes, set across from the referring copy. Though now hyphenated, the shorter-measured lines still sport an inelegant rag.

This schema was evidently introduced with the 1970 edition of *Thoughts*. Another curiosity of Rand's overall handling of his books was that he then strayed from this layout — which was to become the template for all his books — to take a slight detour for *A Designer's Art* (Univers! Helvetica!). Was it a stutter?

It's the norm for designers to tinker with their approaches across incidences of the same artifacts. A new book is an opportunity to reconsider its form and function *ad infinitum*. It's what designers do. Even if — probably *especially* if — you're Paul Rand. What's at issue isn't the simple fact of

Rand directing changes in his work. It's the inconsistent inquiry afforded his products in comparison to his outsized reputation. Paul Rand is simultaneously the most *and* least scrutinized practitioner.

7: House-organ

Self-scrutiny is also notoriously unreliable. Artists aren't trustworthy analysts of their motivations or perceptive of the actual reasons for their accomplishments. If an artist meets with success when wielding a specific creative program, then it's natural to attribute said triumph to the system.

Rand deftly described his philosophy and its application and how it influenced clients and audiences. But as was observed in his later years, when corporations turned to design Rand regarded as inferior, he was at a loss to explain it. Other than to declare said companies' CEOs foolhardy. A faulty diagnosis on his part didn't occur to him.

Just as designers themselves are unreliable witnesses to their work and times, so are the profession-centric authors to which the field entrusts its history. Though Steven Heller dedicates an entire chapter to "Paul Rand: Author" in his lauded 1999 monograph, he makes no mention of the second, substantially reworked edition of *Thoughts on Design*. Heller skips to *A Designer's Art*.

Celebration is the order of the day with *Thoughts on Design*'s reappearance. From the varied commentary in its wake, there seems little in contemporary graphic design that the book didn't foresee or for which it isn't responsible.

It's incontestable that the author was a profound influence on a generation of designers. And it was Paul Rand's first book. However, this doesn't necessarily add up to *Thoughts on Design* warranting regard as the prescient, pioneering artifact that's claimed.

As we've seen, today's commentators are describing a simulacrum. Trying to locate the source of proof for the various encomiums conferred upon the book is often frustrating. Or, for that matter, the basis for most praises bestowed within the design profession.

The mainstream design press is a round robin of opinion, each bird re-tweeting the previous with no checking or sure derivation. In other words, *says who*? Answer: says someone (else) famous.

Assessing the legacy of *Thoughts on Design* is therefore more complicated than allowed. Beyond the fact that many commentators haven't even read the true 1947 version *or* even the reissue, depending on someone *else* having read it and knowing what they're talking about, there's the actuality that said pundits likely haven't bothered to investigate the possibility of other claimants.

8: Novel. But how novel?

The picture of early 20th century design painted by either edition of *Thoughts* and its present-day devotees is that of a fusty, dour expanse of feeble hoopla. Into this turgid marketing hackscape swoops Paul Rand, brandishing the liberating power of European Modern formalism. This one-man funnel cloud of fresh air disperses the stale stench of business bromides, transforming design into an edifying and lucrative dynamo.

As origin stories go, this is fairly archetypical. Particularly for artists (except the lucre part, we look away from that). And plays well in an individualistic culture. But when isn't this derivative scenario of lackeys and lacklustery mapped onto the present day?

Paul Rand's is an inspiring, hardscrabble tale of attainment through prodigious talent and effort. It's no less momentous for its applicability, with differing degrees of fortune, to other design figures in history. And the "hotshot young ad exec on the make" is an established, stock character.

In many cases, categories must be sliced molecule thin to dispense credit to Rand for being the trailblazer. Other designers of his time were producing effective and fetching ads, book and magazine covers, logos, identities, and posters. Placing Rand near the apex of preeminent practitioners is fitting. But giving him primary positioning requires distinctions that distort rather than refine meaning.

The design stage of the time boasted a number of gifted actors alongside Rand in channeling European Modern style. Alvin Lustig and Lester Beall are just two conspicuous names we might conjure. What puts Rand on the top rung? First with a book wins design? *Thoughts on Design* certainly can't claim that distinction. In fact, there was an eminent book on design that saw its reissue the year after Rand puts out his first.

William Addison Dwiggins' *Layout in Advertising*, first published in

1928, "was considered the standard text on the subject," according to his bio for Art Directors Club Hall of Fame. His book was just one publication in a wide-ranging and extensive writing career that ranged beyond profession-related material. Rand was well aware of Dwiggins' text, including it in the "Select Bibilography" of his final book *From Lascaux to Brooklyn*.

Dwiggins was also an advertising designer, book designer, type designer, typographer, letterer, calligrapher, illustrator, theorist, historian, playwright, master marionettist, and more. In its existence as a discreet discipline, graphic design hasn't produced a figure that comes closer to a status as its Renaissance man.

Ironically, between the respective books, each man's title is more suited for the other. Where Rand speaks almost exclusively of the graphic arrangement of advertisements, Dwiggins examines a variety of products, from "blotters" to billboards. "This book discusses the operation of putting an advertising project into graphic form," begins the Preface, "For the purposes of the argument 'advertising' means every conceivable *printed* means for selling anything."

In 200 pages (including index), Dwiggins crafts an authentic how-to guide that is detailed, specific, clear, and clear-headed. He first discusses the physical components of design pieces, and the process of printing and constructing them. His presentation of design is holistic, confronting the individual concerns of doing design along with the practical. Instead of offering his own work or that of others to elucidate his principles, he fashions speculative sketches.

Dwiggins is opinionated yet aspirational, refusing to lecture or impose his particularized vision. Readers are encouraged to develop their own critical sensibilities and personal voices: "… the writer has not assumed to give directions. He has aimed, rather, to help the practitioner compile his own book of directions. The help that the text may be expected to provide, then, will be along the lines of evocation — or *education* in the root meaning of the word — drawing out of the receptacle what was already there. If it succeeds in enlightening the student of graphic advertising as to methods of attack and analysis it will have done one good thing. If it then inspires him to build up his own structure of judgments and

standards, based upon the exercise of his own faculty of criticism, it will have accomplished its aim."

The promotion of diverse approaches balanced with an unwavering commitment to craft as a critical component of making design is thoroughly contemporary and far-sighted. *Layout in Advertising*'s instructions on organization, ideation, layout, and typography are as applicable today as they were in 1928. Only an updating of its visuals and some period idioms and references would be required to put the book back on the shelves.

In comparison, *Thoughts on Design* is vague, officious, and disinterested in the actuality of design practice; its process and physicality. Rand's design is about the surface. His prose is stiff and struggling, reliant in large part upon the words of other, non-design writers to elucidate his notions. Dwiggins is smooth, conversational, playful and confident. He writes with conversational authority.

9: Logical import shapes the map

Beyond issuing his book earlier, Dwiggins has a better claim at being design's alpha than Rand. *Layout in Advertising* addresses everything Rand is given credit for initiating. Rand's original first paragraph quoted above sounds as if he was reporting on Dwiggins' main points.

What about "the role of typography in terms of both amplifying and complementing a message?" Dwiggins has you covered: "Printers who advertise indulge in a great deal of talk about the *expressiveness* of this type and that, about making typography fit the crime .... One is inclined to doubt the truth of these arguments .... it isn't so much the types that give expression to a mood as it is the way they are put together .... In the pursuit of novelty it is probably wiser to depend for that quality upon a way a normal type is handled rather than upon an eccentric type. It is dangerous to play pranks with the actual reading process itself — with legibility .... "

The almighty logo? *On it.*

Dwiggins opens with a jaundiced eye on the marks of his time: "A trade-mark — the usual trade-mark — is a necessary evil. It is utterly indigestible." He then zeroes in on the essentials: "A proper trade-mark needs to *mean something*. At its best it is an epigram — a tense and pungent summary of some significant fact about the business. The words to be stressed

are 'epigram' and 'summary.' A trade-mark that attempts to illustrate a process in detail, for example, fails on both accounts."

Missing from *Layout in Advertising* is the European Modern-inspired fetish about the abstract symbol and Gestalt principles. Again, spurning trendiness, Dwiggins offers timeless advice that doesn't require multiple modifications.

Another aspect of design where Rand is bestowed a foundational role is validating humor throughout the profession. According to Michael Bierut, "Rand's essay on humor ... really had a lot to do with setting the tone for a whole school of design and the tone of advertising that would follow." If tightly aimed on advertising ("advertisements were dominated by exclamation points and all these explicit overwritten evocations of convenience, modernity, product performance"), Bierut's assessment may be sound. However, a few sentences later, Rand has suddenly "introduced humanity" to design.

Though evidence of Rand's humor continues to elude me (if present, it's so dry as to be desiccated, and a far cry from wit), advocating in favor of drollery is always welcome. But it's a stretch to stand Rand above all comers in using a light touch, to say nothing of "introducing humanity."

In *Thoughts*, Rand himself cites another effectual use of humor, and in an arena less expected to display it than advertising: "... as an aid to understanding serious problems in war training, as an effective weapon in safety posters, war bond selling, morale building, humor was neglected neither by government nor civilian agencies during the war."

Before getting carried away with Rand's supposed instillment of humor or humanity into design, we must keep in mind that it was all strategic: "Readership surveys prove the magnetic force of humor as applied to visual presentation, whether in advertising, editorial matter, or miscellaneous design problems." It wasn't comicality or personality for its own sake. It was just another powerful tool of persuasion to sell goods, just like the abstract symbol.

By contrast, humor suffuses all of Dwiggins' work and is ever-present in his writing. In 1941, he self-published the pamphlet *A Technique for Dealing with Artists*, a tongue-in-cheek manual advising businessmen how

to manage designers. Sample chapter: "How to Lower the Conceit of an Artist." In *Layout in Advertising*, his prose displays his typical spritely tone that doesn't need to explicitly instruct designers to lighten up. (Although, a subheading in the "Technique" sections asks "Why so serious?") In humor, Rand was playing comic catch-up.

In terms of "humanity," Dwiggins promoted a plurality of approaches and self-empowerment that was alien to Rand: "It must be pointed out again that the method of design indicated by these expressions is only one of a number of methods successfully used in advertising layout. The procedure advocated is not unique. The methods are almost as many as the practitioners. There is no established and standard practice that can be quoted to aid the student of layout — he will need to evolve his own method of design under the tutelage of his own convictions, his taste, and his experience." People came first for Dwiggins. And he allowed for Rand, but not vice versa.

This statement about the basic principles of graphic design would comfortably fit into either book: "If the reader of this text should be inspired to make a statistical analysis of it, he would find certain words used over and over again: logical, simple, simplicity, pleasing pattern, controlling line, blank space, space design, unity .... "

Layout in Advertising also stand out for concluding with a ringing declaration of personal ethics: "... there are projects that undertake to exploit the meaner side of the human animal — that make their appeal to social snobbishness, shame, fear, envy, greed. The advertising leverage that these campaigns use is a leverage that no person with a rudimentary sense of social values is willing to help apply .... "

Repeatedly, tenets commonly identified with Paul Rand are found in Dwiggins' book. Foremost is the big *M*: "'Modernism' is not a system of design — it is a state of mind. It is a natural and wholesome reaction against an overdose of traditionalism. The average citizen calls it "futurist" or "cubist" or just plain crazy — and doesn't understand it, or doesn't want to; but notices it, nevertheless."

The respective Modernisms of the two designers' diverge. Rand's creative gaze is fixated eastward, drawing his immediate inspiration from

the European Modern strain, then of that continent's artistic and intellectual histories. At times, the only American Rand seems able to abide is someone like expatriate E. McKnight Kauffer, who wrote the introduction to *Thoughts*. No such limitation is displayed by Dwiggins, whose internationalism included identifying with his home country's creative legacy.

As he danced around "advertising art" and it being an "easily accessible means of æsthetic enjoyment," Paul Rand's goal was to elevate design and the public. The unfortunate result was to fashion *Thoughts* into an ersatz art history text, adopting the form of such books while misapprehending their substance. He then compounded the error by refashioning the book — and all that followed — into a self-declared "primer," complete with the condescending manner it entailed.

Another sad legacy of *Thoughts* is that with the veneration of Rand's epigrammatic prose, graphic design snuffed out a nascent critical sensibility. Design might have built an inimitable literature upon Dwiggins' varied and engaging writings, one that invited deep and diverse investigations. Today, that kind of writing is fugitive and often dismissed in the field.

Instead, design prizes short, subjective bursts of assertions whose authority largely rests not with the cogency of argument, but the author's level of professional achievement. Rand surely hoped that his books would garner respect for design activity from thinking, visually perceptive people. By hewing to his example, design ensures it won't be taken seriously outside its boundaries.

Bill Dwiggins related to his audience as an expert but still a fellow traveler. He confronted design as design, a uniquely Modern mode of representation. Dwiggins' work embodied the formal ideas Rand wore on his sleeve. Were we to draw a Venn diagram of the two designers' books, there would be substantial overlap. But *Layout in Advertising* would almost entirely consume *Thoughts on Design*. The difference is what happened after, and where we are now.

How Dwiggins was shunted aside and largely forgotten by a profession that should still extol him was bluntly articulated by Jeffery Keedy in his 1997 essay "Greasing the Wheels of Capitalism with Style and Taste or the 'Professionalization' of Graphic Design in America."

Corporate design and its enablers were elevated to the pinnacle of design activity and activism. There was no higher calling than to be able to call the client's head honcho direct. In short, money talked — loud and about logos ... and still does. *Real* designers shill for moneyed interests. Everyone else is walking.

Having turned his back on commercial striving, the career path of W. A. Dwiggins, though rich with formally accomplished, effective design, didn't fit the new mold. (From Hingham, Massachusetts? *Please.*) It didn't help that he declined to adopt the European style of Modernism and referred to designers like Paul Rand as "Bauhaus boys."

A simpler reason for Dwiggins' fall and Rand's rise is that many contemporary, prominent designers had personal contact with the latter. For former students, lecture attendees, or occasional lunch dates, Rand was an immediate, living exemplar. Dwiggins is a dated, distant abstraction.

However, it's now a categorically "eclectic" era where varied models of design practice and performance are expressed and applauded. For instance, individuals can again combine ingenious decoration with idiosyncratic writing and be praised for it. WAD stands as a predictive figure that designers didn't know they had and needed. We'll always have Paul Rand.

10: What we choose to see

In its concision, *Thoughts on Design* continues to act as both perfect mirror and blank slate. On Rand's sparse surface, designers perceive their reflected aspirations *and* project their desires. Meaning isn't found *between* Rand's lines. Sparsely set, meaning is to be imposed *upon* them. For my money, Michael Bierut's homilies on Rand's writing are far more affecting and lyrical than anything his hero generated. I just eliminate the front man.

For untold designers, the actual *Thoughts on Design* is literally and figuratively ideal. Were this new edition a faithful reproduction of that 1947 volume, they would probably impose the same lessons on *that* text and declare it equally portentous. Provenance and chronology are transcended: *only* Paul Rand could write the hallowed words and he *always* wrote them.

I realize my mistake about the book was more profound. I wasn't consulting the wrong text so much as using it incorrectly. The cadence, the

short verses, the avowals, the rote repetition, it all adds up. *Thoughts on Design* is more than a book; it's the design profession's liturgy.

Having revealed its true nature to us, there's only one suitable response: *Amen.*

*My thanks to Marian Bantjes for alerting me to the likely Adolph Loos reference after the initial posting of this essay.

𝒰 & 𝓂-ℬ

Nothing is perfect; perfect is nothing.

In his last year, Josef Müller-Brockmann gave a lecture in Mexico on his work. The renowned Swiss designer brought down the house with his final slide, which was blank. "This is my best piece of work," intoned Müller-Brockmann. According to biographer Kerry William Purcell in his 2008 monograph, *Josef Müller-Brockmann* (Phaidon), the statement was meant, "as if to illustrate how the reputation of designers always reside in their potential, not their past realizations."

Purcell's reading may be correct. And the declaration certainly wasn't tossed off. For the second question of a 1995 *Eye* magazine interview (no. 19, vol. 5) at around the same time, Müller-Brockmann was asked what work he regarded as his best. The response: "The white reverse sides of my posters!"

That *Eye* interview was my first encounter with Müller-Brockmann's own words on his art. I was taken aback by the declaration. Perhaps it was only puckish humor on the renowned designer's part, riffing off his reputation. His answer can be interpreted many ways. Sardonic or not, I thought the answer spoke big, blank volumes about Müller-Brockmann.

It managed to simultaneously claim as exemplary all his works and none. At the same time, it tersely combined both humility and conceit. I felt it to be the definite statement of a quest not for an expression of the

ultimate communication but of formal purity. It was also an astonishing irony. For Müller-Brockmann, the most articulate design was one that literally said nothing.

The incident related in Purcell's biography hasn't served to change that first impression. Müller-Brockmann's oft-caustic self-deprecation offers proof of a sort for Purcell's interpretation. That combined with Müller-Brockmann's relentless search for the essential design expression. It's a pursuit that encompasses and defines the designer's life.

Purcell's biography came at a particularly relevant time. Müller-Brockmann's importance to graphic design and visual culture makes him a suitable subject of recurring study in any era. However, the 2000s saw a purposeful, large-scale return to the formal attributes of the "Swiss International Style" of design of which Müller-Brockmann was the leading theorist and performer.

Josef Müller-Brockmann has a defensible claim as the 20th century's most influential visual artist. The formality he made iconic transformed visual expression internationally. Fine artists may have a hold on high culture regard but Müller-Brockmann is more widely disseminated within culture.

It might be said in any noted graphic designer's biography that the subject's recognition within popular culture falls far short of that figure's impact. Biographies of designers remain rare, especially if not autobiographies. There's a significant backlog of historical figures in design deserving of examination while we enjoy an over-abundance of monographs on early-career contemporary practitioners.

The lives of creative people aren't conducive to affecting biographies, or shouldn't be. If the artist is at all dedicated to the craft, time should primarily be spent working. Pretty thin drama. Any escapades must occur during off-hours with questionable relevance to the work. For designers, sample extracurricular activities typically comprise of drinking, drugging, wrangling with clients, browbeating students, and giving innumerable far-flung lectures extolling the supremacy of one's concepts.

With an ascetic like Josef Müller-Brockmann the going's even tougher for the biographer. A fitting chronicler of this subject may be a writer conversant in subtlety and minutia, wringing maximal meaning out of minimal

gestures. Nicholson Baker, author of *U and I*, an intensive-obsessive appreciation of John Updike, may be the man. Perhaps there were bacchanalian excesses that go undocumented in Josef Müller-Brockmann, but it seems unlikely. The latter three spectacles are, however, well represented.

With his biography, Purcell has turned in a well-researched and respectful product. Properly, the volume is geared toward the design neophyte: many details will seem obvious or repetitive to a design-aware reader. This is unavoidable as Müller-Brockmann's ideas are embedded within design's DNA. As with his posters, Müller-Brockmann honed his doctrine through years of rigorous explication and is left to quote extensively from Müller-Brockmann's autobiography.

Purcell's role is then to provide historical and professional context. Additionally, he broadens Müller-Brockmann's own self-abridged personal and creative narrative. With the expanded portfolio, it's illuminating to have rarely-seen illustration, exhibition, and set design works. Unsurprisingly, things the artist dismissed as unskilled or unacceptably subjective are lively and deserving. While no patch on the marvels to follow, they deserved recoup as more than curiosities.

When the famed concert posters take stage, the book sings. For the connoisseur, their splendor is self-evident. The work embodies its proof, confirming any rationale offered for their being. Time (and replication) dulls awareness of how startling these posters were (Purcell provides the obligatory complaints of baffled concertgoers) and still can be.

Though Müller-Brockmann scorns designers resorting to "splash," in their own way his masterpieces spatter abundantly. Subject matter, artistic intent, and an ideal historical moment produced æsthetically profound pieces that manage to be both intellectually contemplative and visually stunning.

Purcell stumbles over his own exposition of Müller-Brockmann's accomplishments. These passages are frustratingly abstract and dense. Purcell's analysis is in keeping with the Modern form-based, dialectical structure claiming objectivity. The works, however, are no less open to interpretation as any other broadside. Purcell's lone step outside the Modernist frame is a fleeting and obscure statement that "a final

meta-language is forever out of reach." Otherwise, "universality" is presented as a tangible, obtainable state. A design's "essential character" is discernable and inarguable. Though delivered as self-evident, these assertions are mysticism alchemized into fact.

An authorized biography is an unlikely showcase for a substantive critical examination, especially a contentious one. However, some questioning of Müller-Brockmann would be welcome, if not obligatory. For instance, Purcell chooses to ignore that a substantive challenge to Müller-Brockmann's agenda came from within Swiss design in the form of Wolfgang Weingart. This neglect is simply bad history and suggests Purcell is engaged in hagiography.

Some objective affirmation might be provided for the designer's claims. Instead, the book obediently supports the patronizing and apocalyptic tenor of Modernist designers: all other methods are shit and civilization hangs on each font choice. Müller-Brockmann's tacit dismissal of anything non-Constructivist and a preening self-deprecation quickly grows tiresome.

The strength of Müller-Brockmann's philosophy is its internal consistency and rigorous application. But its essential flaw is that while regarded as objective and neutral due to its mathematical basis, Müller-Brockmann fails to acknowledge that this status is still but one option among many. Many geometries are employed to describe our world, each mathematical and objective, each internally consistent. If you stay within a system, you get the right answers. You just can't cross between or combine geometries.

If you accept the premise of Müller-Brockmann and his conceptual adherents, his system alone is rational. Any other design sensibility is irrationality. The reality is that there are separate rationalities. Literally, different perspectives. Other systems exist that are just as scrupulous and purposeful. Müller-Brockmann believed he was describing the world in his philosophy. What he crafted instead was another simulacrum, another metaphor.

As did many Modernist designers of his generation, Müller-Brockmann thought he pioneered a formality that resided outside of time. Instead, his principles were wholly of its time. The formal foundation of

Müller-Brockmann's philosophy is the grid: "In his own words, the grid expressed a 'professional ethos,' supplying the "designer's work...[with] a clearly intelligible, objective, functional and æsthetic quality of mathematical thinking.'" The grid's ordering function and representation of societal memes is accurate. But the latter aspect was far from fixed throughout time.

As described by Jack H. Williamson in "The Grid: History, Use and Meaning" (*Design Discourse: History, Theory, Criticism*, The University of Chicago Press, 1989), and at greater length by Hannah B. Higgins in *The Grid Book* (MIT Press, 2009), the grid structure has a long, complex history. The arrangement has been imbued with and promoted a variety of meanings. Müller-Brockmann's utilization spoke to its historical moment. History belies the transcendent virtues he claimed for the grid.

Purcell emphasizes Müller-Brockmann's ethical profundity, but its foundation is shaky. In the book's introduction, Müller-Brockmann is proclaimed a trailblazing advocate of "socially accountable design," decades in advance of "the flurry of books on ethical graphics published in the past decade." Is the rationale for this decree the designer's decades of work for altruistic or socially active organizations? Was it his stance against rampant consumerism and the reification of corporate design practice?

No and no. It's because Müller-Brockmann was a tireless advocate of design "where the form should reflect the content and the content the form." In other words, he relentlessly, unashamedly, and daringly championed himself.

As a practitioner, Müller-Brockmann was conscientious and honest. But his vaunted moral stance was based on his rigid adherence to a formality he considered preeminent for any and all clients. This was no more than the rest of a field condemned as being critically short of such values.

Indeed, the design profession is portrayed as an expanse of conscienceless hacks. This is an unconscionable slur against a multitude of practitioners past and present also possessed of integrity and commitment. These postures demean countless designers and Müller-Brockmann's achievement. Instead of diminishing Müller-Brockmann's accomplishments, a broader critical examination could illustrate its true dimensions.

As is the fashion with most designer monographs, other eminent practitioners are given cameos to affirm the subject's ascendancy. Purcell goes top shelf, trotting out Paul Rand at various points to embrace Müller-Brockmann as his peer. To drive the point home, Rand is given the book's final words, eulogizing Müller-Brockmann with a "geometric analogy." Müller-Brockmann manages to one-up the American design idol, wresting an IBM book commission away from Rand, who, while "supposedly very unhappy," is magnanimous over a loss on his home turf.

Subsequent events have not been kind to Müller-Brockmann's status as seer. His predictions are marked more by wishful thinking than a clear understanding of culture. His forecast in 1971 in *History of the Poster* that "factual knowledge and powers of judgment and discrimination based on credible information will impel advertising in the direction of objectivity" may still be realized but has, so far, been wildly off the mark. Müller-Brockmann's own objective advertisements — such as a late 1950s campaign for Nestlé dried milk rendered in his distinct austere style — seem like *Print* magazine "Humor Issue" parodies of the International style.

Purcell glosses over inaccuracies, continually pressing on to the next project. Design seems almost to die along with Müller-Brockmann, just as no creditable work (outside of his protean peers) is produced during his life. A meaningful appraisal of Müller-Brockmann's legacy would observe and speculate upon the revival of the austere Swiss style in the 2000s, as most celebrated in the work of Swiss design group Experimental Jetset.

On its face, this revival may be evidence of the enduring quality of Müller-Brockmann's approach. But in the statements of the many young European designers reanimating the austere approach, there is an ambient nostalgia. They hearkened back to a previous era, insisting upon the continued relevance of this purest expression of modernism. And there was none of Müller-Brockmann's authoritarianism. Theirs is a deliberate, conceptual quotation of Müller-Brockmann and his influence.

Contemporary designers have steered clear of proselytizing the style with the zeal and fundamentalist fervor of Müller-Brockmann and his peers. Plus, the revivalists demonstrably embrace pop culture, channeling the Beatles, Stones, and Sonic Youth to mellow the stark mood. (Rock

the grid!) The upstarts' verbosity about their concepts equal Müller-Brockmann's, yet, conversely, the new products often are more interesting to think about than actually look at.

It remains the special hell of Modern designers such as Josef Müller-Brockmann that their narrative has been overridden and overwritten by Post-modernity. While the young Moderns invoke the idealism at the core of the drive to essentialize design, it's also, if not more, all about those cool forms. So it is for everyone. Especially Josef Müller-Brockmann.

The great designer was committed to his design. That passion was his kink, the excess Purcell's book details. If design is like a relationship, it was, with Müller-Brockmann, a three-way: him, his design, and us. And it's our proscribed and passive role to observe mechanically and feel abstractly.

Fuel full pull poll pool cool cook book

FLAP

"Peter Miles, Damon Murray, and Stephen Sorrell pursue an exploration of graphic media in this, their first major publication. Formed at the Royal College of Art in 1991, Fuel design group came to prominence through their eponymous independent publications. Despite limited availability, these collectable editions succeeded in questioning convention within a magazine format. As well as publishing their own acclaimed magazine, Fuel have, over the last five years worked on high profile media campaigns for clients including Levi Strauss, MTV and Virgin Records. They are based in Spitalfields, London."

FACT

The concept, art direction, design of *Pure Fuel* is by Fuel, with text by Richard Preston. Over twenty-five other individuals are listed as contributors. The book has 208 pages in full color, is 10" wide by 12.5" tall by 1" thick and weighs 3.125 lb. It was published by Booth-Clibborn Editions (London) in 1996 and costs US$50.

THEM

It's British Invasion time in graphic authorship. Most noise about the topic has emanated from the States, both theory and supposed practice. The near-simultaneous release this year of two books from design groups

working in England seems an almost concerted attack on the authorship charts. Fuel's *Pure Fuel* and Tomato's *Process; A Tomato Project* invite comparison not only for the proximity of their release dates but also for their ambitions. Both groups formed in 1991 and have high profiles in progressive British design for their distinctive output and aggressive self-promotion. To continue the pop music comparison, the two groups are like the Oasis and Blur of British design. Minus the sniping.

Tomato has a leg up on Fuel since its collaborative includes members who have been working in design since the 1980s. Also, the group currently numbers three times as many members. *Process* could be considered Tomato's second book, after 2000's *Mmm Skyscraper I Love You*. Tomato has also been distinctly vocal theoreticians about design. *Process* represents a declaration in word and deed for their concepts.

Fuel isn't as well known but has garnered significant attention, such as the feature "Both Ends Burning" in *Eye* 11, vol. 3, 1993. Except for press notices such as this, the group is largely unknown in the U.S. Having the opportunity to produce a book so early in its career makes *Pure Fuel* a singular subject for consideration. For many designers, notoriety overshadows the specific ideas. As can be discerned in the rare quotes given in the *Eye* articles and the evidently authorized second-person interpretations featured in its book, the nature of *Pure Fuel* and the overall intent of its designers should focus attention on the work and not the relative inexperience of the group.

LIKE

Pure Fuel is presented as a manifesto of the group's design sensibility. As with Tomato, Fuel has at first glance rejected the traditional monograph. Rather than solely revisiting past client-commissions, the two groups offer its books as original, self-directed works. While both have thus sought to move away from the typical retrospective, they haven't completely erased the impulse.

Certain material is recycled or was previewed in other forums: Fuel has reprised its self-published "magazines," while the "inthisworldtogether" insert first published in *Emigre* 40 (1996) reappears in *Process*. *Pure Fuel* also begins with a 16-page portfolio of previous works to "introduce

the thought processes behind Fuel and (contain) an outline of their development."

Because of their self-initiated status both books are candidates for the slippery realm of graphic authorship. Content derives from the designers but neither book is self-published. The prominent and oblique remnants of conventional design monographs, however, place the books in a state of flux. This indeterminate state may be a constituent aspect of graphic authorship. Certainly, for Fuel, who stress "ambiguity" as strongly as Tomato intones "process," such uncertainty is both tool and goal.

Pure Fuel is design as content. The introduction leaps to this assertion before all others: "In a society which favours the written word for the dissemination of ideas and opinions, the visual is easily misconstrued as mere decoration." By examining Fuel's artifact, we have an opportunity to describe a different, distinct identity for graphic authorship. While asserting a role that may regularly be called authorial, Fuel never employ the term "graphic authorship." Any debate about the expression is ultimately immaterial in reading *Pure Fuel*. Graphic authorship is of more interest for the response the concept has generated than as a model for activity. This being said, *Pure Fuel* does provide glimpses of processes that I would propose as marking a new design activity. In many ways, it is a status Fuel attains more by accident than intent.

WORK

Pure Fuel appears to be an expanded version of one of the group's magazines. Alongside its commercial projects, Fuel gained attention in the U.K. for a series of self-published, limited-edition magazines. The seven works, each bearing a one four-letter-word title (*Girl, Hype, Cash, Dead,* etc.) usually conform to a standard paginated print format but have also included a T-shirt. These works introduced the Fuel æsthetic, described in *Pure Fuel* as "their uncompromising brand of graphic design-no frills, edgy, appropriated and naïve .... "

Apart from the force of this approach on its own terms, it provided a distinct difference from how British design was perceived at the time. As Rick Poynor described in *Eye* (in a quote reprinted in *Pure Fuel*), "The raw visual treatment has real freshness and force after a decade of sugary style

in British graphic design." ("Both Ends Burning," *Eye* 11, vol. 3, 1993.)

While unquestionably legitimate, Fuel's design approach is assertively not that of true naïfs. The group has chosen to work with a limited palette signifying an unfussy, direct approach. "Decoration can be confusing," Poynor quotes Stephen Sorrell as saying, "There's no need to flower things up. We are interested in an undesigned look." More than ten years past Robin Kinross' "The Rhetoric of Neutrality," we must recognize that Fuel have chosen a graphic strategy as loaded as any other. They have remained firmly within the province of professional design. More stylized, for instance, than the cut-and-paste approach of Jamie Reid's graphics for the Sex Pistols. Fuel's manipulation of the rhetoric of "undesigned" and "immediate" serves to differentiate themselves from contemporaries Why Not Associates and Tomato. Fuel is, though, as much stylists as those they react against. Perhaps more so.

Comparing *Pure Fuel* to the group's previous products is problematic. I am relying on reproductions of selected pages from these earlier works for a distant, Fuel-selective experience. Due to the magazines' limited availability, and Fuel's upstart status, it was presumably deemed necessary to include the introductory "history" section to its book. Such a move may be expected and welcome under the circumstances. But it is, on any terms, a concession from a group trading on an image of being uncompromising. The section undercuts the intended openness to interpretation to assure us that these guys aren't just in off the street. (Were it not for the com-mercial work, this book wouldn't have been commissioned.) Fuel's work overall shows a high comfort level with commercial demands. A marketing concession may not be seen as a concession at all. It's just being a designer.

Striking all prefatory remarks does not guarantee a clear slate. In a vi-sual world that includes appropriators such as Richard Prince and Sherrie Levine, we are far past the point where work can speak for itself. And how different is Fuel's history from an artist's monograph sporting a multi-page listing of exhibitions? The issue is not the dissonance of self-aggrandize-ment (though the extravagant claims for the book cannot be put aside in evaluating it) but the completeness of intent. Fuel's ostensible strategy is ambiguity and open interpretation. The prefacing in the overview chooses

directions for the reader and sets up expectations.

MAKE

Pure Fuel is a conventional, chapter-organized book predominantly of images, interspersed with various texts. Images are mostly photographic but also feature color illustrations and pictograms. The chapters all bear one-word titles: "Function," "Leisure," "Chaos," "Spoilt." No explanatory text enlarges upon the meaning of these terms. The headings may well be arbitrary and substituted with little loss of meaning. An "Index" is provided which provides terse, ordinary descriptions of images or a series of pages. The effect is an illusion of traditional structure without providing a narrative framework. It may also exist as another convention of books that Fuel seeks to distort to unspecified effect.

The photographs and illustrations surround and play off brief texts comprising conversations, first- and third-person narratives, or resembling advertising copy, speeches, and instructions. On their own, they are imaginative, evocative, and concise. Banner captions also adorn many images or are set on facing pages. "Prevent Contact with Eyes" slashes diagonally across a photo of an elderly couple dancing. "Pure product is a product with no application" meets a diagram of a combination clothes-dish-washer-refrigerator-oven. "Real Fruit Flavouring" is set beneath a reproduction of what the index identifies as a homemade bomb. Scattered throughout the book are snatches of poetry, signage, and slogans.

Pure Fuel is made by the art direction, the interaction of the text and image elements. Rather than evincing an ambiguity or generating possibilities, most of Fuel's juxtapositions are diagrammatic. The experience of turning to the index after reading pages is often deflating. A dream-like story is paired with six pages of photos showing people napping. The Index informs us that a two-page spread painting of a coffin is "Dead." It is the book's final section. Rather than demonstrating extremity or an eclecticism, the text/image interactions just seem quirky. The art direction is rarely as inspired as the stories and often detract from their potential. Aiming for ambiguity, Fuel manages vague.

Fuel's formal talents are considerable. Their handling of text and image is varied and sure. Within their self-imposed limitations, Fuel manage

a consistency while thoroughly exploring the permutations of a few elements. Text and images usually appear against stark white backgrounds. When used, solid colors will occasionally bleed off all sides behind elements or be used as frames or panels. Fuel keeps things moving, demonstrating the possibilities inherent in an approach frequently shunned as stolid. Here, the group makes a persuasive case for the viability of their formal method.

Their method includes use of traditional typefaces. A condensed, bold Times is the principal face for *Pure Fuel*, with a Grotesque spotted for contrast. Fuel has expressed a belief that using familiar types will point the reader toward the images and draw less attention to them. While an arguable point, it is muddied by the variegated treatments that text receives. Copy varies in outlines, size, alignments, and measures. Again, it is an able, expressive handling but hardly plain. The result is not so much that type turns transparent but that the fonts become identified with the designers.

To set up camp in such occupied territories merits attention. Fuel has forged a distinctive style out of the basic design set and artistic gestures. Their process is one of reclamation and repackaging. Depending on your perspective, the recycling can seem witty or a usurpation. One example is another signature visual device of Fuel: their rough, line-art pictograms. The symbols obviously parody and seek to expand upon common emblems. Fuel's illustrations are strongly reminiscent of artist Matt Mullican's graphics that study corporate and vernacular symbology. Mullican focused attention on his variations by removing them from context, while Fuel manipulate their symbols in a design setting. The recirculation of imagery through these contexts blurs any sense of origin. Are the commentators commenting upon comments?

SNAP

Imagery is central to *Pure Fuel*. Most pages are given over to full-bleed photographs or groupings. The selection, juxtaposition and assemblage of imagery makes up a large part of Fuel's art. Photography is the lead instrument in Fuel's design performance.

The imagery also explores the rhetoric of the immediate. Most photos demonstrate a studied spontaneity that's widespread in contemporary

fashion photography. Unglamorous subjects and subject matter are documented in ordinary settings under harsh and available lighting. Though brief, the photographic style that is preponderate in *Pure Fuel* has a distinct lineage.

The style finds its origin in the work of Nan Goldin and her influential 1986 book, *The Ballad of Sexual Dependency*. This collection of photographs was a diary of Goldin's "tribe:" her family and friends at the margins of cultural and sexual mores. The photographs are stark, voyeuristic portrayals of these characters that often intrude into the tawdry and startling. Goldin's subculture portraits have now been thoroughly commodified and mainstreamed by numerous fashion photographers. Fuel has invested in this imagery of stylized contentiousness, made familiar and toothless from repetition.

With *Ballad*, Goldin produced a book of her photography that went beyond the monograph to be a work in its own right. Other artists have since explored this medium, creating their own works of graphic authorship. These books approach the art/design intersection from a direction opposite to that of Fuel and provide a sharp perspective.

Jack Pierson is one such artist who has released two books-as-artworks. Pierson's publications are meaningful for comparison because they are graphically sophisticated; the artist has worked as a graphic designer. With Goldin, he shares an interest of documenting daily life and dramatizing the mundane. *All of a Sudden* is an entirely photographic book, comprised only of full-bleed photographs. Meaning here may be regarded as wide open. Unidentified individuals in unspecified or ordinary settings engage in unknown (in)activity. Narrative is simultaneously suggested and denied.

Pierson's *The Lonely Life*, is more reminiscent of the traditional monograph and *Pure Fuel*. It features the usual introductory appreciations by art writers prior to Pierson's content. Documentary photographs of his gallery installations are combined with page-encompassing photographs. Prominently featured in the installations and in close-up photos are words comprised of 3D signage lettering. Pierson's texts may be framing or commenting upon the imagery, much as Fuel's chapter headings. His jumble

of type styles suggests movie marquees and decaying signs on shuttered buildings. Pierson's handling of text and image displays an awareness of the impact that the codes of design can have upon viewers.

Fuel's work ventures into the territory of these artists and must meet the same standards. Unfortunately, Fuel's production fares badly in the depth of its intellectual investigations. While this may seem a standard criticism of design work, it is ameliorated by Fuel's significant advantage in being designers.

What designers possess is a more profound appreciation and ability in the grammar of design. Most fine art works that feature text and image are graphically unsophisticated. This art-artlessness is not merely in its formal aspects but in the awareness of how design resonates and is content. Design is the dominant visual medium of our culture. It is on design's terms that most visual production is interpreted by the public. Designers, therefore, should recognize a unique opportunity to define their own terms. Fuel's deficiency is in setting no terms, in unrealized potential.

OURS

As a title, *Pure Fuel* is bluntly accurate, though it's not the solipsistic navel-gaze the title might suggest. The members make cameo appearances in some images (one, a composite headshot of all three). The graphic authorship is performed an apparent social commentary on common themes like alienation and consumerism. The book is, therefore, about Fuel as much as a band's eponymous album with songs about alienation and consumerism is "about" them. Or, an artist's exhibition with works detailing alienation and consumerism. Fuel doesn't seem to be describing its own state of mind; it's observing.

A theme of contradiction recurs throughout: the cover image of flames issuing from a fire-extinguishing pail, a concrete lifejacket, a Jell-O helmet. The basic inconsistency of language is proclaimed. Objects express and contradict their function. Fuel declare (again, through Poynor) that they are "trying to have it both ways." Though easily read as a pejorative, it is meant to show how blurred the boundaries are between art and commerce. It is in this domain that Fuel seeks to operate.

At times, *Pure Fuel* resembles a fusion of an issue of Benetton's *Colors*

magazine and the Marshall McLuan/Quentin Fiore collaboration, *The Medium Is the Massage*. But as social commentary or cultural investigation, *Pure Fuel* is thin stuff. The book is far more interesting as a pure design statement: can graphic design be its own content? This is the question of graphic authorship. The debate so far has been constrained. However, it has touched on a unique development in the appreciation and production of graphic material.

The most prominent attempt to outline the graphic authorship issue has been by Michael Rock, in his *Eye* magazine article, "The Designer As Author," (no. 20, vol. 5, Spring 1996) and subsequent lecture on the same topic at the "How We Learn What We Learn" conference in New York in spring 1997. Though oft cited, Rock's essay is conventional and limited.

His overview never strays far from traditional conceptions of design activity, the designer's role within it, and the literary theory debate over authorship. Rock's conclusion is unsurprising: "designers (are) designers." They're not authors, auteurs, or artists. Though they desire and may attain a higher level of involvement, designers only undermine their claim by adopting the authorial banner.

This analysis overemphasizes the importance of the term "author." The irony may be that the designers most deserving of the title have little interest in it. In addition, the process designers undertake to create the work — and the role graphic design plays within it — is only glanced at. Emphasis is upon the final product and the designer's stylistic trace.

Though diverse in the types of works he considers, Rock curiously omits a major work of the time from his inventory. Ignoring Elliott Earls' interactive CD work *Throwing Apples at the Sun* is puzzling due to the attention afforded the work and its unique one-man-show origin. As an artifact of graphic authorship, Earls' project could declare itself as a defining example of the genus. What *Throwing Apples* also does is elude and overstep the categories Rock creates for graphic authorship. It may have been that including the work would upset Rock's argument. *Pure Fuel* and *Process* also rest uneasy in this formulation.

The debate over authorship has been a prominent influence in design for more than a decade. Some designers who have claimed graphic

authorial status have also championed the postmodern critique and setting up an incongruity. But this self-canceling state does not hold for all
aspiring graphic authors. And a claim to that status may be accompanied
by a novel conception of creative process. One might be called an author
and be both flattered and uninterested.

Literary theory's translation into graphic design terms, as many critics
have pointed out, is dubious. Design involves both text and image and
their interrelation. For many designers, use of the term "author" is only
a metaphor to point towards a new role in the creative process and the
search for a new language. Since Foucault and Barthes are writers, it's
understandable that they obsess over "authorship." Designers should be
aware of these writers' critiques while recognizing the limitations. As design is inextricably linked to other cultural productions, it's meaningful to
look to other disciplines for insight on how those cultural products come
about and are perceived.

IDEA

Graphic authorship may be part of a larger shift in creative production. Comparisons of design to literature and film reveal more flaws than
is useful (film theorists abandoned the design-popular "auteur" theory
altogether). An area that has demonstrated a marked change in creative
roles, technological revolution, and wide-ranging cultural import is popular
music. Here is a model that provides healthier possibilities in appreciating
design's cultural role. It is also a field that has had a heavy influence on
design, not only for being a progressive client.

Brian Eno has been an insightful commentator on music and culture
(and, not coincidentally, design). A paraphrasing of his comments given
over a number of years in various interviews, describe a new paradigm in
music. And possibly in design.

Eno identifies the true innovation of contemporary music as timbre.
This may be described as the sonic attributes and qualities of recorded
music, separate from the notes. It is primarily spoken of as the use of the
recording studio as instrument to sculpt sound. Particularly in classical
music, musicians traditionally have been concerned primarily with fidelity.
The score is to be performed as accurately as possible and the acoustic

properties center solely on clarity. In other words: a sender/receiver/no-noise situation.

Popular music, arising with and because of technological innovations in recording, explores additional dimensions of sound. Sound may be manipulated via an array of effects on the specific instruments and in the recording process. A common example is the echo chamber. The notes are the same, but a sonic environment has been created which affects the listener's emotional response to the music.

What this opens up is emotional properties of sound and a new grammar. As Eno explains, he can put a Dwayne Eddy guitar solo on a song and get double credit: first for the inherent quality of the performance, and secondly, for the associative resonance that is brought by the particular tonality of the guitar playing. You think, yeah ... the fifties. Early days of rock 'n' roll. Poodle skirts. Hot rods. *Rebel without a Cause*, etc.

This sonic realm doesn't exist for classical music but is the primary concern of contemporary musicians. Traditional composers work only with ordering notes. Contemporary musicians are interested in creating new sounds, unique sonic experiences. For classical listeners, feedback is only bad sound. It is non-music. However, for millions of others, that "noise" carries and is information.

A major outgrowth of this shift in how music is performed and perceived is the creation of new roles within the music profession. The "producer" has come into prominence, though the activity of the individual holding that title varies widely. Also, engineers and mixers, the former technicians of music, have come to the fore as artists. Are these people musicians? Is a performer whose music can never be reproduced "live" and samples extensively a composer? Is it creative to "remix" a song? Does it matter?

An analogy to design can be constructed. Fidelity, clarity, and noise suppression have all been historic concerns of graphic design. Now, with the influx of computer technology and cultural turns in how visual material is perceived, roles are breaking down and mutating. Designers are probing the areas between and around text and image, performing the rhetoric of design, exploring the grammar. In a way, the evolution of the "designer"

itself is a sign of this cultural shift, predating the change in music.

This is the area in which graphic design authorship resides. Design has been in the culture long enough for its grammar to become apparent. The vernacular obsession is the recognition of a design language that can be manipulated. Most designers are engaged in a prosaic handling of design's grammar. Instead of starting from zero, designers regularly follow established formats to crank out magazines, brochures, annual reports, and so on. It's why everything looks like everything else. A "graphic author" seeks to access and expand upon the grammar of design to produce unique, self-determined works.

VOTE

This context of graphic timbre is the one where *Pure Fuel* shows the most promise. The theme of social commentary in *Pure Fuel* may be regarded the same way that "love" is a frequent theme of pop songs. It isn't that the composers are being insincere but that each song isn't a direct outgrowth of a personal experience. Most tunes are truly about verse-chorus-bridge. *Pure Fuel* is design using social commentary as subject matter.

The problem arises if Fuel is claiming a position as cogent commentators. As such, its observations are usually Correct (cap C intentional) but trite and derivative. It is difficult to imagine a heated political debate arising around *Pure Fuel*. It's hard to discern what Fuel's positions are if they exist. Fuel's shallow and uncertain takes on pressing concerns are likely counterproductive to debate. Again, the group's sincerity need not necessarily be questioned, however, its treatment begs that conclusion.

Fuel is not alone in this predicament, striding into a trap that has claimed many victims in fine art: to be serious artists, you must address a serious topic. (Tomato has selected another established serious method: high intellectualism.) After the collapse of the overheated art market of the 1980s, artists turned to "issues art" to (re)claim legitimacy as vanguards of culture. Artists swarmed over various social problems to provide content for their productions. Often, the works became "commentaries" merely by alluding to certain social situations. Simply placing a crucifix on your work (or immersing it in your urine) became a commentary on the Catholic Church (though Serrano insisted — perhaps disingenuously considering

other work in his œuvre — that his notorious *Piss Christ* was about the qualities of light and color seen through his micturation).

To be doing important art, an artist now had to be a social commentator. Works were professedly about prejudice, intolerance, and child abuse, et al. and not about artists making salable pieces. The result was a glut of self-congratulatory and unconvincing works, which provided little respite or solution for the weighty problems they supposedly addressed. The apotheosis of this movement in the U.S. was the 1993 Whitney Biennial, which focused solely on such work. Even by the standards of this regularly rebuked exhibition, the show was resoundingly condemned.

This is not to say that controversial topics are off-limits to artists inexperienced in a particular adversity. It's to point out how "social commentary" has become rote subject matter for artists. Artists always need to address some particular topic to be considered "serious." An "innovation" may be defined as when an artist is able to expand the definition of what is considered serious art. Various unlikely subjects have been put forth as being conduits to enlightenment on the human condition: portraiture, landscape, and abstraction. Each has produced revelations (and still do) but are now predominantly the domain of formalists.

Unfortunately, many designers transpose artistic concerns to their field rather than forging a unique design identity. If serious art is socially aware, so must be serious design. In attempting to differentiate themselves from the "sugary stylists," Fuel has adopted the rhetoric of graphic immediacy and cultural investigation. Their work suffers when compared with other design works presenting commentary. Placed alongside the posters of the Guerrilla Girls, for instance, or a Barbara Kruger work, Fuel show themselves as naïfs in intellect, not in design.

Another concern that is frequently overlooked in issues-oriented work is the forum in which the work is encountered. True radicalism likely lies not in the subject matter or handling of material but by whom and how it is marketed. The real difference between art and design is the market into which the creator enters. How activist can art be when it is isolated in a gallery out of sight and with a price tag beyond the reach of most people? And are they buying it for the commentary or the æsthetic

qualities?

Pure Fuel was not contracted for by Booth-Clibborn as a political document. It was published as a slick design tome to sell to a category of designers attracted by the critical/stylist buzz around Fuel. That *Pure Fuel* costs $50 and is found on the Graphic Design shelves of the bookstore is the end-be-all of its status as a social commentary. Though it's much more affordable than your common art gallery object. Another advantage for design.

RAVE

Designers can and should be creating works that delve into commentary but it demands choices many designers are loath to make. One is to talk about themselves in the first-person.

As in traditional monographs, Fuel allows others to describe the group and its work. In other recent books by controversial designers such as *Emigre: Graphic Design into the Digital Realm* (1993) and David Carson's *The End of Print* (1995), the principals hover just off-stage, being quoted by the stated authors of the text. An odd dislocation results, which may be born of an attempt at objectivity or humility. The design, however, is so manifest that such deference seems misplaced.

Process breaks from this pattern with first person narrative throughout: Tomato interprets itself. The final essay of *Process* argues at length on the perils of separating creator from interpreter and calls on artists to speak up. Fuel distinguishes itself by a total textual absence: no quotes, no direct statements. All writing comes from outside sources. This conservative aspect combines with other conventions to make *Pure Fuel* less than the uncompromising work it claims to be.

Having decided to remain mute about itself, why have any explanatory text? The boldness of the claims made about Fuel on the dust jacket and in the introduction place a great deal of pressure on the work. Since they have presented the total book as its work, Fuel must be comfortable with the explication and value statements.

Most are superlatives. We are to witness "elements of the everyday and the shocking, which leave the viewer alternately confused and enlightened." *Pure Fuel* "encourages the audience to form its own opinion on the

content. By juxtaposing unexplained, or simply inexplicable, visual and verbal fragments they orchestrate an ambiguous manifesto in an attempt to reanimate the act of reading. Meaning, whether communicated through words and pictures, is never simply fixed."

Along with being highly contentious, these statements have become the buzzwords of a progressive design. Their terse, declaration-of-fact presentation hollowly echoes more investigative designers. The claims become a list of ingredients rather than a proposal. Because such terms are so well known in the market for which *Pure Fuel* is intended, such condensation is possible. Designers may not need their act of reading reanimated but designers selling design books need to reanimate the act of designing. Or at least give the appearance that they are. The possibility is remote that the design crowd buying *Pure Fuel* will be shocked or confused by the content. By Fuel's choice, everyone else is unlikely to see the book.

REAL

Does the very existence of *Pure Fuel* undermine its claim to be extreme and provocative? Booth-Clibborn has invested significant resources into this book and rightly expects a return. It obviously believes there is a market: a demographic interested in design with a cachet of challenging the status quo but with definitive credentials in the field. *Pure Fuel* does stumble into a provocative area of graphic authorship but is hedged. The ambiguity is less a response to a cultural situation but a blunting of tough questions involving commercialism and production.

How daring is it to be indeterminate? Wouldn't a forceful, articulate, socially conscious position be truly extreme? Fuel's boldness exists only within the narrow confines of standard graphic design practice. Here, glossing over ethical concerns is commonplace. What usually passes for values is insisting on timely payment and proper attribution. How contrarian is Fuel's obscurity? We are left with wholly conventional self-promoters, talented and shrewd. These have been the ends of mainstream design for some time.

The clients that designers work for are always telling. Typical for "progressive" designers such as Tomato, Fuel's work has primarily been for businesses heavily invested in style. Its client list is a roster of usual

suspects: youth-oriented fashion, designer footwear, techno bands, MTV. These clients are not de facto objectionable but it is worth considering why certain designers naturally gravitate here. Both Fuel and Tomato skirt the significance of their associations. Fuel employs known ironic gestures of anti-fashion. They burn the client's product in photographs, or play with themes on the evils of consumerism.

Tomato momentarily encounters this dilemma in the final extended text segment of *Process*: "... it's ironic then that personal work and experimentation ... should find its voice and space in the world of commerce." The discussion goes no further. The essay veers off again into the abstract, cerebralized mode Tomato regularly employs. The real question of what is actually occurring when businesses hire Fuel and Tomato is left hanging. Commerce is not buying into these designers' theories of ambiguity or process. They are purchasing style.

Tomato admirably seeks to expand and defy creative boundaries. But its process always ends when the client calls, though a particular visual exploration may not. From its text, it seems as if all the members of the group could get caught up painting on velvet if its process led them there. (This "process," though repeated like a mantra, is never explicated in a practical working situation.) If so, will Tomato say No to Nike if they come asking for a TV commercial? Will it instead offer a rendering of the Las Vegas Elvis? If process really rules, its list of dissatisfied clients and rejected commissions should be long.

Tomato is, however, attempting to engage a debate and take public risks with stated ideas. *Process* is an engaging demonstration of what might be possible with a new graphic hybrid. *Pure Fuel* also shows the potential for this new work but it's questionable if the creators are able to or interested in pursuing it. Fuel's use of theory so far has been a veneer. Otherwise, its aspiration is to be Big Name Designers. That's no less legitimate than wanting to write interminable essays for *Emigre*. It is up to Fuel to decide where its ambition lies. Locating oneself in the artistic/commercial matrix need not be straightforward.

It would help Fuel's claim of social concern if it was engaging clients with social interests. (Memo to designers: Amnesty International isn't the

only activist organization out there.) Fuel's considerable talents might aid a number of organizations desperately in need of attention-getting graphics. If the group is shy about leaving popular culture, there are musicians whose ideals would mesh with Fuel's style. Association with an agit-prop group like Oysterband would dramatically upgrade Fuel's awareness and spiff up some packaging.

LAST

With their books, Fuel and Tomato insist upon and deserve a new perspective in evaluating their work. The chosen direction of design as content is valid. Their results differ but share an inability to get fully with the program. Tomato might work an exchange with Fuel: the former provides a reading list while receiving instruction on how to stop making sense. Trying to have it both ways cuts two ways. What's available to Fuel and all designers is a myriad of possibilities. The obligation is thinking beyond the page, into the world of actions. How you do it is not as important as what you do with it.

Fuel has perhaps crafted a more telling identity than they realized. The final page of *Pure Fuel* shows their signature emblem: a mirror-image gas pump, feeding on itself. Fuel's energy, its product, propels itself, endlessly circulating, with no outlet. It is good that designers are looking at themselves more closely and empowering themselves. But the gaze must be exacting. And outward. What is revealed when two mirrors are facing?

ENDS

Don't read me
I am boring

The arguments these artists mount to the detraction of beauty come down to a single gripe: Beauty sells, and although their complaints usually are couched in the language of academic radicalism, they do not differ greatly from my grandmother's haut bourgeois prejudices against people "in trade" who get their names "in the newspaper." Beautiful art sells. If it sells itself, it is an idolatrous commodity; if it sells anything else, it is a seductive advertisement. Art is not idolatry, they say, nor is it advertising, and I would agree — with the caveat that idolatry and advertising are, indeed, art, and that the greatest works of art are always and inevitability a bit of both.

— Dave Hickey, "Enter the Dragon"

As a showcase for previously released Sagmeister material, *Things I Have Learned In My Life So Far* is an improvement over his first book, *Made You Look*. However, the compilation aspect is a minor similarity between the books. The focus exhibited by *Things* can be partially attributed to presenting a themed series of works. But Sagmeister also continues to come into his own as an artist. So much so, in fact, that he deserves his own category: metadesigner.

What's significant about Sagmeister's work, and makes him a

"metadesigner," is that he's not very original, as that term is classically used. He lifts freely from a wide range of designers and artists (in this book, he channels his post-Hipgnosis sensibility through Ed Ruscha). Sagmeister recognizes that the history of art is a history of appropriation and adaptation. And, more importantly, that graphic design is now a distinct language operating in culture, with its own idioms, tropes, and representations. Metadesign is graphic design taken to a higher level, self-aware and self-referencing.

This is one way that Sagmeister represents another crisis for the Modern movement in design. He's jettisoned or contradicted nearly all of Modernism's directives, not out of a contending doctrine but simply because it's dull and confining. Never mind your literacy-warrior typography and "ugly" graphics; it's Sagmeister who's killed off the Modern design movement. With kindness.

Things is not a standard codex but more a variation on the AGI/Mike Doud/Peter Corriston package design for Led Zeppelin's 1975 LP *Physical Graffiti*. Instead of that package's New York tenement, here you peer into the die-cut head of Sagmeister.

The cover concept is so simple it feels patronizing to explain it. This is the mark of Sagmeister's work: it's not the originality of complexity of the concepts, it's the lengths he will go to realize it.

Within the sleeve are 15 separate booklets with different cover designs that may be shuffled to the front to produce a different pattern within the designer's face. Each of the booklets features a typo-pictorial staging of one or more of 21 declarations of Sagmeister realizations. Most are fairly self-evident ("Everybody (always) thinks they are right"), some ironic ("Trying to look good limits my life"), some I'll have to take his word on ("Material luxuries are best enjoyed in small doses.")

The dramatizations ("illustrations" is too meek a term) of the statements are a catalog of visual representations. The book is the print equivalent of a David Byrne mix tape: a *cumbia* followed by a New Orleans brass band next to a North African chant up against a chamber orchestra work alongside some funk. Sagmeister will perform his own compositions, for instance, shaping words himself out of AC ductwork or twigs. He'll also

step aside for guest soloists such as Marian Bantjes forming words out of sugar.

Things is a testament to eclecticism. Sagmeister actively lunges down Modernism's throat and yanks it inside out. His contrarian formula for relating to the broadest possible audience is to adopt kaleidoscopic stylistic variety. Rather than synthesizing the Universal, he's asserting subjectivity as the way to communicate widely and accurately. If Sagmeister indulges *himself*, he connects with *you*. In his quest to not be boring, the only boundaries are his personal taste. Otherwise, Things is a triumph of "it works if you make it work." Everything is up for grabs.

Beyond the cover sleeve, no attempt is made to represent the statements in its attendant imagery. Disconnection is the declared strategy. Significantly, it's here that Sagmeister gets wobbly in his justification: "Even though I am, in general, not a big fan of ambiguous design ("the viewer can take whatever she or he wants"), in this instance I thought I would leave the system open and create room for the audience to relate." This rationalization suggests the need for a 22nd statement: "Don't make distinctions without a difference." Sagmeister's design may not always look like a Cranbrook special but it's quacking like one.

The sentiments that the book is built around are simultaneously heartfelt *and* meaningless. They're textual hangers to drape the graphic indulgences upon. Sagmeister possibly sees his salvation from Ambiguous purgatory in the ordinariness of the phrases: no clever word play, puns, or double meanings. Sagmeister's list may also push back against a perceived pressure to be "serious" in his work. Someone else (like critics?) wants him to have a (gulp!) theory. No thanks, he'll just pull something from his diary and run with it.

For a picture book that isn't a monograph, Things is damn wordy. In addition to Sagmeister's extensive explanatory texts, the book boasts three guest essays. Psychologist Daniel Nettle, Guggenheim Museum curator Nancy Spector, and omnipresent design writer Steven Heller contribute tracts in their specialty areas (happiness, art, and writing genial forwards to design books, respectively).

Since the featured imagery was originally deployed in other contexts

such as ads, and is being reprinted for the book, *Things* can be regarded as a "making of" documentary. Sagmeister's text resembles a director's commentary track on a DVD bonus disc. His attention is almost exclusively on technical details and anecdotes. The text has no in-depth analysis of design.

Sagmeister proclaims that the book's intended audience is non-designers. Evidently, they appreciate or require voluminous liner notes. Sagmeister prefers the books where the designers get chatty. And the popularity of those behind-the-scenes DVD extras supports a populist approach. However, this being a book of graphic design raises the question of explicatory overkill, if not negation.

Perhaps this is simply my personal preference to enjoy work without the artist constantly whispering in my ear. (I'm still of two minds about printing the lyrics of songs in albums and CDs.) I feel I may almost trust Sagmeister's work more than he does. A real area of risk may be for him to restrain his impulse to coat his work in a syrup of "talk normal" banter. Save it for the lectures.

The voluminous text points out another schema in the book. Why trot out Spector and Heller to speculate on Art and Design if you're not up to something? The weightiest aspect of the text is ruminations on the relationship of those two disciplines. Sagmeister introduces the topic then, unfortunately, hands off to Spector and Heller. Of the three, Sagmeister is briefest but has the best grasp of what's going on culturally. His exceptional instincts lead him to the essential truth; art and design differ only in the segment of the marketplace in which they operate. The essential activity is the same. They just answer to separate validating structures.

But what Sagmeister gets wrong isn't really his own claimed insight. Usually, his art borrowings have merit. Here, however, Minimalist sculptor Donald Judd is approvingly quoted that "Design has to work. Art does not." Going to fine artists, however well respected for insight on art, is the last place to visit for reliable commentary on graphic design.

That fine art is relieved of the necessity of actively pleasing an intruding clientele would be news to Christoph Büchel or Richard Serra. It all depends on what your definition of "work" is. Much of the design in this

book "worked" no harder than a Judd piece. Sagmeister's clients have gone from agreeable (some rationalized connection of client content to the panoplies is required) to indulgent ("do whatever you want").

His briefs were open-ended. The clients were buying "a Sagmeister" not commissioning a graphic designer. Wrangling over matters such as budget, siting, and content is typical for art installations. And though art buyers may not specifically commission an artist to make a kind of work, they regularly place demands on the type of piece they'll purchase. They also return art to the gallery without qualms.

Sagmeister, usually a voice of sense and sensibility about art, here takes an uncharacteristically romanticized view of the enterprise. It's puzzling why he bothers to wade into the morass at all. He should trust his instincts and not differentiate. It unfortunately leads him on a path away from his full potential as a transformative figure.

Not that he's actively applying for the job. He's too savvy to get bogged down in grandiose gestures. Every aspect of his work is downplayed and soft-pedaled. He admits the statements making up the book are "almost banal." The whole project began as a spontaneous riff, initiated under deadline pressure. In the contemporary coinage of non-admission concession: it is what it is.

Sagmeister is refreshingly self-effacing and upfront about his ambitions. The extravagant claims come from the textual hirelings (I'm making them for free!). One claimant is psychologist and author Daniel Nettle. His essay on happiness is fine until it specifically addresses Sagmeister's phrases. Nettle inflates their meaning more than they are worth. While it's good that scientists are studying happiness, the reported findings aren't exactly revelatory. They easily fall into the category of reports like "Men are attracted to women they find comely." But now we have metrics!

Nettle means well but overstates the case. An artist keeping a diary with reflective thoughts isn't headline news. Despite this, Nettle comes close to having a point if he juxtaposed Sagmeister with fine artists over the emotional tenor of his work.

Art for the last century, and contemporary art in particular, continues to scorn æsthetic pleasure and emphasize the baser instincts and actions

of humanity. To use a generalizing, musical metaphor, art regularly embraces atonality. Graphic design promotes melody. Uplifting messages in art grow scarce and suspect as you get to the rarified heights of the field.

To cast aside the joy aspect of human existence is plain dumb. Though it usually does so clumsily, graphic design has carried a banner of beauty (with an effort like "Cult of the Ugly" being the clumsiest). Sagmeister's dogged pursuit of happiness is a welcome contribution to a pleasurable counterforce.

If there's an artist that Sagmeister resembles, it's Yoko Ono. Her work is frequently simple and affirmative, making it stand out in the avant-garde art world which was her initial attractant to the oft-cynical John Lennon. I treasure my copy of Ono's *A Box of Smile*, a small plastic container, that when opened, reveals a mirror at its bottom. The piece rarely fails to generate the intended reaction. Simple, commercial, literally insightful. And with famous works such as *Cut Piece*, Ono was willing to make her self part of the art. Being cut also figures prominently in Sagmeister's portfolio.

The essayists who speak directly about Sagmeister and art are Nancy Spector and Steve Heller. Despite the fact that Sagmeister consistently insists that he's not making art but graphic design, Spector offers an art history lecture on artists dabbling in the advertising/print world.

Spector's discourse on these art movements is irrelevant. It's not the lineage Sagmeister's coming out of. Her comparisons serve only to demean the designer's real, relevant activity. Spector can't get her mind around graphic design being substantive in its own right. Only when it resembles what "real" artists do does she count it as deserving recognition. A telling comment is when she labels Sagmeister a graphic designer "extraordinaire." This precious term smacks of condescension. Would Frank Stella be called a "painter extraordinaire"?

Conversely, Steve Heller simply doesn't get art. He repeatedly commits a fundamental art critical error: drawing comparisons based on surface similitude. In the course of three pages, Heller stumbles through 20th century art to align Sagmeister with Futurism, Dada, Fluxus, environmental art, conceptual art, word art, Pop Art, and his own contra-historic confection, the "epigram school." At that pace, he may as well

have continued on to Surrealism, neo-Geo, Lettrism, concrete poetry, or neo-Pop, to name a few. Heller's effort is not to provide insight as much as encrust Sagmeister with high-art accolades.

Incredibly, Heller dedicates only a sentence fragment to associating Sagmeister with something or someone specific in graphic design: Tibor Kalman. No other reference to the field is made. No mention of design movements or philosophies. From Heller's text, a reader should assume graphic design to be a homogenous, ahistorical practice, bereft of any significance when discussing its most storied contemporary practitioner.

If Sagmeister is to be linked to the contemporary art marketplace, more relevant artists can be found than those presented by Spector and Heller. Sagmeister's confessional nature suggests Gillian Wearing's *Signs that Say What You Want Them To Say and Not Signs that Say What Someone Else Wants You To Say* (1993). Her title is an apt summary of Sagmeister's entire project.

Wearing's photographic series documents people she met on the street who she invites to hold handwritten signs expressing their chosen thoughts. They are simple expressions of individuality and the tension between private life and public display. They're also exercises in giving and getting voice in contemporary (media) culture. Sagmeister stands in for Every(wo)man in his work, while Wearing puts her/him center stage. Both projects feature bland statements that are made profound (and strange) by their presentation. An additional spin on the art/design/commerce interplay comes with the "appropriation" of *Signs* for a Volkswagen ad campaign, among others.

The greatest failing of Spector and Heller's essays is that they don't question the popular conceptions of art and design. As it would require them to question their own establishment views, it's no surprise they go the traditional routes. For them, artists remain privileged for their experiments in the design realm, over graphic designers. The assertion is exactly backwards. Sagmeister isn't inserting himself "unabashedly" anywhere he hasn't always been. At the least, he's reclaiming usurped territory and showing them how design's done.

An oft stated failing of graphic design is that it must derive meaning

from some other source. Graphic design can only be the means to a meaning. This supposedly holds it back from being a fine or even liberal art. But Sagmeister's work suggests that graphic design may, in fact, be able to stand on its own. We must open up our definition of "meaning" even further than we have so far.

Paint is long established as having meaning *as paint*. Abstract painting is where the vehicle became the driver. Why not graphic design? A unique aspect of graphic design is its manufactured, multiple nature. The various material effects — inking, varnishing, die-cutting, paper stocks, embossing, bindings, *et al* — are expressive in consumer culture. They are extensions of physical representations such as a rough paper edge signifying "immediacy" ("torn from today's headlines!")

Sagmeister's métier is exploiting and celebrating these mechanically generated production effects. Though he's regularly noted as not having a signature style, this exploration of physicality is essentially the same as style. He's not the originator (Peter Saville and Ben Kelly's sleeve design for the first Orchestral Manœuvers in the Dark LP is the purest example) but has made it his distinct expression.

The popular estimation of Sagmeister in the design profession is right on: he's an artist *as a graphic designer*. Unfortunately, he continues to be mis- and over-praised by an insecure field stuck on the Modern conception of "originality." (See Peter Hall's text for *Made You Look* for the definitive example of this.) Sagmeister doesn't do anything new. He does *better*: wringing new articulation out of timeworn graphic tropes.

A subject for concern is if Sagmeister abandons the public art aspect of graphic design. To do so would be to echo art's service of exclusive clients. Forms may change but the framework of capital remains. Sagmeister's insistence to be counted within the populist medium of graphic design is negated if his artifacts are estranged from a mass audience. "Blurring the boundaries" is a meaningless, restricted diversion if the design market economically functions the same as that of art.

What is potentially transformative is if Sagmeister challenges the connection between elite practitioners and the moneyed culture. As a producer of rarified commodities, he'd be just another facilitator of celebrity

and capital. Good for him if he breaks into the art market. But will it be a triumph of stardom and networking, or graphic design?

Things is a positive indication in that regard. It's Sagmeister the designer, making signs to and for everyone, out in the everyday world, not being boring, generous and mischievous. It's more fun than "art," and, perhaps, better for you.

Character references

When Rudy VanderLans announced that issue 69 would be the final *Emigre* magazine, he emphasized via a "reminder" from partner Zuzana Licko that it wasn't the end of the company. Considering the magazine's primary role in determining Emigre's identity, and that the journal was its namesake, the notice was necessitous. The foundry that had become the core business would continue developing and vending type.

In addition and importantly, the specimens that promoted their typographic works would continue to be produced. VanderLans had separately declared a commitment to continue these print pieces. The pledge placed Emigre in a distinct minority. We're in a time that has seen a marked decrease, if not total abandonment, of foundries issuing physical type catalogs. Whether it was a decision based in pragmatic marketing or a nostalgic nod to the Unended Print, VanderLans' avowal was welcome amongst aficionados of everything Emigre. The magazine was an acceptable but tough loss. Having to also bid farewell to the catalogs could have been devastating.

While *Emigre* magazine was a fundament in its firmament of products, it was always only one aspect of a constellation of printed works that grew up around it and the foundry. By VanderLans' estimate, the company has generated close to 200 printed artifacts, comprising catalogs, specimens, posters, brochures, postcards, pamphlets, and other printed

ephemera published since 1984. All converged in the magazine and spun off from it.

Foremost amongst those ancillary works were the specimens that introduced individual or a selection of faces, and the annual inventory of the Emigre library. In the magazine's heyday, the boundaries between it and the specimens blurred. For many designers and some critics, *Emigre* magazine was little more than a glorified type catalog. Curiously, and revealingly, the distinctive critical content is downplayed, if not dismissed. The pioneering type design and marketing originalities are highlighted. Zuzana Licko's typographic innovations have been evidently easier for the design field to assimilate than the ideas set in her landmark faces.

The appraisal of *Emigre* magazine as glorified type catalog denigrates both the journal and the full-fledged specimens. Emigre absolutely made, and continues to make, glorified type catalogs. But they *are* the catalogs.

Emigre's type specimens are the intersection of its two signal accomplishments, the magazine and type design. They are also the most representative artifacts of the partnership of Licko and VanderLans. The reputations of their other products understandably overshadow the catalogs. While the magazine and type have received considerable attention and documentation — most recently in the *Emigre no. 70* anthology — the specimens go largely unnoted.

Both for their connection to and fusion of Emigre's more celebrated work, and as artifacts in their own right, the type specimens are worthy of separate attention. All the aspects of Emigre's contributions to contemporary design are present in form and content. If, as Rudy VanderLans regarded them, issues of the magazine are considered graphic "albums," the specimens are the "EP's" and "singles."

Emigre's specimens are notable for the negotiation of practical considerations and creative idealism, the essence of all graphic design. They demonstrate an adept dovetailing of these concerns, crafting a format that stimulates desire then provides an efficient vehicle for satisfying it. A balance is struck between providing an enthusing context for the type while not overwhelming it. Though far from "neutral," the framework is evocative and clear.

This framework has become more involved than embellishing the traditional catalog display. A rethinking of purpose and presentation is evident across the history of the pieces. Emigre's specimens advance upon earlier examples of the form that utilized it to advance a wider conceptual agenda on how typography is defined and practiced.

A precursor is William Addison Dwiggins' specimens for his new type designs. His were more realized, progressive publications centered on type display. A simple necessity was embraced as opportunities to explicitly express his typographic philosophy.

Dwiggins' "Emblems and Elektra" specimen eschewed the rote alphabetic exercise to put forth a manifesto. "How is one to evaluate and assess a type face in terms of esthetic design? Why do the pace-setters in the art of printing rave over a specific face of type? What do they see in it? Why is it so superlatively pleasant in their eyes? *Good design is always practical design.* And what we see in a good type design is, partly, its excellent practical fitness to perform its work."

That final statement is purely subjective. But as is often the case, the distinction of the type design supplies affirmation for his rhetorical position. Plus, you get a measured dose of Dwiggins' delightfully idiosyncratic abstract illustrations.

Along with spurring a surge in digital type design, Emigre's catalogs sparked a spate of inventive promos from a variety of short-lived and established foundries. Simply having the specimens was a practical necessity that isn't attributable to Emigre. But the venturesome contexts adopted by many of the other foundries owe a debt to Emigre's examples.

Often, the specimens were the most — sometimes only — interesting aspect of these other type designers' efforts. As abstract works, separated from their sales imperative, they were engaging artifacts, parading wild, unfettered graphic novelties riffing off the theme of character sets. As proffers of usable type, they were far less viable. Simply put, I'd rarely imagine ever using faces from these specimens. But as elements in an "artist's book" of Roman characters, they were engaging marks.

That the faces were disposable didn't lessen the charm of the specimens, which could get baroque in concept and hyperactive in the number

and variations on a theme. Another intriguing exponent of the surge in specimens was that they provided scarce examples of graphic design by individuals known foremost as type designers. Jonathan Hoefler's *Muse* publication lasted the one issue but was succeeded by a few catalogs that shared the same delightful classicist sensibility. Much as I admire his typefaces, I'd put money down for more Hoefler print objects.

The earliest Emigre specimen I own, "Signs of Type," is similarly unique for its rare "Design: Zuzana Licko" credit. Absent the notice, the piece might easily be attributed to her partner in its presentation of her low-rez faces illustrated with bit-mapped scans.

The overall design sensibility of Emigre specimens naturally moved in parallel with the flagship magazine. Roughly, specimen history can be divided into the pre- and post-4-color eras. Pre-color, the specimens proffer VanderLans' distinct formal sensibility but are straightforward in text and concept.

The phrases set in the faces are descriptive of the type's features and formal rationales. Or, as with Dwiggins, propound terse typographic manifestos: e.g. "Typefaces are not intrinsically legible; rather it is the reader's familiarity with typefaces that accounts for their legibility. Studies have shown that readers read best what they read most."

With the advent of full color publication — the time leading up to and after the end of *Emigre* magazine — the specimens bloom as deeper, broader artifacts in their own right. A preservation principle seems at work. The energy of the magazine couldn't be destroyed, only channeled and adapted into another form. One of these alternate outlets was VanderLans' book projects: *Supermarket*, and the *Palm Desert/Cucamonga/Joshua Tree* music trilogy. And the specimens also received an additional infusion of vitality.

Specimens became small journals in their own right, offering broader speculations and investigations of type design. Short accounts of a face's origins and the designer's intentions regularly appear and expand. Experts such as John Downer provide extended essays on topics related to typographic revivals.

The text examples become extended haikus or proffer full-on stories.

Writer David Barringer was commissioned to bring his fluent prose to the two volume "Little Book of Love Letters." Other republished texts feature early-20th century writers on subjects like the geography of the U.S. southwest, a VanderLans obsession.

Other specimens give the type designers the opportunity to frame their creations in artist-book quality promotions. The late Frank Heine crafted two amazing booklets for his Tribute and Dalliance faces. Mark Andresen wrote and illustrated a VouDou tale for his Not Caslon booklet. Jeffrey Keedy generates a visual/textual polemic for Keedy Sans. Elliott Earls does Elliott Earls. VanderLans himself imagines eccentric and elaborate historical markers for the Historia specimen.

The ultimate and ongoing charm of the pieces transcends their status as product catalogs. However attractively designed any specimen may be, it is as disposable as any graphic design artifact, if not more so. That the specimens' primary type product is essentially unchanging presents a significant design challenge. Change is mostly through accretion: the addition of new faces to the library.

In broader terms, a common charge against graphic design as a discipline is the unapologetic disposability of its product. The overwhelming majority of graphically designed artifacts are properly characterized as ephemera. What then the products for a graphic design audience? Is the factor doubled? VanderLans' fancy flights confront these realities and serve a very pragmatic purpose: how to make the same collection of forms fresh.

The particular genius of these works is their beautiful functionality: an equal balance of abstract æsthetic qualities and clarity of use. The feature in the specimens that best expresses this balance was the now discontinued order form. Their layouts were also divided across the introduction of process color. Within these diversities, they've remained fairly consistent: an incidence of an inability to improve upon perfection.

The forms are the most succinct expression of VanderLans' design approach (his "inner classicist" in Rick Poynor's description), an articulate and resonantly apparent structure. As formal compositions, the order forms residing somewhere between El Lissitzky's "prouns" and Sol LeWitt.

Pre-process, the layouts were all right-angular, sectioned by thick rules that strategically extended beyond the form's basic framework. With the introduction of color, circles came into play, accenting in hues and shapes. Actually writing on the forms didn't ruin the effect. Rather, it became a lively, improvised vernacular accentuation.

Often, the underlying structure of VanderLans' layouts are visible and made decorative graphic elements in its own right. (See *Emigre* 40, "The Info Perplex" issue for his most elaborate expression). This strategy has tangential relation to designs that display a visible grid, as can be seen in a number of classic Müller-Brockmann posters. VanderLans' structures, however, are more flexible and colorful. Their agile geometries are efficient to their task of segmenting and structuring space.

If enthusing over an order form as a counterpart to signature works by renowned artists isn't grandiose enough, I'll take a step further. As previously mentioned, many of the booklets stand amongst the finest artist books of any era. The Hypnopædia specimen, for one, is a marvel of pattern and color that rivals many painters' output. Not to mention its status as a triggering expression in the "rational/decriminalized ornamentation" movement now in full flower.

More than this, these specimens provide one of the best examples of graphic design demonstrating content in its own right. It's a near universal tenet that graphic design is an applied activity, possessing no substance upon its own. But when considering these catalogs, they can be "read" the same way that abstract painting are.

A color field painting by Mark Rothko is "about" color, physically about paint. These specimens are about character forms, physically about type. The specimens transcend the mundanity of words to express ideas of the representation of language. We can contemplate the letter as we might upon the hue of blue.

It is a charge, a challenge, I regularly place upon my students, and ultimately upon all graphic designers. Is this discipline of graphic design worthy of contemplation on its own terms? Might you pick up any graphic design artifact and enjoy it for the pure joy of its unique status that straddles and fuses form and function? Can you pick up and delight in a

type specimen as you would a painter's (or sculptor, or photographer, or what have you) monograph? Not seeking professional "inspiration" but sensual indulgence?

Graphic design artifacts are like nothing that came before them. Their motives and intentions are unlike any creative form now or since. And this stature is best represented in forms like type specimens. They speak volumes of potential, in the works they will conjure into being, and what they suggest for how we regard our past and current print culture.

A thorough documentation of the Emigre's specimens is a valuable undertaking. Like the entire Emigre enterprise, the boundary was sometimes crossed to encompass booklets for its nascent music label, and some non-paginated pieces (though excluding posters). I've focused on the type aspect of these pieces, though most may be rightly considered catalogs for the entire Emigre product line. Whatever you want to call them, enjoy.

A viewer's guide to periodic literature

An unfortunate aspect of graphic design's history is the field's estrangement from writing. Whether it's outright hostility to the word or simply a predilection for the visual, design regards literature warily. Literature readily returns the favor. The origin of this rift is the Modern promulgation of the idea of a discrete "visual language." Unfortunately, this effort required demeaning that other, established language. What emerged was a contentious division as injurious as it's artificial.

One result of the split has been the stunting of a distinct graphic design literature. Theories and histories of design's activity are still scant, especially compared to the (other) liberal arts. But while the suspicion of text is ingrained in the field, it's never been universal. The past two decades in graphic design can be seen as response to diverse attempts to realign and integrate the disciplines. A major action along these lines was the introduction of literary theory in the early 1980s into graphic design thinking.

At about the same time, a new forum for contentious graphic design work and thinking emerged: *Emigre* magazine. Apart from the specific opinions expressed in its pages, *Emigre*'s very existence worked to bridge the design/literature divide. The importance and necessity of writing in and on design was regularly championed and demonstrated. Design couldn't stand apart from the word, nor can literature disdain design.

Design is where literature manifests physical form. An author takes the first and most essential step in making literature corporeal. But it's not the last. Even if you believe — as many do — that to set words into type is (or should be) a straightforward exercise, we can discuss how standards of typesetting originated. And why many designers choose to diverge. *Emigre* magazine provides a distinctive opportunity to discuss literature's physical nature and import.

If you look at an issue of *Emigre* magazine in its final incarnation, you would correctly assume that it was a literary magazine. The majority of pages are dedicated to texts presented in a conventional, bookish format. A discerning eye would spot contemporary aspects enlivening a usually staid genre. Prominent amongst them is the occasional non-standard and plainly irregular text typeface. The design says *this is a magazine for serious reading*. Only a brief section at the end is given over to graphics.

This last variation of *Emigre*'s format, which progressed from assertively alternative toward an increasing convention, is both further departure and a return. An all-text art publication isn't unusual. Critical theory that stands apart from evaluating specific objects is long established in art. But in design, it's virtually commercial suicide. It is, however, true to its principles, and the material published. Throughout its history, *Emigre* matched form and meaning.

Emigre began as a self-published, cultural tabloid. Wanting an outlet for their creative work, a small group of expatriates invented their own forum. The first issues have the requisite fare: stories, poetry, scripts, interviews, photography, and illustration. *Emigre*'s distinction was its founders' status as immigrants to the U.S. (providing the direct interpretation for its slogan, "The Magazine that Ignores Boundaries.") And there was the design. The layouts are vibrant collages equally determined by a deliberate D.I.Y. æsthetic and a limited budget. The design here says: *this magazine is different*.

Every magazine and design artifact takes a stance on how content should be represented. Though not expressed as such in its text, *Emigre* magazine immediately challenged the "serious" presentation of serious literature. It asserts that the physical nature of the characters can't help but

affect the reader's expectations. Designers count on it. Critiquing the verities of design will be *Emigre*'s constant theme for the twenty years.

Within the field, *Emigre*'s move to an emphasis on graphic design as subject matter (with issue 9) is taken as a transition. *Emigre* themselves state as much in their materials. This is good marketing for the publication within the profession. Unfortunately, it limits *Emigre*'s wider regard, relegating it to the status of trade publication. But culture continues to be *Emigre* true subject matter. Only now, culture is scrutinized tangentially, through an innovative study of design activity.

Emigre eschews the professional-orientation of design publications expressed in *Print* magazine. This restricts *Emigre*'s field of vision and expands it. Graphic design is the subject of every article but the insights intend to reach beyond design. And they recognize that design is an active, often defining player within culture. Even if one wishes to make a commercial determination on the efficacy of a design strategy, you must confront this reality to gain a meaningful answer.

Design is another "text" that we read: sometimes incoherent but never neutral. *Emigre*'s art direction reflects this, doing more than packaging its contents alluringly. The magazine is taking on the world, and the whole history of representation. At the least, it's honest advertising, advocating its ideas through its form.

Due to the variety of writers *Emigre* featured, those ideas are diverse. Their convergence is in a challenge to design orthodoxies. If not given entire credit for establishing a graphic design literature — one that, within its pages, is wildly variable in form and quality — *Emigre* can claim a sizeable chunk of it. It became a locus of design writing, a place where all paths converged.

Emigre harbors sympathy for many of its writers' stances. However, the magazine's core belief is of the necessity and value of an open dialog, and a design literature of substance. Designer/editor Rudy VanderLans openly admits to disagreement or dislike with some of the material he publishes. He also candidly muses (in issue 47) on how "[m]uch of my more expressive layouts in earlier issues were the result of being insecure about my writing and interviews. Such layouts were used to strengthen (or

obscure?) the perhaps inadequate writing."

This frankness is a regular feature of the magazine. While actively sponsoring new design writing, and questioning the received wisdoms of the field, *Emigre* remained self-critical. The typographic debates raging within its pages — and across to those of other journals — are impassioned but problematic. Debaters often talk past one another, speculating in abstract terms. Disagreement festers over a small percentage of design work — both as a category, and in actual pieces printed overall. From the essays, devastating illegibility and irrationality — or oppressive blandness and conformity — can result from minor shape variations in a letterform. *Emigre*'s editorial voice is frequently one that's idealistic but practical.

Though some design arguments may be taken to absurd lengths, to dismiss them totally is myopic. The fact that literature is a material artifact is frequently overlooked. We're long past the dominance of the oral tradition to sustain literature. Readings have made a comeback, but as part of the author's book tour — just like the concert tour it emulates.

Literature is often regarded as non-corporeal; an essence that takes many forms. A wide variety of creative people are regularly included in the "literary" circle. Writers plus graphic novelists, musicians, DJs, and performance artists all can be celebrated for their literary pursuits. The implication is that literature is transcendent. It can occupy a diverse array of vessels. The physical manifestations of literature are, therefore, irrelevant.

The importance of the materiality of literature is not just the province of book collectors or designers. Prominent writers have devised or demanded specific typographic handling for their words. William Faulkner first requested that different colors of ink be used to differentiate the thoughts of the separate characters in *The Sound and the Fury*. As this wasn't practically possible at the time, italics were employed instead.

James Joyce insisted that quotation marks never be used in his published texts to indicate when a character speaks. He opts for a European convention of placing an "em" dash at the beginning of the sentence containing the quote. This makes Joyce's prose additionally challenging to read. It becomes difficult to differentiate between characters when two or more are in dialog.

These writings are expressions of Modernism that can be found across the arts. The material characteristic is an integral part of the artwork. For instance, the painting declares that it's paint on canvas. Design is the substance of literature. The formal arrangement carries meaning in addition to what's expressed in the words.

Dismissing the typeset of the text, the cover design, or the paper stock as mere marketing concerns understates the situation. We live in a consumer culture where literature is product. The impact of the design doesn't end when the book is purchased, nor does it mean that the design was successful. Ideally, literature would be evaluated on its own merit: the essential words shorn of materiality. But this is an impossible condition.

The motivated reader may reach a state of pure appreciation, as in being unaffected by materiality. It can, ironically, trigger a devotion to the object. Enthusiasm for first, or particular editions, of books is common. And publishers lavish the most design attention to the classics.

Literature's increasing movement towards engaging its physical- ity — its design — is represented by some of the most publicized writing of the past few years. Dave Eggars' *McSweeney's* is a fiction collection that changes format with every issue. In the worlds of design and artist's books, Eggars' productions are familiar and tame. But in mainstream publishing, they're fashionably exotic and PR friendly.

Jonathan Safran Foer's novel *Extremely Loud and Incredibly Close* also intrudes into the designed. Foer employs typographic tricks (including the colored ink that was denied Faulkner), pages intentionally left blank, and a photographic flipbook coda. Originating from the literary end of the arts spectrum, Eggars and Foer's projects are given the high cultural credence denied to designer-involved literature. That they're not designers make them acceptable. In the literary mainstream, it's still possible to have *too much* a design awareness and imagination.

An example is *VAS: An Opera in Flatland*, a collaboration by writer Steve Tomasula and designer Stephen Farrell that was published in 2002. It's one of the most effective demonstrations of the materiality of literature, and the potential of design as literature. The book's design elements are integral to the experience, and symbiotic with the text. The book can be

rightly considered a new literary genre. However, on the literary side, it has received limited attention.

Meanwhile, some of Tomasula and Farrell's earlier collaborations were published in *Emigre* magazine. In addition to introducing a greater appreciation of design in (and as) literature, projects such as *VAS* might serve to make designers more appreciative of writing. Through its different incarnations, *Emigre* magazine furthered both causes.

In 1940, William Addison Dwiggins contributed an idiosyncratic article to the premier issue of *Print* magazine. "The Five Hundred Years: A Time-Problem and Its Solution," was a fiction that took the form of a report claiming to have discovered a history of letterforms and printing from the year 2440. It was an imaginative and uniquely literary approach to contemplating graphic design.

Dwiggins was a prolific and versatile writer, critiquing graphic design in practical terms and as a cultural force. His writing created a potential and a challenge for the field. For decades, both went unappreciated within design.

Though unique in their achievement, *Emigre* can be seen as reclaiming and extending Dwiggins' legacy. Design and literature are inseparable, each dependent upon and defined by the other. Though designers are notorious for prizing the image over the word, it's no coincidence that often design's foremost practitioners are and have been effective and dedicated writers.

The web may be the force to truly test the significance of literature's materiality. Whatever happens in the short term, the physical word, rendered in type on paper or screen, will be with us for some time. Unless we return to an oral tradition, or develop a telepathic one, we'll keep on seeing and reading.

file under nowhere

Rudy VanderLans' books, like many of the locales they picture, occupy places between recognized and well-traveled routes. Those places are real, have been given names, and noted on maps. But they are known more as areas away from development, as pass-throughs, or pass-bys. If you want to be somewhere, you keep moving. If you decide to stop and set up shop, expect people to roll past, convinced it's nowhere.

VanderLans' books inhabit a publication interzone. They're books that are difficult to categorize easily, or shelve. To give them their full due, they must be regarded as book-works: compound entities whose ultimate subject is what books are, and can be. Though constituted primarily of photographic images, they are far more than the standard collection of discrete prints. Because they are artist-initiated, a simplistic label for them would be "vanity monographs." Yet they are intently personal and the result of a singular vision. The books reside somewhere between mass-market publications and artist books. More eclectic and personal than the former and more accessible (and often more affordable) than the latter.

To varying degrees across his six volumes, VanderLans' books orchestrate images, sound, texts, typography, layout, and their construction as codex forms to make their impact. Other artists are called upon to provide some texts and the music on CDs enclosed in *Palm Desert*, *Cucamonga*, and *Joshua Tree*. However, their contributions are usually commissioned

for the specific project and sharply focused. From a graphic design perspective, we're in the realm of "graphic authorship." As denizens of that indeterminate domain, these books are model citizens. Though, admittedly, it's pretty open country.

An analogue for properly regarding these books is that of phonographic not photographic albums. Record albums originally served as simple, straightforward collections of individual songs. They were live performances consigned to vinyl, attempting to replicate the live experience. You gathered together enough tunes to fill out two sides, put the hit single first, got back on the road.

It was Brian Wilson who helped change all that in 1966 with *Pet Sounds*. The milestone Beach Boys' album was conceived as a whole, its individual tracks outlining a rough portrait of a young man's emotional and physical journeys. With the record, Wilson raised the stakes for what pop music records could be. All while having indelible melodies and stunning arrangements.

The metaphor of the record album is apt for all six books, more so the first three. Music is a literal aspect of the *Palm Desert/Cucamonga/Joshua Tree* trilogy, and its motivating and defining element. Music plays a lesser role in *Supermarket*, and is absent as an evident component in VanderLans' most recent works, *Pages From an Imaginary Book*, and *Bagdad, California*. These latter volumes are more "bookish," more conspicuously engaging the codex tradition. They are the "concept albums," where a coherent story is announced up front, and played out across the songs.

The *Palm Desert/Cucamonga/Joshua Tree* music trilogy is the most perplexing to locate for the typical reader or bookstore owner. However, they are simple in intent and approachable in execution. These books abide amongst traditional photo collections, artist books, special edition music CD releases (e.g. R.E.M.'s 1996 release *New Adventures in Hi-Fi*, with its ambiguous landscape pix by singer Michael Stipe), and renowned author/photographer collaborations such as James Agee and Walker Evans' *Let Us Now Praise Famous Men*. The trilogy books have elements of all of these yet swerve off to make their own trail.

The individual photographs may be and occasionally are separated

from the book context and appraised as discrete prints. Within the books, the images are by turns landscapes, snapshots, cinematic stills, and indices. They serve as part of a dynamic that has elements playing off of and reinforcing one another. Though photographs may be given independent presentation, they resonate more in concert with the typography and activated by the page layouts. The visual elements are like the instrumentation within a song with the images playing lead.

Other productions outside the graphic authorship circle could make the argument that they engage the book as book as fully as VanderLans does. Claimants include children's books such as Eric Carle *The Very Hungry Caterpillar* to anything that has stuck a CD into the package. What set these books apart are the sophistication of the effort and the mastery of its producer.

Often, the confluence of media and techniques in those other atypical books fail to rise above gimmickry. VanderLans' inventions are focused and no ingredient is "default." He is keenly aware of the rhetoric that even paper stock provides. This is the discernment of the designer, but utilized as metaphor. The maker of these books loves books.

An obvious, readily acknowledged influence on VanderLans' work is Edward Ruscha. Ruscha's book titles told you everything you needed to know about the contents: *Some Los Angeles Apartments*, *Every Building on the Sunset Strip*. Ruscha's first, *Twentysix Gasoline Stations* (1962), introduced a deadpan humor for the mundane buildings it documented, but leavened with respect.

The artlessness of Ruscha's books was carefully composed and the blatancy guileful. His books are artifacts of their time, both as artworks and documents of an era. The 60s were marked by the reaction to the dominant art æsthetic of the time: heroic, process-oriented, abstract expressionism. Ruscha, like his pop contemporaries, was deliberately debunking many of expressionism's claims. The subjects of his art are casually rendered banalities.

In the four decades since *Twentysix Gasoline Stations* and its sequels, the "typological" photography project has become a cliché. Aspirants are determined to blandly document every category of artifact produced

by humanity. A case of repeat until profound. As is often demonstrated, these artists neglect the historical moment that brought the progenitor books into being. Ruscha's wit and personal connection to the subjects is vital to understand them. That they were chosen not via some æsthetic rationalization but because he simply passed them in his travels is also overlooked and difficult to match.

While the influence of Ruscha is prominent, VanderLans is making his own way. Ruscha designed his books to achieve an "instruction manual" look, evincing a refined sensibility. VanderLans' designs also employ the rhetoric of design but to a different end. The choice of materials is intentionally evocative of books from an earlier era, yet are not slavishly imitative or aspiring to simulacra status. While indulgent in detail, they skirt preciousness through the form's consistency with the concept.

Our historical moment also define these books. They would not exist without the technological developments that made bookmaking possible on this scale of detail. The "D.I.Y" impulse that is manifest across the arts, bringing forth 'zines, independent record labels, myriad web logs and other sites, and much more is also significant. Our society is open as never before to "average" individuals being relevant cultural participants. In addition, there is an acceptance of personal narrative in the public literature. The memoir has supplanted fiction as the ascendant literature.

An extensive library of works concerning the Southwest and the desert already exists. VanderLans acknowledges this by including a photograph of some of these books as a frontispiece in *Bagdad, California*. As a photographer, he is haunted (in *Supermarket*) by numerous, renowned precursors: "And when I look into the view finder all I see are Ruscha and Baltz and Baldessari and Hockney and Frank and Friedlander and Misrach and Deal and Evans and Owens and Lange and Wessel and Weston and Adams (Robert and Ansel)." Is there anything new under the burning sun?

Making three books of homages to obscure musicians seems a thin premise. But it's certainly no worse than photographing gas stations. However, as with any number of creative works, the subject is a trigger, a starting point for a personal meditation. This basis for making art is long standing, and has included high and low sources. To "read" the book

literally is to be obtuse. A criticism of *Palm Desert* was that it failed to provide a well-rounded portrait of Van Dyke Parks. Such complaint misses the point entirely.

Though these books are a testament to VanderLans' commitment, he manifests directionlessness. He has the desire to create books but an uncertainty of what to make them. This is heard in *Supermarket* ("He ... asked what I was photographing ... I told him I'd find out as soon as the photographs were developed.") and in *Bagdad, California* ("One of the guys wants to know what purpose it serves to make a small book about a non-place like Bagdad, and I have difficulty answering the question. I mumble something .... ")

This is an enduring, pressing existential question for the creative actor: How do I make a subject mine? VanderLans' answer is in his manipulation of the physical and conceptual elements of the books. Rather than "popularizing" his subjects, his approach is as decidedly individual as the sources. They become "true" to their sources by being determinedly true to VanderLans' distinctive imagination. And also, by his indirect presence in many of the photos: the frequent shots that include in his car's windshield, mirrors, or hotel rooms.

Supermarket expands upon the music trilogy. In construction, it is those books writ large but without the tunes. Instead of using the musicians to frame the geographical exploration, it's a travelogue on its own terms. Like the areas it traverses, the book is sprawling, taking us from city streets around L.A then out into the desert. Images are set with text: VanderLans' observations about by the scenes.

Pages From an Imaginary Book spins an offbeat cover story to (re)contextualize its coarsely rendered, monotone landscapes. It claims to be a poor copy of a lavishly unproduced tome called *Desert Rhymes*, making it a Borges picture book, with 'real' pictures and places. Spreads with pairs of place names ("Sawtooth Range," "Dead Mountains") are alternated with pages having a single, coarse-resolution monochrome landscape photo. Every page item, whether image or name, is assigned a "Figure" designation. And while the book is not the lavish production desired, it's a limited edition of 250.

Bagdad, California is the simplest and briefest of the books, a photographic survey of a map location with no "there there." Monochrome images are paired with a diary-like exposition. As with the numerous signage studies in *Supermarket*, *Bagdad* seems to exhibit a particularly graphic designer regard in its "souvenirs." Many are typographic in their form. But this interpretation may be determined by knowledge of VanderLans' design day job.

The author's voice is a vital element, though it is often uncertain. So is some of the photography. The unassuming nature and directness of the commentaries match that of the images. Subtlety is paramount in every aspect of the books. No message or interpretation is forced into the book or onto the locations. VanderLans, in the manner of Stanley Kubrick's film making, seems to be perpetually "finding his book," having meaning arise from the process, with only a few boundary stakes planted to anchor himself.

If anything, at times a firmer intention is desirable in the books. VanderLans' restraint seemed to blur into passivity when confronted by the west's expanses and the abundant desert literature. The books became exercises in how to (re)package an assortment of essentially similar images of nothing in particular. Yet while the offbeat nature of these works can't wash away such concerns, they raise significant questions about their applicability.

This may be the ultimate correlation between the geography and the books: both resist easy definition and delineation. Containing the land is futile; you can only impose arbitrary frames. The desert breaks down signposts. Its rhythms are different from those of well-trod areas. You must situate yourself, and look closely at your surroundings for a long time. All while awed by an enormity. You have to recognize that you're not nowhere, give up searching for something that isn't there, and surrender to what is.

References:

Typologies: Nine Contemporary Photographers, essays by Marc Freidus (curator), James Lingwood, and Rod Slemmons (Newport Harbor Art Museum, Rizzoli, 1991).

Visions of America: Landscape as Metaphor in the Late Twentieth Century, (Denver Art Museum and Columbus Art Museum, Harry N. Abrams, 1994)

Sea Change

My longest-running magazine subscription is for *The Atlantic* (Monthly), going back some 20+ years. I can't recall exactly where I first encountered it, likely someone I was staying with or visiting frequently had a subscription. Though I was just out of art school, I ponied up for my own when my borrowed access ended. However tight my finances got, I kept the magazine coming. I felt a little extra connection as it was prominently and resolutely headquartered in Boston, where it was founded and I lived.

As I listened only to music on the radio, and watched little TV, *The Atlantic* provided me a regular connection to the serious, adult world of ideas, politics, and culture. I appreciated the depth and breadth of its topics, and the length at which its feature stories investigated subjects. Whatever sophistication I have about politics and an intellectual life derives in large part from reading *The Atlantic*.

It also played a revelatory role in my creative life. A 1988 article by David Owen (all his stuff was great, I missed him when he moved on) introduced me to the term "ephemeral states." From the short piece on imaginary countries and their colorful founders, I evolved a conceptual center for all my imaginative pursuits.

In a way, I never really felt I was supposed to be reading it. From its' advertising, I recognized I was miles (and $0000s) from the target demographic and I'm hardly much closer now. Akubra Hats from Australia?

BMWs? Private banking? By sending me an issue, it felt as if the magazine was slumming. Maybe I'd luck out and become a well-known artist. The only ad I've identified with over more than two decades was a surprise 1991 fractional-page promo for R.E.M.'s *Out of Time* (Warner Bros.). I almost expected to find the ad had been tipped-in over a "real" one just in my copy.

Both *The Atlantic* and I are long gone from Boston. It's remained a constant as I've swerved through career and life changes. It's undergone a number of adjustments in direction and focus on its own with as it worked through publisher and editor changes. Over the years, my attention and interest has flagged at times. But I stuck.

If I'd noted *The Atlantic*'s design, I recognized it followed the mainstream design styles of the times, with a better application. The magazine design was serious but not dour, in keeping with its devotion to culture and entertainment. There were always elements I particularly appreciated, often illustrations, and some that seemed stale.

Lately, I'd liked some of the iterations it had been making on its layout. It was great to be able to haul an issue into Typography class and show them hanging punctuation in a monthly journal. If there was anything in the design that consistently bothered me it was the covers. The face of the magazine was usually dull and too frequently unsightly. And the masthead? (Shrugs.)

And so the latest issue comes in the mail and I find *The Atlantic* has undergone a redesign. Not only that but my magazine opted for a top-shelf renovation by Pentagram, specifically Michael Bierut and Luke Hayman. Like the magazine's ads, the choice tells me I'm still way out of the demographic. Selecting Pentagram is a bit disappointing to me, for the safety and brand-namedness. It's unsurprising, as Bierut has worked tirelessly to be one of the field's most Literary designers. If not him, I'd expect the next choice to be Winterhouse.

That the resulting design would be creditable and defensible goes without saying. But the new design makes me feel even more estranged than the adverts. Along with the rationales Bierut provides in the new issue on the redesign, I'm sure there were pragmatic, demographic ones that are unstated. For me, the redesign is, at best, a lateral move. But elements of

the magazine I appreciated before have been purged. And that I'm somewhat let down may be good news for the magazine.

If I had to guess at a pragmatic, unspoken demand on the redesign, it was to trend younger. That seems a safe assumption for any product, especially one that's been around for 150 years. If so, I feel doubly old, as while I can admire the redesign as a design artifact, it doesn't particularly appeal to me as a design aficionado.

What makes me feel old on its own is how big and bold the graphic elements have gotten. Rules are single and thick, and the title face (Titling Gothic) is a Condensed Black with squinty-eyed counters. Even the text face, Hoefler&Co.'s Mercury, looks bulked-up from the magazine's previous face. Bierut regards Mercury as "elegant," which, in comparison to most faces, can certainly apply. However, I'd toss in a modifier of "spiky" or "jaggy," with that (and, hey, now that I read the founders' own description of the face, I see they use 'spiky,' too.)

It's a nice typeface and I think Hoefler&Co. are probably incapable of producing a dud font. Its curves are a bit too "taut" for me, here.

In addition, the layout clears away what were evidently deemed "graphic tricks." The sense of "urgency" in the design that Bierut hopes to achieve (balanced with "ideas") predominates, and the result is kind of bland. A sense of constant to-the-chase-cutting is across the pages. There was a sense of contemplation I found in the previous design that has been cleared out. It's all text, rules, and a cordoned-off gallery of hit-or-miss "image arguments" (to paraphrase the editor) sprinkled throughout. To me, the magazine now looks like the "homework" look, Bierut sought to avoid (though I'm still furrowing my brow over that descriptive).

If there's any graphic whimsy to leaven the overall tone, it's in Felix Sockwell's miniscule illustration buried at the bottom of the table of contents.

How this makes me feel old is that, like that R.E.M. ad, I wonder if *The Atlantic* knew I just got my first pair of bifocals recently (maybe Michael B. got it off my Facebook profile) and everything had to be graphically demonstrative. I'm also off-put by the funeral, white type on solid-black background opening page to the Features section. It's like a memento mori

to the old magazine, or to a way of reading.

One element that's a solid genius move is the revival of a long-standing masthead (the issues from the 1950's employing the masthead are the pick of the lot). I can only hope it'll be given some breathing room in the future. The first cover is a jumbled mess of a layout, and then down to the fitted-text composition. The left-hand vertical band makes practical sense to eliminate waste but adds to the clutter here. The use of this masthead makes me wish that that sensibility had been brought inside the magazine. It's a wonderful idiosyncrasy that deserves more play. Then again, for most, it may have seen as a nostalgia-wallow.

But the punctuation still hangs and the content makes me put everything aside when the new issue comes in. I won't complain to the editor about the remake but I won't be celebrating it either. As Bierut says, the new design will evolve and I'm content to wait and see. From this outlier on your sub list, *The Atlantic* could use more idiosyncrasy, curves, and graphic entertainment. See you next month.

Welcome the interruption

Projects like Kevin Lo's visual/literary journal *Four Minutes to Midnight* (*23:56* from now on) evoke Steve Baker's essay "A Poetics of Graphic Design?" The 1994 text appeared in the Andrew Blauvelt-edited *New Perspectives: Critical Histories of Graphic Design* and is one of the most intriguing essays written about graphic design criticism. It proposed a unique method of representing design activity.

Baker drew upon the writings of French feminist writer Hélène Cixous to propose a "more imaginative form of critical writing." It would "...take(s) its lead from Cixous's demonstration that the visual and verbal need not always be kept strictly apart, but can escape to each other's territories and beyond." This "graphic design poetics" would be a critical method that evaded the "'masculine' linearity" prevalent in criticism and multiplied meaning. Before that, graphic design's nature as a hybrid form of text and image interplay simply calls for a distinctive form to discuss it.

Baker affirmed his article was only "very provisionally gestured" toward what a graphic design poetics might be. Which, depending on your viewpoint, made it either literally nothing to consider or an inspired provocation. As a fan of contention, I've long been favored the latter. As a profession, graphic design asserts definition, not uncertainty and open-endedness. Practicality and practicability are keynotes. An eventual mystery is invoked . Why will a talent will select this color or typeface over

that? But only within the field.

As the overwhelming majority of graphic design activity involves crafting prosaic artifacts, a "poetic" graphic design study begs a label of double pretension. The first pretense is, for many practitioners and outsiders, criticizing design at all. Utilizing it to consider more challenging, or less standardly commercial, graphic design products at least removes the initial incredulity.

This brings us to 23:56, a limited edition (300), independently published journal by Kevin Lo and John W. Stuart. It's a paperback-sized soft-cover book. Contents are an assembly of submitted and composed elements, curated more than edited.

The theme of the issue is "Radical Beauty," something I know from messages soliciting material (and announced on their web site) but unstated in the book itself. Submissions are subject to reconstruction and combination with other material. This process is beyond the typical adaptation that graphic design does traditionally. By-lines are provided along with a list of contributors but it can get fuzzy who's done what. The book is paginated but not indexed.

Formally, the layouts move between classic, straightforward representations of texts (stories, verse) and "expressive" treatments tending toward layering, bleeds, and fragmentation. Writers can get very touchy about how their copy is presented; however, even the most intrepid settings evince a respect for the word.

23:56 is a descendant of *Now Time*, the L.A. cultural magazine that lasted only four issues from 1992–95. The publication (three of the four issues designed by ReVerb) was similarly a varied blend of formats and content, marked by an arresting farrago of typography.

For the design aficionado with a 'progressive' leaning, 23:56 is a satisfying, well-crafted typographic and compositional piece. The typography utilizes a limited base set of stylish contemporary faces, which imply "serious reading" without being staid.

However, there is a constant sense of menace and gravity about the content. The monochrome page inking is surely an economic decision but it contributes to a sober sensibility. On the title page, the issue numeral

"10" is rendered in skulls. The title itself indicates suspense and is literally "dark." Not much light at four minutes to midnight.

The issue as a whole mixes light and dark: day is invoked along with night. A tempering and counter-pointing of emotions occurs throughout. But shadows are always looming. For instance, the color cover design is primarily sunny and bright. Against a vivid green background, a deft collage of images resolves into a pleasant image of a seated woman in a floral dress. However, a fragment of text extends from behind a grey-scaled turned-away face overlaid with a text fragment that, like a thought balloon, jarringly declaims in a graceful, serif italic "... laughing 'fuck them!'"

What keeps the content from becoming oppressively dour is the stylish (in every good sense of the term: considered, æsthetically affirming) design, particularly the typography. Though it's bad news for the writers, I'm content to let the typography to move me on its own, like melody. The texts become lyrics whose purpose is to add the human voice element and not be distracting (or dumb). In this sense, it's off point to enjoin them to "lighten up, dude!"

The open call solicitation makes 23:56 a grab bag, hit or miss collection of images and writings. The quality is variable but never embarrassingly low. What's significant is that there is, throughout, a marked consistency of tone and outlook. Memes of struggle, resistance, troubled desire, and doubt threads through all the texts. The imagery begins light-hearted — a photographic sequence of a woman (girl?) blowing bubbles gives way to more enigmatic and disturbed graphics.

The public politics that are implicitly (and explicitly) espoused are earnest, liberal-progressive, centered on resistance to intellectual control and corporate hegemony. The personal politics negotiate classic themes of estrangement, regret and yearning for intimacy and the language to foster it. These politics are intertwined within the texts, and their collation within the book.

Many of these expressions, in image and text, seem familiar, often expected. At some point, I knew I'd encounter documentary evidence, here photographs from Kosovo and Afghanistan, which keep it all publicly real. Eventually, I'd encounter the personally frank, in the form of erotic — but

tasteful nudes (here, always women). Eventually, some comics set at the end, complete with some character cussing.

It comes close to a template of progressive literary art journal. The result can be a sameness, a set of predicable expressions repeatedly shuffled. This is, to a degree, a simplistic reduction few publications could endure. Yet, in reading the issue, there was an absence of surprise. It was admirable, pleasant ... but comfortable.

My notion of beauty wasn't radicalized. If anything, it was affirmed and gratified. The theme could have acceptably been exchanged for any number of concepts. It may be that I'm really jaded and/or there's no more axis to extend on what's considered "beautiful." We can only loop/twist back in on ourselves like a Klein bottle.

The consistency of attitude and the relative ease factor raises the concern that the "architecture of resistance" becoming codified, diagrammatic. 23:56 serves as a call to and document of a community. Establishing an identity is important. But fashioning tropes and clichés of "alternative" content is as insidious as the hegemony of the corporate/consumerist mainstream. Do we exchange one uniform for another?

I don't want to overstress this point, as I worry more about no think than group think. What's most important is that a project like 23:56 continues to hang in there. As a graphic design artifact, it's thoughtful and finely crafted. If it's a "uniform" of resistance, it's a damn good looking and tailored one. I can only applaud an effort that is surely a financial (and often emotional) burden. There's little external affirmation in these kinds of efforts. The reward is pride in keeping to one's principles and the delight gained in bringing your ideas into form. It may be my own predilection but I have more faith in the product of those impulses than commercial determinism. That faith is that the 23:56 will knowingly and willingly explore and adapt in response to real needs of community.

Meanwhile, I don't know about the viability of a poetics of graphic design. Artifacts as subtle as 23:56 deserve a criticism that's similarly imaginative and expansive. As part of this speculative poetics, Steve Baker proposes utilizing ekphrasis. This poetic device (here Baker quotes Grant Scott) "... might be a 'featured inset' which 'digresses from the primary

narrative.'" It's a "strategic ... form of interruption."

I don't know if this is a poetic graphic design criticism you're reading. But consider my discussion of it your interruption.

Conversations with notable graphic designers

How to Think Like a Great Graphic Designer (Allworth Press) is a collection of interviews presenting 20 noted graphic design-related figures ruminating about their activity. In her introduction, Debbie Millman disclaims the book's title but it's fairly descriptive, being instructive by example rather than recipe. Since the book makes no pretension of compiling a definitive list of contemporary design "greats," I won't fuss overlong (for me) over the arbitrariness of the designation.

What *does* constitute graphic design greatness? All of the interviewees are practically accomplished graphic designers (save John Maeda, who has renown but simply isn't a graphic designer by the field's common standards). However, the jury's out on the long-term significance of most of these practitioners. That many other designers could claim equal or greater stature compared to those selected doesn't spoil the book. Still, it would have helped for Millman to, at least briefly, outline her criteria.

Again, a curve isn't necessarily being drawn that would be thrown off by alternate choices. The common trait attributed to all the interviewees is "high levels of empathy" that makes them able to "logically, poetically, and telegraphically transfer ideas from one mind to the other." Besides being a tad mystical for my taste, the description suggests I may want to wear my tin-foil hat if I ever attend a Design Legends Gala. Some more demonstrable and mundane abilities may first be ascribed to these worthies without

lessening their real accomplishments as producers.

These arguments are ultimately beside the point. This is a book about and for graphic designers who are already sold on the standing of the interviewees. The biographies provided on the designers are cursory, lacking full context. An increase of *showing* over *telling* would make a more convincing portraits. If someone is possessed of great wit or an engaging spirit, it should be made manifest in the subject's own words.

It's obvious from the text that the reader will expect no justifications. Millman isn't engaged in sanctification (and, for their part, the designers don't actively sanctify themselves) but I couldn't help wondering what happened to the great design *bastards*. They exist, don't they? And considered great by some?

While I would sieve out a portion of the modifiers in the text, it's the interviewees' words that are the heart of the book. At this level of the field, it's given that these people are articulate. *And* practiced at talking about themselves. Remove a third of these designers from the lecture and conference circuit and ... well, the remaining two-thirds would need twice as many interns as they picked up the slack. So, the challenge of this book is squeezing something fresh out of over-examined people.

On this count, Millman does a fine job. Having a group that tends toward the garrulous helps but has its drawbacks. Millman prompts with a light touch and checks her enthusiasm, letting it work for her. Some of the questions are familiar but the interviews are accomplished with admirable restraint. They may not be the "deep(ly) psychological discussions" promised in the introduction (more confrontation would needed to pull that off) but the book is no worse for it. Simply put, *How To Think* was an enjoyable read and I learned stuff about everyone featured.

The best favor *How to Think* does for graphic design is demonstrating the variety of personalities, approaches and opinions amongst its practitioners. In other words, it showcases some healthy friction. Millman doesn't directly challenge her subjects' opinions or natures but the "greats" go at each other across the pages. It's good to read Neville Brody claiming Stefan Sagmeister is "extremely wrong" on a topic and saying *why*. And early on, Carin Goldberg succinctly defines and disdains designer *schtick*,

which is later performed by its master, Chip Kidd* (replacing the bulk of his text with a rim shot sound-chip would eliminate the middle man and prove no substantive loss).

How To Think is a good mid-range discussion, between a critical 'scoping and the typical lecture Q & A . It's best filed under "Conversations with Notable Graphic Designers." And it is small praise to simply credit Debbie Millman for bringing a smart, new interviewing voice to design.

What I would like to see from her next is a long-overdue project for the field: giving voice to the "regular" graphic designer. The real picture of graphic design is the legion of non-"great" but thoughtful (and sometimes not) practitioners crafting our visual environment. Millman's own empathy for all designers is considerable, evidenced in this book, her Speak Up posts, and *Design Matters* shows. Interviews of the kind offered in *How To Think* with the "regulars" might do more to raise awareness of graphic design outside the field. Then again, it might not. But Debbie Millman could be the one to give it the best shot.

* *Note:* Carin Goldberg does not name Chip Kidd (or any other designer) as a purveyor of *designer schtick*. The interpretation and identification is entirely my own.

The good just is

If designers have a central precept, it's that their activity creates economic value for commercial interests. Practitioners regard this as their predominant purpose. Within design, even among students, this pecuniary capacity is considered self-evident. But the eternal lament among design professionals is that business isn't grasping this certainty, or only does so erratically. Design is largely regarded as a frivolous afterthought.

Failing to outline the exact mechanism by which this value addition operates has hampered design's cause. It has instead proffered the testimony of prominent executives such as Thomas Watson — "good design means good business" — as evidence, which has proved not to transfer or extend successfully. Though illustration more than argument, Apple's market dominance due to celebrated dedication to design has also become a staple citation.

Still, little traction has been gained in getting business to understand design's import, and in securing designers an influential seat at the corporate table. If anyone should be able to recognize and articulate the argument for design as a primary component of financial reward, it would seem to be economists, who ostensibly study and propose business best practices.

That's not happening, either convincingly enough or at the necessary scale. As to designers' fluency in speaking about economics, many regard

themselves as adroit if they've operated their own shop. That's about it, and business isn't relating. Meanwhile, when designers encounter economic concepts such as "ROI" (Return on Investment), they instinctually recoil. Design education and theory have also failed to take into account economic forces and justifications.

Design and the Creation of Value (Bloomsbury Academic) by the late British design historian John Heskett is a long-overdue attempt to address the estrangement between economics and design. As Sharon Helmer Poggenpohl says in her afterword, "Economics and business understanding are missing links in design practice and education and few have the interest or are capable of going beyond basic comprehension." Heskett attempts to forge those links and direct ways forward.

Because it focuses on design's core rationale, my impulse is to pronounce this short, posthumously assembled volume one of the most important texts *ever* offered on design, arguably the field's essential book. In addition, separate to its specific content, it also stands, in Poggenpohl's words, as "a scholarly gift" to design education.

The book was assembled from notes for a seminar Heskett last offered in 2009 at Hong Kong Polytechnic University along with related draft and incomplete manuscripts. Heskett contemplated forming the material into a book but never actively began the process.

Editors Clive Dilnot and Susan Boztope have done an exemplary job of shaping the disparate and fragmentary material into a coherent and substantive whole. Rather than detracting from its impact, the book's sketchy status adds a level of immediacy. Both Heskett and the editors regard this study as just the opening of a wide-ranging, extended discussion. The book's incomplete condition may act as a more inviting prompt for additional research.

Heskett's stated intention is practical: "This book is about how design can add and create economic value for businesses and other organizations." Its specific audience is "designers and managers of design" to present as the case with businesses for design being an "integral element in firms' activities."

Immediately, Heskett acknowledges discussing the relationship of

design and economics as a "minefield, " due to the "deep schism of mutual incomprehension [that] separates them." Neither field is adequately
versed in the other's concerns. There seems little appetite on either side to
remedy the situation.

Fortunately for us, it's Heskett that sets himself the task of chart-
ing the landscape of economic theory and its implications. He is a lucid
and engaging guide, summarizing the major economic theories without
sacrificing nuance. (Dilnot and Boztope provide two affirmations from
economists on Heskett's competence in their area).

Dinot's introduction provides a detailed and candid assessment of
the book's achievements and limitations. The transparency and comprehensiveness of his notes are immensely valuable beyond this particular
study. Rather than limiting the appreciation of Heskett's work, or channeling readers' expectations, Dilnot's opening provides important context.

Part one of the book, "Economic Theory and Design," moves
through the major schools of economic theory: Neoclassical, Austrian,
Institutional, New Growth, and The National System. Each is outlined
deftly in text and diagrams how the theory presumes commerce operates.
Further readings are provided for those wishing a deeper dive into the
theories.

Neoclassical theory is the one that readers will be most familiar, as
it constitutes the mainstream of economic thought. Devised between
the world wars, its terms and premises are what "economics" is popularly
considered to be.

Neoclassical theory features the familiar concepts of markets, goods
and service, supply and demand, and Adam Smith's "invisible hand."
Design's inability to gain respect in business derives from its status within
Neoclassical theory. Or, more accurately, its total absence.

Neoclassical theory is a "static" model, concerned with what *is* and
not with what *might* be. Neoclassical theory doesn't concern itself with the
devising, planning and manufacture of a good. The good just is. Heskett
presents design as concerned with change, an action of devising preferred
from existing states.

In this way, Neoclassical theory contemplating design is like science

speculating on what happened before the Big Bang: there's no way to know so it's pointless to speculate. Within Neoclassical theory, it's seems impossible for design to ever gain a hearing. "... if markets and products are as constant as depicted in Neoclassical theory, this as best reduces design to a trivial activity concerned with minor, superficial differentiation of unchanging commodities, a role, indeed, that it does frequently perform. At worst, it contradicts the whole validity of design."

"Dynamic" theories such as Austrian and New Growth offer design the most potential for respect and inclusion. Heskett outlines three areas of "concern" for designers in current economic thinking: technological opportunity, innovation, and its functioning within institutional structures. Emphasizing these aspects may improve design's argument for inclusion.

More than locating design's possible role in the various theories, Heskett uses design as the key means to evaluate them. Each theory is subjected to critique, weighing its merits intellectually and practically (does it conform to actuality). In his analysis, Heskett assigns design a profound role in his analyses as a decisive test. Design's situation in each theory stands as a key intellectual and practical proof of its contemporary viability. Here, Heskett may be paying design the greatest compliment it's ever received. Design and the matter of value may serve as an indicator and prompt for (in Dilnot's words) "change and evolution" in economics.

Part two, "Design and the Creation of Value," is briefer and examines design and economics from the others' standpoint. The chapter inverts the approach of the previous chapter, to directly tackle the book's central premise. Heskett provides a skillful summary of his arguments, providing numerous opportunities for subsequent scholarship to expand upon the ideas.

Throughout the book, Heskett speaks as an advocate for design but is just as frank about the field's intellectual shortcomings. Foremost is design's often-curt dismissal of economics' concerns. "From the point of view of designers' attitudes toward economics, there is mistrust of the dominance of numerical calculation and financial management in corporate administration, something perceived as alien to how design functions. Setting aside the irrational aspects of what is indeed frequently

an exaggerated, defensive reaction, and the deficiencies of some designers in clearly articulating their ideas, there is nevertheless substance in such perceptions." Still, this perception shouldn't lead to the frequently whole-sale rejection of economics' measures of design viability.

If popular economic theory is challenged for slighting what does and may occur prior to the sale of a good, Heskett also considers the lack of study of post-sale factors. The "user" is a complex construct in its own right, and "user-centered" design is brought on to assert it's potential as "a key operational concept in introducing values, in a broad sense, to ensure that any technology is appropriate for any targeted group of users and, as far as possible, based upon an assessment of a wider pattern of repercus-sions in social, cultural, and environmental conditions."

Heskett's interrogation of terms throughout is unfailing, especially "value." Though profitability to a producer is naturally given prominence as how "value" is defined, it's not to the exclusion of broader, intangible con-siderations. Ethical and personal constructions are acknowledged. Value judgments exist in an artifact's planning, production, acquisition, and use. Each circumstance demands its own consideration.

Hovering over the discussion throughout, but never named, is the practice of branding. "If goods help us construct personal meaning and have social relevance, these are obviously important considerations in how value is created," Heskett states. Of the many implications of his text, branding's rhetoric and impact is possibly of primary significance. Here is the most culturally profound and lucrative expression of constructed personal meaning.

These ineffable and individual value assessments are the hardest to chart. An appealing aspect of the Heskett's writing and his approach to the topic is a humanism that prevents people from being the automatons frequently described in economic and design theory. Heskett forthrightly acknowledges a broader meaning for value and design.

As design can serve as a test for economic theory, consideration of value may enhance and enlighten our understanding of design and economics. According to Dilnot, value may serve as a "third term," a "new object and new language that belongs wholly to neither field," that

following Roland Barthes use of "text," could illuminate both fields.

The fragmentary nature of this book can prove frustrating, as dense and elusive ideas are given relatively short shrift. And as inclusive as Heskett is, there are boundaries and conventions to a number of his declarations. His view of art (under Appendix 2's "Æsthetic value") seems decidedly romantic:"the outcome is a surprise to the artist and the result created in dire straits." The art marketplace would be possible a more fecund ground to explore value generation.

Under "Moral value," Heskett is at his most terse: "Moral or ethical value seems to have limited relation to design." That single sentence begs an extended exegesis. And under "Intrinsic verses extrinsic value," he finds that "It is difficult to identify any intrinsic value of design." As someone that purchases many record albums solely for the packaging with no interest in listening to them, I seem to elude that claim. Perhaps this only reinforces the ultimate personal nature of value. But once again, branding raises its head.

As to the value of *Design and the Creation of Value*, it's pronounced and plentiful. For practitioners, the book lends substance to long-standing contentions. The potential is for designers to become conversant in the language of economics and to understand the derivation of its ideas. Greater still is the potential for design to transform the practice of its major patron.

For educators and researchers, the book succinctly describes the commercial landscape where design is publicly performed. Though centered on economics, it provides numerous prompts and directions for further significant research. Heskett, Dilnot and Boztope have presented design with a truly essential text, one that, to be relevant, practice and education must engage.

12 views of 120 posters

1.

The poster is a graphic conundrum: a unique space where the surface is, not only meets, its edge.

2.

The poster's status as a primary, mass medium of cultural exchange has long since passed. Any cultural form that boasts an era of activity described as a "golden age" has moved into senescence, if not irrelevance. The perspective is backwards and looking up to a peak. Unlike the metal, this intangible gold lives a half-life, decaying over time like a radioactive element. There's energy but a progressively declining affectiveness and effectiveness. Conversely though, its aura grows stronger. If we're to honestly contemplate the poster, we need to acknowledge this reality. However, the poster isn't unique in this status nor does said status remove it from serious consideration in the cultural conversation. The poster may be losing charged particles but can still enlighten us. From readily available evidence, it's still energizing generations of designers to make posters — and audiences in their response (though, as always with graphic artifacts, that response is problematic to quantify). Poster output is still high, perhaps greater than ever, and not simply because there are more makers at work.

3.

Has the Internet, ironically, saved the poster? Given it new life? Our

virtual global forum is a boon for the display and dissemination of posters. It's far wider and less constrained than the physical spaces available. Rather than shunted to fringe public areas such as construction hoardings, which may be physically prominent in the very center of public spaces, but are categorically ephemeral, posters can be center stage, and accessible at any time. The interval between realization and display is far shorter, with a greater assurance of a wider audience. Infinite galleries can be erected and opened to view. But while termed posters, many of the contemporary works are wholly digital. Having no substance other than pixels, one of, if not the, key attributes claimed for the poster is wholly absent: materiality.

4.

Crafting a poster is a gesture of seriousness, whether you're a brand, a band, or a political movement. The simple action of making a poster, regardless of the actual content, is symbolically important to the latter two. It's a declaration of intent to join or start a social conversation. *We're here.* An idea may be expressed verbally and spread through repetition but is still evanescent. Many political prisoners, though, will testify that even a fleeting, audible expression carries substance and consequence. The substance of the poster though, raises the stakes. As with all design artifacts, it makes thought concrete and extends it into the world of things. The thing is harder to ignore and to deny. So, for their makers, there is an intangible aspect of posters outside of mass marketing: an emotional connection, a thrill of being.

5.

Posters have long been social broadsides, disseminating information and opinion on current events. The increased number of eager participants and the boundless forum of the Web have placed this into overdrive, accelerating commentary via poster production. A principal impetus has been calamity. A graphic outpouring of response now closely follows well-publicized tragedies. The most recent example was the March 2011 earthquake and tsunami that struck Japan. Sympathetic posters burst forth after the calamity with such speed and volume that they seemed the detritus of the killer waves, only washing outward from the rest of the world. Sites sprang up inviting contributions, both of disaster-themed works to

demonstrate solidarity, and to raise funds to aid survivors. As inspiration for diverse graphic activity, the tsunami was a profound trigger. But the ultimate utility and intent of the work wasn't as clear. Clever, well-crafted graphics abounded. Sincerity wasn't an issue: all of the work was done on spec, most with no expectation of recompense. Many were fund-raisers. But was the work about the tragedy or about the poster? Was disaster an excuse almost to design a poster? If charity was the purpose, why not donate directly? And the cause of spreading knowledge of the extent of damage and suffering was extensively documented on video. Could a poster be more powerful than actual footage? If the poster's role is different in such situations, what is it?

6.

This is what the posters presented here are not: examples of the majority. In the poster genus, works of advocacy are a sub-species. All of these works exist against a highly visible backdrop of posters crafted for information. They're so omnipresent; they're invisible to the consciousness. Their mundanity suggests that another, hybrid term be coined to identify them (information + poster = infoster? Inposter?) Mulling over this essay while waiting for my doctor, it's almost with a start that I recognize that it's a poster I've stared at during every visit to the exam room, one diagramming a portion of my anatomy. Hey, that's one too! What can I say about that? My children's classrooms offer little open wall space. Perhaps the walls are painted: it's tough to tell. Within such public/private contexts, posters thrive. They've adapted well to the interior environment, almost run wild in numbers. In form, they're boisterously polite, adherents to the bourgeois principles of good design.

7.

Does materiality matter? What is claimed is that the poster's cultural substance comes from its physical substance. The poster can be felt, is tangible. This aspect is put forth largely to differentiate between digital forms of communication, those dependent upon contemporary devices such as laptops, iPads, and smart phones. For the older generation calling forth the poster's physicality, there is no romance in silicon. Romance is all that supports the idea that materiality is the poster's strength.

8.

A primary cause of the poster's decline from relevance is that it has been practically legislated out of public existence. Starving it of display venues effectively bans the poster. In the cause of public order, unauthorized posting has been banned in most localities whether it is municipalities overall or the individual establishments within. Meanwhile, the permissible zones from posting are few. Like graffiti, posters fall into a conflicted area where free speech and the public order collide. Extemporaneous graphic expressions aren't seen as healthy exponents of a vibrant First Amendment. Instead, they're regarded as indicators of anarchy, examples of decay that must be eliminated in the "broken windows theory" of civic tidiness. The poster can doubly deny and affirm, where the messages sent by the poster's existence and that of its content, collide and collude.

9.

The poster is the most conservative, traditional artifact of graphic design. There is no form as established and widespread as the marking on a single sheet of paper. Unless you're inscribing directly onto a natural or built structure. Books may make a creditable claim to an original status, however, codex forms, while encompassed by graphic design, also transcend it, occupying their own distinct category. While the poster is an established, establishment form, it is commonly associated, as with this exhibition, with radicality and progressive thought. "Protest poster" is nearly a redundancy; the association is so strong of the poster to political ferment.

10.

During these auric eras, the apices of the poster, we may also witness its destruction. This was when the distinct poster artists, such as Lucien Bernhard (the object-poster, Sachplakat), occupied the form, wedded it to a new commercialism, and elevated formal adventure. The poster became an exponent in a wider æsthetic agenda that paid lip service to, but ultimately displaced commercial concerns. Amongst the poster's most accomplished performers is Swiss designer Josef Müller-Brockmann, the standard maker and bearer for the high Modernist International Style of design. Here was the ultimate expression of this formal adventurism.

The forms were all, the "subject" of the poster, essentially irrelevant. The poster lost an immediacy and spontaneity. It became the province of the pros. The ground rules for poster achievement changed and migrated to and became like lawns manicured within an inch of their lives. Lush and beautiful, though.

11.

It's in its immediacy that the poster still channels and exhibits power and relevance. For the flaws in the popular view of the poster and its material nature, there is a fundamental, tangential truth. For all the manifest visual pleasure of the commercial poster, it's the unstudied, spontaneous works that define the form and prove the most affecting. Many of the revered posters of the sixties, such as the 1969 Art Workers Coalition poster of the My Lai Massacre, are crude pieces, the antitheses of the reigning, high-Modern style. This reality is often glossed over by commentators, as championing these political works undermines their fundamental taste-making arguments on what is proper design. It's possible, if not necessary, to embrace the diversity of æsthetics. However, the poster becomes the most noticeable place to detail, in the poster's status as primal artifact of design, the inconsistency of mainstream design thought. Commercially determined notions of apposite layout, defined and proscribed by marketing concerns, seem twee and extraneous when confronting these powerful, pointed posters. The formulas and tropes of graphic design fall away. The profound works make their own rules, and in their wake leave us asking, "what just happened here?"

12.

It's a paper cut like a knife.

Re: Song Cycle

If rating the rockers don't you panic.
It's music democritically romantic.
Two ears the gear were required to dope out
what gets them inspired. 'Til some
sea shore dude and four 'Pudlians collude
three chords into tine art.

Essayers now have to get smart. 'Bout stuff
you must read in a book.
We can't just delight in pop hooks.
Now I'm fretting my favor to do this.
Of Charles Ives and Mahler I'm clueless. So in rhyme
I'll opine plus tongue torqued tide
score 'round the Parks and zone out.

Re: Cycle

The U.S. has absorbed and appropriated countless cultural influences. What is distinctly "ours" becomes difficult to determine. There are many American musics. Jazz is frequently declared to be our only unique music. Following this claim is the obligatory irony of how unpopular it is in its native land.

Rock-and-roll and country-and-Western also conjure images of

Americana. And this evocative power is one that many musicians continue to employ. Less used and more challenging are two musical styles that originated elsewhere but dominated by the U.S.: the musical theatre and movies. The defining eras of these sounds are as ingrained in our imaginations as the conventions of film noir. Few musicians have meaningfully brought these themes to popular music. Unsurprisingly, these few began their work in the musically-experimentive 1960s. It was a time when artists were digging into American popular culture of earlier eras. It's also material that these musicians hailed from or moved to the L.A. area, locus of the film industry.

Van Dyke Parks' nonpareil minstrelsy embarks
upon this elite motif discreet.
The quintessensible virtuoso's '68 album
uno as orphic opera extraordinary.
The theses in situ: sonicycles of integumental
hymnography, commonalty, nuncupative vagary.
When verbiating Van Dyke Parks we must considerate
the native throng and the costs along.
Unique in furthering a streak
of American music he belongs: the orchestrated
contemporary popular song. VDP is straight with tunes
which predates both diapasons priorly alluded.
His larks harks and with life imparts
the celluloid and boards-trod score. *Song Cycle* as first
foray; accompanying the flickering personal display.

What's Up In Laurel Canyon, Doc?
Original moniker for Waronker: *Looney Tunes*.
Classic Warners sign, though do say me
s'more Merrie Melodiedy.
An earful of cheerful,
not an agog gong show.

The Child Is Farther Than the Band
Song Cycle is relatively brief, running just under 33 minutes. Individual songs time in the pop song range of between three and five

minutes, though three clock in at under two minutes. The perfectionism inherent in the time and effort required to produce those 33 minutes definitely set a tone for the labor-intensive process of later records. Then again, Parks had the immediate example of Brian Wilson spending $50,000+ over three months to make a 3:35 "Good Vibrations."

Wilson's drug-dazed, paranoiac musical genius is an unspoken, uncredited influence throughout Parks' record. If only for mentoring Parks, taking him on as his lyricist for the aborted *Smile* project, providing encouragement and confidence, Wilson's craft hovers over these grooves. When asked if he had any musical influence on Wilson, Parks response is succinct: *yeah, I wish*. Wilson can be heard in *Song Cycle*'s sound effects, the curious treatments of voice and instruments, and the astounding, intuitive mood and tempo shifts, as unveiled in "Good Vibrations" and "Heroes and Villains," their first collaboration. Parks' album contains the true "pocket symphonies" complete with full orchestra that Wilson spoke of making. Discussion of the lost *Smile* album always regards *Smiley Smile* as the salvage. It may be that *Song Cycle* was Parks' reclamation of that potential, by necessity made away from Wilson.

Joyce to the Whirled Record

Song Cycle is constructed as a suite of songs: movements within a larger, two-sided work. The album's title certainly suggests this. Parks throws open all the conventions of a record in *Song Cycle*, formerly and structurally. A hint of what's to come is clearly indicated in the credits and song lyrics on the back of the record jacket. Alongside Parks' Joyce-lite stream-of-puntiousness lyrics, a song called "Laurel Canyon Blvd." appears twice, once on each side. Side one concludes with an eponymous track "Van Dyke Parks," credited to the Public Domain. The song consists of the sound of crashing waves and distant voices warbling "Nearer My God to Thee." The flip side then reverses the title and composer credit for a straightforward (or as straightforward as this LP gets) vocal with musical accompaniment.

Song Cycle operates at its own paces: dramatically and unexpectedly shifting tempos, melodies, and direction throughout. Some seem spliced together from smaller songs within songs, while musical quotations from

other composers spring forth and are subsumed. Lovely instrumental figures appear then segue or are abruptly terminated. The piano kicking off his adaptation of "Donovan's Colors" or the treated harp on "The All Golden." Soaring string sections swell up then careen off on tangents. Triumphant brass provide glissandi and impulsion. Sweetly plucked harp is a frequent lead instrument, hobo harmonicas drone. Amidst the mix is Parks' nasal voice, crooning lyrics which follow their own entangled path, guiding then veering off the music's path. The alliterarity lyrics are a crafted tease of settings scenes and biophonography.

Song Psychol

Where there are lyrics to a song, there will be the attempt to discern the meaning of the songs, then by extension, the entire album. Also, the more distinct the lyrical style, the greater the feeling that the words are fraught with significance, especially personal. While elusive in their meaning, Parks intends them to have significance while indulging in polysyllabic variegation. As with the music, once the particular rhythms of the words becomes familiar, the sense is discerned. The evocations are again of an American present reflected in times gone by.

As with the "Van Dyke Parks"/"Public Domain" song title reversals, the album title also suggests a similar inverted reading. On the cover the "*Song Cycle*/Van Dyke Parks" credit is printed twice, side-by-side, reading up then down in blue and red. The separating slash mark prints opposite of the type color. It seems another suggestion of the musician both playing and being played by the music. *Song Cycle* appears as a two-way musical biography. To us the listeners, this record is Van Dyke Parks. And who is Van Dyke Parks? A musician: a man made of music. Parks reveals and toys with the idea of the art as poise for the person, stringing us out with massed violins and violas as far as we will go.

Low Coin

For many musicians, the first album is their singular achievement. For others, it is a sparse framework for heights to follow. Often, a label-imposed gloss or restraint strives to beg sales. *Song Cycle* is in a small select company of unique debut efforts by solo artists. Challenging, adventurous and assured, it ranks with other landmark first albums to follow swoon:

Richard Thompson's *Henry the Human Fly!* (1972), and Brian Eno's *Here Come the Warm Jets* (1973). Each are virtuoso performers on their instrument (Parks piano, Thompson guitar, Eno synthesizer), pursuing uncompromised personal musical visions soaring in the face of commercial considerations.

> Tendered the twine,
> Mr. P.'s incline is to strike up
> the biggest band in our land.

Wax Æsthetic

It may be that *Song Cycle*, for all its many virtues, firmly established Parks in the cult-critical favorite category marked by worshipful reviews and microscopic sales. This no more lessens Parks as an artist nor should it glorify him. And while he doesn't disclaim *Song Cycle*, it is worth noting the aspects of the album which don't appear in subsequent releases. For some, particularly the unique lyrical approach, he has unequivocally stated that the reason for the shift is that he wishes to be more accessible and commercial. Knowing his sarcastic and ironic sense of humor, such statements may mask another common desire: to move on. However, in thinking of the role of the musician in a commercial culture, Parks' comments belie any charge of willful obscurity. In some ways, Van Dyke Parks after *Song Cycle* is a testament to how unnoticed you can be while making some of the most accessible, joyful, and melodic music around. Much admiration goes to artists who dare to be difficult. What of those being uncompromisingly tuneful when discord may pay better? Like Parks pal Harry Nilsson, who at the height of his early 70s popularity puts out *A Little Touch of Schmilsson in the Night* (1973), an orchestrated album of standards (e.g. "I Wonder Who's Kissing Her Now," "It Had to Be You," "As Time Goes By"). All classic songs, elegantly rendered, some twenty years before Sinead O'Connor's *Am I Not Your Girl?*

One of the stories attached to *Song Cycle* is its abysmal sales figures. Unlike the Velvet Underground, those other 60s alternatives, every one of those few thou of purchasers *didn't* go on to form a band. Likely because it's tough to find all those cello players for your group *and when someone did, we got ELO.* However, his music hasn't gone unnoticed

by contemporary musicians. In a *Ray Gun* interview of Parks and Brian Wilson, pop perfectionist Matthew Sweet cited Parks' Datsun commercial score as a major dinfluence.

Disc Misc.

My description of this *(picks up CD)* isn't the thing, it's a something else entirety. Only *this (taps on CD)* can be *this* in reality. So if I talk about music, I literally only talk *about* it: around, aside, tangentally. Making an oblique attack could in fact bring you closer than any direction.

Lonly in a careen
as idiosympatic has Parks
could an LP s'much like *Song Cycle*
be insidered consistent
yet out-standing.
The LP dreams distinctly of its times,
of venturous gained,
virtuous strain.

One thing *Song Cycle* definitely is *not* is a rock-and-roll record in terms of instrumentation. There's no rhythm section. The ratio of balalaika players to guitarists is 3:1, the axmen not only eschewing power chords but power, playing acoustically. What *Song Cycle* shares with other popular music of the time is the experimentation, the expansion of possibilities for recorded music. Where other artists were grafting orchestrations onto R&B-based songs or occasionally enlarging their influences to the song-writers of the stage and movie musical, Van Dyke Parks constructed his music entirely from these sources. In addition, he played up the artificiality of records while making something distinctly personal.

Eponymous Lex

Song Cycle reads as both literal, description of the contents of the record *and a punning one at that* and the suggestion of an epic, like Wagner's "Ring Cycle." Grandiose music describes tales of the mundanities of Van Dyke Parks' life. Locales feature prominently, notably of Los Angeles: "Palm Desert," "Vine Street," "Widows Walk," "The Attic." When not describing his world, Parks introduces his friends: "The All Golden" is

a tribute to Steve Young. When he's not dispersing into the public domain, Parks is assuming mysterious alter egos. A single version of "Donovan's Colors" preceded the album, attributed to George Washington Brown, who on *Song Cycle* is tacked as the track's pianist.

Song Cycle manages to be one of the most elusive yet personal artistic statement put on record. His album initiates with a address direct to the appreciative listener, set to music. A tryst failing listing on his racket jacket. Instead of opening to the first track "Vine Street," the album fades in with an unreleased Steve Young bluegrass version of the folk tune "Black Jack Davy." After a minute, the song fades out. Parks then emerges like the CD M.C.. Over strings gently swaying, he sings like he's confiding something between him and the listener. It's a persona précis in musical key before he strikes up the show:

> That's a tape that we made
> But I'm sad to say it never made the grade
> That was me, third guitar
> I wonder where the others are

[Strings end, grand and tack piano duo starts]

> I sold the guitar yesterday
> I never could play much anyway
> A curtain drawn back to reveal another curtain.

Song Ellipsisical

It's a given hear, it will seduce your ear and mind. With a surprise every staff — on the next track or even the consensual second of the song. Let it play you, given way to a setting of eternal Hollywood, country, and rhyme. Nothin's like it. But it's a one night music stand. Can we see how this particular pot pourri could reevolve? The cycle unbroken, off to uncover America, ringing a northern death knell.

Once done, is done. First talk in tongues. You soon settle singerly for one.

The world at yr Cornershop

Imagine walking the streets during a bazaar, street fair, or some other festive gathering where celebration mixes with people's everyday activities: strolling, shopping, errands. Perhaps you're in or near an urban park during a festival or parade.

Music animates the air: blaring from boom boxes, spilling out of open doorways, buzzing from loudly tuned iPods, spouting from amps broadcasting musicians on an unseen bandstand; the mixture resounds and rebounds off surfaces and buildings near and far. Blend into this canorous mixture an undercurrent of the speech and song of the milling public, numerous conversations, announcements, ads, chants, shouts, cries, calls. At first, you're not quite paying attention, simply letting the sound wash over you. But gradually, perhaps even suddenly, a realization occurs. You're listening to a single, spontaneous song.

At first, the atmosphere seemed a formless audio mélange of diverse musical styles: rock, pop, funk, punk, folk, psychedelia, soul, R&B, reggae, AOR, MOR, electronica, house, gospel, hip-hop. Now, as you walk, the resonances of this locale have transformed into an album. The disparate styles flourishing around you have somehow strangely, wondrously come together. No matter how far or in which direction you walk, or whichever new style rises in the mix, the songs hold true. The underlying rhythm constantly transmutes, threatening dissolution but is held together by

one prominent feature. Carrying above the street rhythm is an ambrosial woman's voice, guiding you through the changes. You don't know the language in which she's singing, can't understand the words but are transfixed, nevertheless. Staggered at first, you start to dance.

This is how I visualize Cornershop's latest album, *Cornershop and The Double 'O' Groove Of* (Ample Play). For me, a new Cornershop album is a cause for celebration, first because of their infrequency: six records in 20-ish years, seven if you count the 2000 "Clinton" side project *Disco and the Halfway to Discontent*, plus an assortment of EPs, singles, and remixes. Conveniently, the music contained on each album is an ideal soundtrack for festivity, no matter your mood or melodic persuasion. And Cornershop is the quintessential celebration of popular music through both space and time. Its albums sound like nothing else out there. Because like no one else, Cornershop sounds like everything else out there.

Cornershop and The Double 'O' Groove Of is another singular and captivating turn in a career defined by defiantly unconventional moves. In the context of typical music world hype, that's not saying much. Claims that a band commits some form of artistic transgression are commonplace, if not obligatory, for street cred. The rock-n-roll-rebel meme still rules, even as the music has fragmented and mutated. The contravention of choice is to cross over, leading to a surfeit of style sippers and genre skimmers.

Yet even against this backdrop, Cornershop quietly (they receive nowhere the amount of press as lesser nonpareils) manages to be truly inimitable in their sound and approach to music making. Adventure and invention abound in their records.

The short history of Cornershop is of a raucous British guitar-based agit-pop group that quickly transmutes into ... well, everything. The core of its changing membership has been college chums Tjinder Singh and Ben Ayres, with Singh serving as producer, principal songwriter, and usual lead vocalist. Its greatest intrusion into popular consciousness was their 1997 LP *When I Was Born for the 7th Time* (Wiija) and its smash single "Brimful of Asha." The record was a landmark of sonic invention and adventure, through the astonishing assortment of musics incorporated into its mix, to

stretching the definitions of what constitutes a "song." Tracks that on first listening seemed throwaway trifles or a clashing blend of elements became revelations of insistent, compelling cross-cultural grooves. Singh's sonic imagination seemed limitless, especially when he quadruple-downed on the follow up (and Cornershop's masterpiece to date), 2002's *Handcream for a Generation* (Wiija).*

For its efforts, Cornershop has dutifully received credit for clearing a "World Music" path for acts like M.I.A. and Vampire Weekend. More than bringing acceptance to World Music themes, Cornershop does the greater service of demolishing the brittle, patronizing label. In a relentlessly cited era of globalization, Cornershop stands as a healthy example of pan-global perspective and possibilities.

The challenges the band presents to popular music, its audience and industry, are as audacious as those they assume for themselves. Foremost is a determination stated by Tjinder Singh, "The only thing that all our records have in common is that each one tries to sound utterly different."

Creatively, there isn't a more formidable task a band can assume, requiring the broadest musical palette imaginable and the ingenuity to use it. However, that's nothing compared to the considerable commercial risk inherent in Singh's declaration. It negates the possibility of establishing a signature sound, a major aspect of economic viability. You might tinker with your sound but not overhaul it wholesale. Due to its frequent guest vocalists, you can never be sure you're listening to Cornershop unless Singh's voice is the lead. Keeping an audience guessing if it's even you quickly leads to the question, will you have an audience? A creative risk without a marketing risk isn't a risk.

Not only do Cornershop albums each have distinct personalities but are unpredictable from track to track. And then the songs can swerve off on idiosyncratic angles. Amongst it all are offbeat but unerring production touches (sound effects, dialog, children's choruses, samples). It's a testament to Singh's talents that the records spin true instead of flying apart in all directions. On its own, Cornershop is the ultimate mixtape.

Cornershop and The Double 'O' Groove Of continues to make good on Singh's resolve. Its particular trait is extending two signature vocal

aspects of the group's albums. A highlight of each has been the Punjabi track, voiced by Singh. With *Double 'O'*, the entire album is sung in the language but by a featured singer. Right away, this is a distancing aspect for mainstream and indie audiences. It's not unprecedented and intriguing when predecessors are considered: see Los Lobos' *La Pistola Y El Corazón* (Slash, 1988).

As front man, Singh has demonstrated no vocal ego, passing the mic to an assortment of guest vocalists. *Double 'O'* spotlights the pseudonymous Bubbley Kaur (a moniker adapted from a lyric of *Handcream for a Generation* track "Wogs Will Walk"), who also collaborates with Singh with the songwriting. Traditionally and contractually vocals have been the defining element of popular musicianship. Switching what's typically a fixture into a variable evinces a significant dedication to making musical choices over personal aggrandizement.

"Featuring" is a standard hip-hop credit line as performers bolster one another's image. With Cornershop, frequent guesting establishes them as more a community than "group," not so much a band making music than an idea of music making. Collaboration is a vital, ongoing aspect: poet Allen Ginsberg, Rob Swift, Paula Fraser, Dan the Automator, Noel Gallagher, Otis Clay, M.I.A., Soko, and Fatboy Slim, are a select few of a panoply who've collaborated with or contributed to Cornershop.

At the heart of *Double 'O'* is Singh's desire to "mix western music with Punjabi folk in a way that wasn't crude." "Western music" encompasses a multiplicity of stances and Singh doesn't skimp, offering ten stylistically dissimilar tracks, unified in accomplishment.

Cornershop deftly evade pastiche and formalist exercises. "I've always thought of Punjabi folk as a precursor to hip-hop," Singh said recently in an interview about his songwriting, "It's beat-based, storytelling, parochial — what's going on around a village. A lot of it is to do with functions – weddings, meetings. Other bits are more melancholy — what has happened to her relatives, or the relationship break-ups. But it's often light-hearted and upbeat."

This succinctly summarizes the textures of *Double 'O'*. The traditional Indian rhythm that kicks off the album's the sassy opener "United

Provinces of India," quickly meshes with funky guitar and scratchy breaks.

As with all Cornershop albums, you never know what's coming up next and how Singh and company will make it work. There's the stately harpsichord that punctuates the soul saunter of "Double Decker Eyelids." The rollicking piano-driven, clattering timber percussion of "The Biro Pen." "The 911 Curry" brassy blasts handing off to analog synth etudes. The sci-fi twiddling synths that open the hyperactive sax bounce "Supercomputed." The regal trumpet samples framing the leisurely march of "Once There Was a Wintertime." The folksy acoustic guitar picking pop of the joyous closer "Don't Shake It." Oh yeah, there's even a sitar snippet plinking through "Double Digit."

The binding force of the set is the varied beats and drum cadences that serve as propulsion, bridge, and soloist. Locked in rhythm are similarly jiving and melodic basslines. But the essential presence in the *Double 'O'* fusion excursion is Bubbley Kaur, Beatrice to Singh's Dante.

In its aural flavorings, the album acts as intersection and realization of intent of two landmark records, 1968's *The Beatles* (Apple) and the 1981 Brian Eno/David Byrne collaboration *My Life in the Bush of Ghosts* (E.G.). The "White Album" is the determinative manifold album, where The Beatles indulged every production and stylistic whim in one sprawling 2-LP set. *Double 'O'* offers the same capricious transitions and escapades.

Eno and Byrne layered appropriated vocals over their composed rhythm tracks, a tactic that was considered at the time by many critics as culturally exploitive. Similarly, Singh has disconnected the lyrical "meaning" of Bubbley Kaur's songs from their musical accompaniment. The results didn't always go down well with her. Kaur speaks of being taken aback even by their initial 2004 effort, the marvelous double single "Topknot"/"Natch." Fortunately, she came back for more shocks.

Singh declines to release even the Punjabi lyrics to the songs, wanting to direct focus to the pure emotive quality of Kaur's voice. By this, the vocal approach comes closer to *puirt a beul*: "mouth music." Other touchstones can be found in British pop with Cocteau Twins or, in an American avant-garde mode, Meredith Monk. While I'm an admirer of the elliptical but evocative lyrics typically found on Cornershop albums (Singh

hands-down contrives the best song and album titles. Sorry, Morrissey), the results here sing for themselves.

Cornershop's music is a studio-only construct. It's wholly designed: constructed, sampled, and assembled rather than traditionally performed. The image Ben Ayres provides of its making sounds more like a designer at work than gigster: "Tjinder would be working like a mad professor in his studio on the tracks when I'd turn up ... it was pretty intense."

Music that's entirely a recording studio creation has been with us for decades. Yet for being compiled, such productions are no less immediate, fresh, honest, and moving emotionally and physically. Popular music has been patently constructed since the advent of modern recording technology, notably so in the 1960s. The "studio as instrument" concept recognizes this reality. However, simply having an arrangement enters music into the "designed" realm, far ahead of recording technology.

The sampling and scratching methods prevalent in popular music can provide insightful models for designers struggling to navigate notions of originality and authenticity in a contemporary creative context.

Design, which suffers scorn as an inauthentic, derivative form, is arguably culture's most vital, engaging visual form. Discussing how an artist utilizes the methods is more relevant than if they pioneered a technique. Constructing originality out of samples is counter-intuitive, and for some, flat wrong. But graphic designers should be contemplating contemporary music's processes to lend context to their practice.

Cornershop is also instructive in the ongoing cultural negotiation of creative identity — amateur versus professional — and the implications of D.I.Y. In interviews, Singh and Ayres continue to insist that they aren't musicians. It's no disparagement of their instrumental abilities to respond amen. Their true status is more significant: music-making people. This subtle distinction has profound implications on one's creative identity. It's about what you're willing to do and how you carry yourself. It's the difference between a job and a calling.

Tellingly, music is the most common subject of Cornershop songs, more than is exhibited in its song titles ("Born Disco; Died Heavy Metal," "Brimful of Asha," "Music Plus 1," "Slip the Drummer One," "Button Down

Disco," "Hip-Hop Bricks," "Wop the Groove," "Who Fingered Rock n Roll," "Soul School," "Non-stop Radio," etc.) Cornershop's amazing reach is due to Tjinder Singh's status as musical omnivore and inveterate record collector. "Brimful of Asha" puts the famed playback singer out front but is a sly paean to vinyl. The tune's a global jukebox inventory of musicians and record labels, where Marc Bolan gets name checked.

It may be another ultrafine distinction to pull the thread of music makers compelled by and reimagining their personal record collection. Here, Singh has affinity with James "LCD Soundsystem" Murphy in self-deprecation, no-BS attitude, disdain for rock star trappings, and dance floor apotheoses. Both readily cite their influences and downplay their talents. Murphy's self-portrait looks a lot like Singh: "I don't believe I'm this wildly original individual. I don't believe that I'm astonishingly charismatic and really need to be heard as an individual voice. I do believe I take music very seriously. I do believe I am a very good manipulator of sound and I'm very interested in how sound affects my body and I do believe that is relevant to how it affects other people's bodies."

In interviews, Singh and Ayres are similarly forthright, wry, but idealistic about their enterprise. Their attitude is a refreshing departure from the ongoing, over-serious rock star affectation and angst that culminates in little more than "look at me!"

Cornershop matter-of-factly demonstrates the unities and common causes in music. They expose the rhythmic and melodic roots then graft new branches. Any action that unifies people is welcome, especially if we can dance to it. Proclaiming music to be a universal language is a platitude with merit, with the provision that music is a universal language of music. What audiences like in music is about more than the aural quality. For good and ill, music is bound up with self-identity. The niche fracturing of the marketplace has contributed positively to the dissolution of labels (my iTunes tells me *Double 'O'* is of the "Pop" genre while its predecessor *Judy Sucks a Lemon for Breakfast* (Ample Play) is "Alternative." How wrong, how right.) But those numerous hybrids all have adherents who won't hazard crossing a line.

It may not be the most representative sampling of Cornershop's

potency in boundary bounding but my 11-year-old daughter hears a lot of its music when we drive together. She's always seemed to prefer singing along to the Indian-language tracks. I'll dial up *Double 'O'* for the additional entertainment of hearing her invented Punjabi harmony. Kaur won't be denied a treasured spot in your brain, given the chance.

In the circumstances of its making and the evidence of the results, Cornershop grants us music that's affirming and expansive. Their particular music may provide creative types some guidance in their necessary obsession with globalism and crossing cultures.

Then again, it may not. We'll just have to settle for some wildly ingenious, infectious tunes.

As its ultimate challenge and promise to listeners, the *When I Was Born for the 7th Time* track "Good Shit" could be Cornershop's manifesto. They're words to live by when contemplating music and graphic design. In the verses, Singh first offers us a challenge:

> *I want each and all to switch your tiny mind on*
> *I want each and all switch on your tiny mind*

before he slips smoothly into the chorus and its earthy, optimistic affirmation:

> *Cause good shit's all around good people*
> *Don't let it get you down, good people*
> *Good shit's all around, it's all about, it's all around*

And, good people, the best shit is found at Cornershop.

*I allege this with great trepidation, as Singh recently wrote on Facebook: "Always been of the belief that when the *Handcream* LP gets recognised then the group would finally be in a position to stop." So fans, please do not like this particular album *too* much.

This is the fourth, concluding section of «Process Music» called "My back pages." Included are memoirs and short stories that offer personal tales, some of which provide oblique perspective on creativity, visual culture and communication. "A portrait of the artist as a young man with crayons" appeared in slightly different form as part of the «Print» magazine feature "What Matters: Inside the Brilliant Mind of Artist Kenneth FitzGerald," February 2021. "The great 3rd grade juice box riot" first appeared as a post on AIGA Design Educators Community journal, January 2014. "The world between" and "Late show" first appeared in «The News of the Whirled» issues #3 and #2; "Memento-Mori" is comprised of three separately published articles in «The News of the Whirled»: "Gatherings" in #1 (1997), "He loved to run" in #2 (1999), and "We pulled his nails" in #3 (2001). "Spinarette" appeared in «The News of the Whirled» #4 (2002). "Blank canvas" was a post at the Ephemeral States blog. "Typeman vs. the fontastical curses" is original to this book.

A portrait of the artist as a young man with crayons

When I was in third grade, I resolved to win an award in my school's next Art Fair.

From an adult perspective, this wasn't that challenging an ambition. But as a child, you work within the goals of your immediate world, and this was mine. St. Joseph's was a small Catholic grammar school in a small Massachusetts town. The competition, in terms of numbers, wasn't great — tens of my peers. It also wasn't fierce: most of the other kids were far less interested in or attentive to creative pursuits. But there was a measure of accomplishment involved. This was before our current era of universal affirmation ("Truitt Intermediate School, *WHERE 'EVERYONE IS A STAR'*"). The nuns — using their own particular measure — were making decisions based on merit, not equally sharing out the gratification.

The resolution was made in the wake of my younger (one year and seven days) sister receiving an award in that year's fair. It wasn't that I disparaged Karen or her winning entry — a portrait of flamingos composed in tempera paint, cotton balls, and macaroni. However, my older (one year, eight months) brother Kevin had claimed a blue ribbon in last year's exhibition. With two siblings being honored for their art, a reputation and expectation seemed to be in play. I drew, painted, and crafted as much as they did. It was important that I establish my own talent.

I experienced typical sibling rivalry; likely exacerbated by the

proximity in our ages and names. Two years behind my sister was another brother — Keith. I needed affirmation before he came along. This rivalry would extend into high school. Following right behind my older brother through the grades, I continually suffered the identification as "Kevin's brother." In it, I interpreted a diminution of my own identity, especially when it came to art, writing, and musical tastes. It doubly burned because I was following his lead. We all were. And it certainly wasn't coincidental that all four of us K children (I had two more brothers whose names began with different vowels) went on to art school — but at different institutions.

But in this instance, I didn't really consider myself in competition with my siblings, or my peers. I was proving something to myself — that I could win an award if I wanted to. Only by having the prize matter could I demonstrate that it didn't matter to me. I was content doing my art and it was almost an inconvenience to be aware of the Art Fair and that recognition from others was possible — or desirable. My mixed feelings about achievement and acknowledgment didn't dissipate with time. In my senior year of high school, my artwork was selected for a statewide scholastic art fair to be held in Boston. When that event was cancelled due to the Great Blizzard of '78, I was mostly relieved.

As I walked through the St. Joseph's classrooms where the art was displayed, I took special note of the prize-winning works. I examined them dispassionately, looking for commonalities. My own art wasn't distinctly different in medium of choice — crayons — or in childhood subject matter. A drawing I can still remember today featured a quarterback with arm cocked back to throw a pass during a football game. Though I was a pro football fan, the artwork wasn't meant as strict documentary. I was loyal to my local team (the then Boston Patriots) but portrayed Green Bay Packers in action. Their vivid yellow and forest green uniforms were more satisfying to represent. And the team's stylized "G" within an oval enchanted my graphic imagination.

In retrospect, my interest in these aspects seems a precursor to a future in graphic design. That I eventually entered the discipline's orbit suggests a proof. However, I regard it more as simply reflecting my media environment. It wasn't until early in college that I'd travel to Boston and,

for the first time, visit an art museum. Abandoning the crayons, I'd soon take to a new graphic obsession: replicating in colored pencils the map of Massachusetts found in the World Book encyclopedia. It was the particular, peculiar graphic elements of maps that attracted me — I wasn't engaged or interested in cartography per se. Eventually, this activity was subsumed in my consciousness to reemerge in my 20s when I initiated a portrait series that employed the flat colors, patterns, and structure of atlases.

My scrutiny of the Art Fair prizewinners yielded actionable information. Subject matter appeared to be the key. The majority of awardees featured either: 1) crowds of people, or 2) religious themes. The popularity of the latter characteristic was obvious, while the former was a matter of brief speculation on my part. All I could presume was that — as I could testify — drawing people was hard. Drawing lots of them demanded special effort. Uncomfortable with the subjectivity required in judging art, perhaps the nuns were seizing on this as an objective determinant of superiority

For the next year, I set myself to the task of fashioning artworks to this calculated brief. And when the next Art Fair was held, I claimed a first prize ribbon. Today, I have no memory of the winning work. That I might have at least created a Sermon on the Mount scene as an entrant — to cover my bases — strikes me as an adult confabulation. Too good of a story. But it sounds a truer note that I fail to recall my first art honor because the work didn't mean anything to me. It was a means to an end.

What I swear is an accurate recollection is what I first thought to myself as I stood before my *be-ribboned* artwork. It stuck because it was the earliest expression of my ambivalent attitude toward public affirmation. I'm always surprised that I declared it so young: *Now I can get on with my own work.*

The world between

To get there, walk south out of Harvard Square because there's no T bus line, toward the Charles. Any perceived Cambridge charm sloughs off as you cross over the river, dissipated on reaching the opposite side, Harvard Stadium notwithstanding. It's just the fringes of Allston. Not really a someplace but a spot within reach of somewhere you need to be. Some zig zagging down a few side streets and you come to the short street dead-ending at the house.

It's a standard starter roommate situation in the area. Four young women, each a few years out of college. Working a variety of first post-school jobs, maybe related to what was studied, usually not. One by one, in the next few years, they'll move out and up. Not a high hurdle to clear. I'm crashed here unemployed and homeless, straining the boyfriend stayover provision.

The house is habitable but troubled. The low rent somewhat indicating the condition. Night shows through joints in the walls. It may well be shingled by petrified masking tape. The structure is beaten by landlord neglect and the parade of tenants. Put as little as you can in, extract the maximum rent. The absentee landlord's main concern is hiding the rent income from his ex-wife. His slovenly brother acts as intermediary, grudgingly performing barely effective repairs.

The upstairs is a higher level of haphazard. A prior generation of

occupants had been given leave to refashion the bedrooms into loft-like spaces with skylights. Purportedly, MIT students, they were enthusiastic but inept carpenters. Theory outstripped practice. Beyond that nothing else is known. But their handicraft begs that they not be engineers. It all seems improvised rather than planned out. Surfaces meet at odd angles or don't join at all. The wood is mismatched scrap, improper for the job.

Beside the house's construction, or lack of it, other aspects make *inside* and *outside* permeable concepts and realities. Squirrels cavort behind one wall of your room, a skittering, thumping daybreak wake-up call. After a time, some wire mesh is arranged in the eaves to close off rodent access.

Then there are the bees. They constantly bump against both sides of the skylight, attempting to fly in or out. The buzzing sounds from behind another wall becomes more pronounced as the weather warms.

Otherwise, it was a benefit to move out of the winter months. The bills are exorbitant when you're literally heating the outdoors. Later, it is learned that the oil tank in the basement leaked. Much of the fuel pumped in ran into the ground.

A nightly call and response is heard: a single bee sounding off, a group echoing the pattern. Cantor and choir. In the morning, they're up with the dawn, off to work, busy as you-know-whats. When the sun strikes the outside wall, the scent of honey is pronounced.

Evenings, pressing ears against the plaster, we eavesdrop on another plane of existence. We spy on a home within a home of desire and searching. In that way, it mirrors our own. To us, they are an invading force, coincident and threatening. We're just background noise to them.

The increasing insect presence in the room makes some action imperative. Your dad has a solution: an injection of powdered Sevin insecticide he has from tending fruit trees. One night, he drills a hole into the center of the wall where the loudest buzzing is heard. The poison is blown inside. He leaves, we go downstairs to watch TV.

When we go up to bed a few hours later, the room is occupied by tens of bees zooming around the room. We elect to spend the night on the living-room sofa bed.

The next morning, the room is quiet. A few bee corpses litter the

floor. Outside, though, a large swarm the size of a cantaloupe hangs from a small tree a short way from the house. Underneath the mass is the neighbor's MG, whose hood sports a glistering mass of more insects, waiting to ascend to the group surrounding the queen. That neighbor's not going to work today. Or, like us, is taking the bus. We watch someone walk unawares toward the car, suddenly stop, then reverse direction.

An emergency bee-handler, the "Bee-Buster," is called and he arrives in the evening. The Hubbard-squash-sized swarm is now entirely on the tree branch which sags under the weight. After shrouding the bees in smoke, the Buster starts vacuuming them up with what looks like a modified shop-vac. He estimates that there are 50,000 bees.

Had we drilled into the other wall, where no sound was heard, they would have come boiling into the room last night. That wall had the comb and the bees. Their sounds reverberated into the empty space. The room was like a guitar. With bees.

Having vacuumed up the bees, the Buster lays out our situation. Insects now driven from the house, the honey will soon begin to soften and flow. "Refrigerator" bees (as the Buster calls them) kept the honey cool by beating their wings on it. They're gone now. We also learn of another type of bee: the "robber bee." They are the stray insects we see entering the eaves.

Reached by phone somewhere far, far from here, the landlord is chagrined. The walls will have to be torn out to remove the likely 1000 lbs. of honey and comb. From another Buster estimate, the colony has been in residence for 5–7 years, with the potential of creating 100 pounds of honey a year. We've driven out the tenant with seniority.

Left in place, the honey will coat the house timbers and attract ants and other insects that will undermine what little structural integrity there is. Because of the poison, the honey is unsalable. This again vexes the landlord, who had foreseen making a killing at the local health-food store.

Turns out a sideline for the Bee-Buster is carpentry and house repair. As he's familiar and experienced—unsurprisingly—in this kind of work, he's hired. We leave in the morning—still sleeping on the sofa bed—you to go to work, me to look for it. We return to find your room open to the elements.

What's left of the walls rest two stories down in the yard. Wood and drywall mixed with chunks of honeycomb lie scattered over the lawn. The floor of your room is sticky and bee corpses rest everywhere. To protect your belongings and recreate a greater sense of having sides, you purchase some plastic shower curtains and hang them across the exposed studs.

I stand at the edge of the room looking down at the debris. As much as I will draw parallels between the bees and me, we both cling to, are dependent on our queen. Though disconcerting, this is all merely an eventful inconvenience. We weren't just blasted with poison then sucked into a vacuum to be disposed of. But my life is not describing an upward trajectory as yet.

We have gained a drama that's about *us*. Something that acted on and can be acted out by us as a couple. A tale to relate within other walls, alternating elements back and forth, responding separately and in chorus to questions. And something is being built.

Late Show

You look up from your knitting to the clock and say to me,

— It's almost time for the end of the universe.

The clock is one of those smiling cat models, where the eyes and tail flick back and forth in unison.

— All right, I say, and put down a magazine I was rereading for the N-th time.

It's always a bit chilly in space, even here, so you put on your most recently knitted sweater and I my dark green fleece jacket. You had spread it on the bed again for the cats so it's as much fur as fleece.

Once outside, we set up the padded lawn chairs (cats rushing out the door as soon as there's a whisker's worth of clearance) and stare up at the black hole's event horizon. Stretched across the surface of this lens are the images of everything that has happened in the universe. Light streams in from every cosmic direction and is trapped on the singularity's membrane of gravity, creating a frozen image of eternity. Normally, you couldn't see the event horizon from within the singularity. You rigged up an arrangement of mirrors that reflected light from the outside universe in and corrected for the distortion. Of course, you didn't do it alone. You balanced on the step stool, adjusting reflectors, while getting directions over the 'phone from your dad, who knows all about lenses (and most everything else it seems). I don't know anywhere as much, not even how to

squeeze that 'phone between my chin and shoulder without disconnecting myself two out of three times.

— Think it will be any different this time? you ask.

— You never know, anything's possible I guess, I reply. Infinite varieties, uncertainty principles, random fluctuations, see it a thousand times and something new each time, all on the next episode of *Nova*....

— Another repeat then.

Chances are it wouldn't be any different this time. The universe expanded outward (why? Ask someone who knows — or claims to) then drew back in on itself. On the way back inward, matter that had cooled down over the eons heated back up as it was sucked (pushed? fell?) into the Primordial Hot-Spot. Everything there ever was and ever could be was squashed down to a diameter small as a subatomic particle. Outside ... well, there is no *outside*, really. Inside that Big Bang Hot-Spot is space itself and time. Then, something's gotta give and we come to the Big Bang Redux. It's as if the Goddess is playing with a big dimmer switch somewhere. She could be next door, one singularity over. Could be.

We've observed countless cycles of collapse and rebirth projected on the gravity lens that is our sky. Actually, the sequence occurred all the time. We could stroll outside and view creation or apocalypse any hour of day or night. We set a regular time — like a favorite TV show — so it wouldn't become commonplace. Plus, we needed to keep watch and make our daily attempt at the Perfect World.

We live on a small planet with a medium-sized sun within a black hole, or, a singularity — a much pleasanter term for the phenomenon. For some reason, singularities are able to ride out the life/death cycle of the universe (why? *ibid*). It may be that they are universes unto themselves. Once inside the event horizon, it's pretty calm. The trick, of course, is finding the way in. Everyone knows the stories: matter stretched like taffy, total annihilation of matter, infinite gravity, even light can escape...and so on. Ours is a standard-issue black hole with all the typical features. I can't give precise details on how exactly we made our way here. Let's just say a motivated cat is a formidable force. And two? More people could be able to do it but wouldn't even try.

Within the singularity, time passes for us at the normal rate but very, very, very slowly to the outside observer (in this case, you). We literally have all the time in the university — quite a few universes, in fact.

For our house, we adapted an early 20th century gas station (Earth dating). Your inspiration was that here in this warmer clime, it would be great to be able to open the bays and let in the cool evening air. I can never convince you I'm in agreement but I always thought it a good idea.

Living within a black hole certainly provides solitude. The quiet has done a lot to soothe the cats' nerves, so frayed after our last move across country. They prefer their stimuli at a safe distance (how a billion light years?) and hate the sound of the doorbell. It's actually a bit *too* secluded, even for us. But not only does it afford us much of what we want now — a place of our own — it provides the opportunity to have everything that anyone could *ever* want. From here, we can make a better existence for all.

In the first fractions of a second of the Big Bang, all the natural laws of the universe are established. Speed of light, gravitation, boiling point of water ... it's all up for grabs. Infinitesimal variations of flux within quintillionths of that first second make or break it all. We could wind up in a universe where objects can pass through one another, travel accomplished instantaneously by thought, ask the cats what they are looking at — and get a reply.

Why not take that shot? we resolved. Everyone talks about the weather but no one does anything about it. So, every "day," we attend the rebirth of the universe to introduce a random element to the process. We have a big bag of lake glass gathered from the shore of Lake Superior that you've never found a use for. I choose one of the sand-worn fragments of discarded bottles and when you see the first evidence of a flare, I skim it sidearm into the maelstrom.

At first, I tossed them directly into the burst. Now, I skip them a couple times, as if returning the glass to the lake. At the sudden motion of my arm, the cats start, tense, and look at me reprovingly. Then they go about their business.

Here now, it's no different. Familiarity was colored with anticipation of something new. Is the universe cyclic or steady state? The scientists

query themselves. We know it's both. Eternity is a constantly flowing stream spattered with small whirlpools, drawing time down into unimaginable depths. And then there's us, a whorl apart containing our little double-binary system (do we orbit the cats or they us?). Above us, the dawning universe.

What will come from introducing a new element into a state in delicate balance? I wonder.

— It's only one piece but aren't we playing dice with the universe? I ask.

— Skip it, you say.

— Okay, I respond, and bring down my arm.

— No, I mean *skip it!*

I toss away one life and await the new.

Blank canvas

One presidential election day, I volunteered to hand out literature at my polling place. It was a first for me. I wasn't sure how people would respond. I'd certainly encounter voters of the other persuasion and political passions can run hot. For company, I brought along my six year old daughter. She wanted to help daddy and I did nothing to dissuade her. I confess that I partially welcomed her as cover in case I encountered an irate opponent. Who could be rude to man with his cheerful, outgoing child by his side? The naïveté of that hope demonstrates my level of apprehension.

I needn't have worried. Whatever their leanings, people accepted my fliers without incident. My daughter enthusiastically joined in. Presented with courtesy — we offered, not imposed — people rarely respond out of kind. I also like to think that us increasingly rare voters try to stick together. It's almost like being in a club.

Another concern was the possibility of encountering some of my immediate neighbors. I was unaware what candidate most of them supported. From the occasional campaign signs I'd seen on lawns, I could guess. Based solely on party affiliation, many seemed on the other side. It was that way with the one neighbor I was certain of. One afternoon earlier that fall, I was outside our house when she pulled up alongside in her car. She said she was off to her candidate's local campaign headquarters to

pick up a lawn sign. Did I want one for our yard?

I thanked her and declined. My neighbor cheerfully accepted the answer and after some brief chat, drove off. Though I backed the other candidate, I was glad for the offer. It was simple courtesy, as if she asked if she could pick up a quart of milk for us.

I didn't talk politics with my neighbors. The topic never came up, and then my New England reserve kicked in. As a college professor, I don't promote candidates in class. I do encourage political participation. While I feel the claims of political correctness in academia are wildly exaggerated, I still scrupulously don't take sides. If anything, I'm for contrarianism. I do equal opportunity critiques.

But I don't think policy really plays much of a role in voting. Identification with a candidate — she's like me! — means more. Politicians I consider evident buffoons will be someone else's statesman. Since we're both looking at the same guy, perception accounts for much. I'd crossed party lines a number of times when voting. But it often felt like betrayal. If I'm indoctrinating anyone with my views, I guess it's my kids. My students seem to already be set in their way.

Back at the polls, some neighborhood friends did arrive to vote. It was a couple with their young daughter in tow. When the girls saw each other, they launched into a happy dance at getting together unexpectedly. Then they raced off to the nearby playground. We adults exchanged pleasantries, without mentioning why we were there. Rather than spoil the impromptu play date, I kept an eye on the girls while my neighbors voted. When they emerged, the kids were still hard at play. As my shift was near its end, I volunteered to keep watch then walk their daughter home.

The girls soon ran back to me in search of new adventure. My daughter enthused about handing out fliers and her friend asked if she could help. Reflexively, I went to give them both a small stack, and then drew back. Would my neighbors want me to be employing their daughter this way? Even if we shared candidates — I didn't know — it didn't seem right.

I dithered for a few seconds then handed them both some fliers. They're only kids, I rationalized. It's no more than play. Fortunately, the girls just handed the fliers back and forth between themselves. When the

friend's mom drove up, I had reclaimed the fliers and my conscience was clear. I also thought that if political leanings were determined at this age, we'd see Hello Kitty in a landslide. It still doesn't seem that bad a prospect.

The great 3rd grade juice box riot

I volunteered a couple years back to help out at my daughter's Emma's third grade picnic. It's a one-hour lunch followed by outdoor fun at the park next door. Because of the 100°+ heat-indexed weather, the picnic was held in the cafeteria. My task was to oversee the beverages: keep them stocked and on ice. Even I can handle that. What I couldn't manage was the melee that spontaneously broke out toward the end of the meal — over a novel drink package.

I was in charge of three coolers: two filled with Little Hug® juice drinks (they're little plastic barrels with peel off lids) on either side of one holding juice pouches: Kool-Aid Jammers® and Kraft Capri Suns®. For about 45 minutes, everything was great. Kids first filed past in their respective classes, grabbed either a pouch or a jug, and moved on. When seconds were announced, children came and went sporadically. I roved away from my post to sit with Emma ("Daaaa-aad!").

Things were winding down when I returned to the coolers, now being overseen by the school's security officer, Mr. Stewart. He was joking with the two or three kids who would come by — who kidded him right back — and knew most of them by name. He urged them to dig deep in the icy water, to get the cold ones.

I was next to one of the Hug-filled coolers when a small girl reached in and pulled out a different juice container, one I hadn't previously noted.

It was about the same size as the Hugs but with a reclosable pop-up top and no label. The girl showed the container (holding a purple juice) to another who asked, "What's that?" On being told she found it in the cooler, the second girl plunged in and emerged with another, filled with a yellow-greenish liquid.

Word of the novel bottles spread instantaneously among the kids milling about. In seconds, there were six or more children squeezed next to each other, bent over the cooler, scouring the ice and water. A crowd of a dozen or more kids pressed in behind them, craning necks, eager for a look at one of the prizes, trying to force their way to the front. The girl who found the first bottle was pinned against the wall in front of me, a look of trapped panic on her face. I tried to clear a path for her while pulling a boy off the floor, knocked down in the rush and in danger of being trampled.

It took four adults to halt the fracas: me, Mr. Stewart, another parent, and a cafeteria worker. Kids were organized into a ragged line to progress to the coolers. Mr. Stewart closed the lid of the desired cooler, sat on it, and announced all the new bottles were gone. Children buzzed around for a while, regretfully making other choices, while casting longing looks at the guarded cooler.

For the last ten minutes of the picnic, Mr. Stewart and I exchanged disbelieving comments on what had just occurred. None of the kids had a chance to *taste* what was in the bottles, and none had a label to say what brand it was. (The girl who got the yellow-greenish one asked later to exchange it because "It's yellow!") The kids had gone crazy over a *container* — because it was different from the others available for an hour.

I suppose there may be a moral here about packaging or branding. If there is, I don't know what it is. Maybe it's just about kids being kids. All I know is next time I participate, you'll find me serving condiments.

Typeman vs. the fontastical curses

To varying degrees, children are influenced by their parents' occupation. The ultimate influence is adopting those pursuits as their own. However, children's rejection of footstep-following is just as storied. For many parents, it's a source of pride and validation for their own choices.

My attitude about my two children's future interests I inherited: do whatever makes you happy. Having my parents' support made me an anomaly among my classmates in art school. But while my wife and I would have followed through on aiding either or both of my kids' choice to pursuit an art career, we didn't actively encourage it. We were generous with applause for their nascent artwork. We also didn't skimp on tales of dad's precarious, serendipitous and hungry course through his art career.

A desire to pursue art never coalesced in either child beyond the usual drawings and paintings. Gestures in that direction were cute rather than coordinated. Kindergarten-aged Emma was provided her own small table and chair to do her work. Picking up on the name of my alma mater, she announced it as her "MassArt table."

As she grew a little older, Emma's creative work became typical: character drawings and static scenarios in a variety of scrap and notebooks. She had a charming, idiosyncratic style that was subsumed when she discovered manga. I was disappointed to see her adopt its mannered style, but it was a relatively short-lived expression. And it was for her

gratification, not mine. Her drawings went private — with one exception.

Approaching her teenaged years, Emma was well-versed in her parents' ways and had a honed snark. One of my small habits was identifying typefaces in television shows we watched. Not all the faces, just ones that were special in some way. After one of these instances, Emma laughingly declared me Typeman, wielder of a particularly useless superpower.

That playful mockery wasn't enough. In short order, she produced a portrait of me as Typeman: "A powerful force in the world of graphic design...able to identify type faster than a speeding bullet!" The figure with upraised arm was readily identifiable as me with the style glasses I sported at the time, some bright green sneakers, and close cropped hair. And though unintentional, it even had a pun.

There's a saying that parents are their children's heroes. I'm fairly certain this wasn't what was meant but you take what you get.

My teenaged son Leaf's bedroom is a mess and he doesn't want to hear about it anymore.

Badgering him about its squalid state tried our patience long ago. So, I did the mature, parentally responsible thing: I stopped looking inside. Somewhat like Schrödinger's Box, it won't attain a state, either clean or dirty, unless I observe. And a cat is involved.

It's not as if his parents are neat freaks. I've frequently identified more paper as my paperweight of choice. When it comes to his school notebooks, Leaf has definitely taken after me in pushing the envelope of how many envelopes can be pushed in a pile.

Gradually over time, a mass of school papers grew behind his seat at the dinner table. It was a compost of largely empty organizers, scruffy notebooks, assignments, exams, lessons, notes. In a paroxysm of organizing one day, I endeavored to sort through the morass and place documents in categories or recycle them.

In margins on occasional pages and on their own sheets were scattered, spindly drawings of airplanes and tank-like vehicles. Usually, they were in action, spewing flame and projectiles, single frames perhaps in a larger story. No individuals were apparent, either piloting or targeted. My guess was these war machines were amalgams of or inspired by historical

sources (he was a WWII buff) and an on-line tank battle game we found him playing one day.

The younger Leaf had done his requisite school art projects but never showed much of an interest outside class. So, it was a small revelation to encounter personally initiated artworks.

The drawings were amusing but unrevealing or special beyond my connection to their creator. But one illustration took me by surprise, altering my sense of Leaf's relationship to my vocation.

This pencil drawing was alone on a torn half-page of ruled composition paper. It was all type and said:

Fuck This
Chemistry Bullshit

Each word was in a distinctly different, almost identifiable typeface, scratchily but carefully rendered. Three were sans serif, one script(!), and contemporary looking fonts. As fond as Leaf is of reading, it's curious that none is a serif. Display was the way. Had one of my design students delivered such sketched detail, I'd have been pleased.

The source of the sentiment wasn't a mystery. Leaf was struggling in the class, due primarily to disinterest in the subject. It was chore to endure not knowledge to amass. Maybe it was. That he chose to immortalize his attitude in typography seemed to speak of a more profound, sustained disdain. The expletives may also been a hint. My reflexive, parental brainstorm was that if he applied as much effort to the coursework as his typographic stylings, blah blah.

As far as I could tell, Leaf's typotastic *cri de coeur* was an outlier. If he had done it at all. Its novelty and ripped-out nature made me wonder if it was an acquired rather than generated artifact. Perhaps some equally exasperated classmate had slipped it to him as a note. Maybe *that* pal was a nascent designer. Proximity isn't causality. I took a photo of the work and put it back among his materials.

When presented with the artifact, Leaf was indifferent to its discovery and mumblingly evasive about explaining it. I told him I found the piece delightful and just wanted to understand its motivation and give him his props. Inadvertently, I'd initiated a design critique, much as I would in class.

That could be fraught enough. Sensitized to student resistance and its diminishing returns, I quickly dropped the matter.

The provenance of Leaf's protest poster will likely remain a small unknown, too problematic a phenomenon to be termed a mystery. Goofing with fancy lettering instead of concentrating on schoolwork is a teenage specialty. My own typographical interest is just coincidental. I doubt he harbors a down-low design œuvre .

Intentional or not, Leaf and I possess a minor instance of intersection, if not inspiration. There will always be the day my son turned to type.

Memento mori

1: Gatherings

Louise Deromedi was born in 1906 in the Tyrol region that today is northern Italy. She came to the United States in 1928 to marry Edward Valentine, a recent widower with eight children. He had written home to his sister, asking if there was a young woman who would come to Pennsylvania and become his wife. The circumstances surrounding Louise's decision are still a matter of speculation within the family. She provided few details about her life in Italy, and the barriers of language and memory make uncovering her history difficult. Whatever her motivation, she became a wife, and mother to children whose oldest was only a few years younger than she. Louise and Edward also had two children of their own. It was with the family of her daughter that Louise — as Louise came to be called — spent her last thirty years.

Following the death of her husband in 1939, Louise held a number of jobs, including owning a bar that served the local coal miners. When the business was sold, she went to live with her daughter and family in New Jersey. She brought few possessions with her and carried the same upon their move north. In her lack of acquisitiveness, Louise was an aberration in her immediate family. Little was disposed of, whether it was mechanical or personal. Within their rambling New England farmhouse and barn, a rich trove of artifacts could provide documentation of the family's past — or

a metal plate to repair a burst radiator. None of this collection, however, belonged to Louise. The treasures she had dispensed with distinguished her. When quizzed on the status of any family article once in her keeping, the answer invariably came back that she had thrown it out. Louise added little to the furnishings of her room. She had no sentiment for cards and correspondence: once read, such missives became scrap paper.

It was only after Louise's death that her family discovered what she saved. Preserved within her prayer book were over 100 religious cards collected over her lifetime. The majority were memento mori cards: pre-printed death notices to which the appropriate name and date were added. The cards represented neighbors and family from the old country and America. Louise had told another relative that she would select a card at random each night and say a prayer for that person. In her last days, Louise imagined all these people alive and young. She believed she was preparing for a gathering that was, at times, her own funeral.

For the people in her life, Louise had great love and generosity. Her lack of attachment to things did not lie in a failure to care for people. Would these cards have such significance if Louise collected many other things? It is their presence in a life absent of such sentiment that their presence is amplified. And it is always a question how we all preserve our memories — especially that of our departed loved ones. What was Louise saving when she kept these cards? What are we saving when we keep anything?

2: He loved to run

Henry Edgar Fitzgerald was born November 9, 1906 in Nova Scotia, the son of Anselm and Mary Fitzgerald. He was one of five children, two boys and three girls. While he would return regularly to a house he kept in Arcadia for many years, his life story was of being an American. He came to Haverhill, Massachusetts at the age of 21 to stay with his cousin. Because of his blond hair, the locals thought he was Swedish. They also teased him for speaking French. He would reply to people in that language though he understood spoken English.

At the turn of the 20th century, Haverhill was known as "Queen Shoe City of the World." As did many others of his background, Edgar (as he

was called) went to work in one of the wood heel factories. At his job in January 1928, he met Blanche Legare. Their courtship was brief: the two were married in October of the same year.

By the time he was 38, Edgar had three children: Barbara, Gerald, and Richard. The oldest was 12, the youngest 5. Under the circumstances, he wasn't susceptible of being called up in the World War II draft. However, his regard for his adopted country was such that he enlisted in December 1943. The decision didn't sit well with Blanche, who would bear many of the consequences of his choice. Though she would always speak with pride of her husband's service, it was also clear that memories brought forth other emotions that went unexpressed. Possible resentments could be detected in the phrasing of descriptions of his army times before his wounding. There was never anything you could call out definitely, yet the impression came that her feelings about Edgar's choice were more complex than she allowed.

One December morning at 5:00 am, she walked with Edgar to the Post Office to see him off to war. He was shipped first to Fort Dix in New Jersey, then Fort Bragg in North Carolina in preparation for the infantry. In the army, Blanche said, he had "the time of his life" among his fellow soldiers. It may be that this was, for him, the time of absolute acceptance as an American. He became an asset in Europe, as his ability to speak French aided the troops in their struggle to communicate with the natives. These were the days he drew from when he related war stories to his grandchildren. Stories of battle were, understandably, absent. He cheerfully spoke of the willing, eager surrender of German soldiers who were much older than he, or teen-aged boys. To them all only he, the French-speaker, could make himself, and them, understood.

As with many infantrymen, Edgar's military career was brief. One year after his enlistment, he was in Cologne during the Battle of the Bulge. Three days before Christmas 1944, a mortar shell hit him. He witnessed his left leg fly ahead of him as he fell into a ditch. It was only here that he would later admit to fear. Terrified that he might be passed by, he yelled out until discovered by paramedics. Soon, he found himself with two legs that ended at or near the knee — the second amputated due to gangrene.

Blanche received a telegram the following month that Edgar was missing in action. Not long after the telegram's arrival, word came from Edgar himself of his survival. There was no telephone in the Fitzgerald home but there was at a neighbor's, who ran to over to get Blanche to take the call. *I got hit*, he informed her, *I lost my leg*. As a kind of consolation, Blanche responded *you're lucky it wasn't your eyes*. Edgar then told her he had lost both legs. *What can you do*, she said was her reply. After the conversation, Blanche cried out for his loss: *he loved to run*.

From a hospital in Belgium, Edgar was sent to Presque Isle, Maine, then Framingham, Massachusetts, then to an amputee center in Atlanta. Blanche visited him in Framingham, driven there by her brother and staying with a cousin. When she traveled to Atlanta to be with him, co-workers took up a collection to pay for her accommodations for an extra week. On her trip to Georgia, she stopped overnight in Washington, staying with a woman who regularly boarded the wives of wounded soldiers.

When Edgar was sent home, his recovery was far from its end. Gangrene remained a constant worry. *I stink, don't I?* Edgar would ask his wife. She would always say no, though the odor of damaged flesh was evident. His legs were encased in iron braces — his "lobster claws" — to shield them as they healed. The braces were awkward and often the cause of pain themselves. Convalescence was slow. Eventually, he was provided with his first pair of prosthetic legs. They failed to restore him to his previous height.

Throughout the remainder of his life, Edgar bore his injuries without bitterness. But the newspaper article in the local paper crediting the Red Cross with his battlefield rescue somewhat rankled. He saved *himself* by calling out despite fright and shock. His positive attitude after his experience resulted in his being sent to counsel other wounded veterans. Eventually, Edgar became Commander of the local chapter of the Disabled American Veterans. In this role, he spoke on radio from Haverhill City Hall. His brogue was so pronounced on radio that his family didn't recognize him.

Edgar made no fuss about his condition, no avoidance. To us grandchildren, *pepere*'s legs and cane were curious but natural — another fact of

the life we were born into. The legs' distinct squeak as he walked, climbed the stairs, drove the car, mowed the lawn, is a fixed sound-memory I can replay anytime. He could easily be gruff but just as readily effusive. On occasion, he would jauntily greet me, a pedantic child, with "Here comes the professor!" To make extra money, he sharpened scissors in his basement workshop, where I watched him for many hours, standing straight at the wheel, dark glasses covering his eyes, furious sparks bouncing off his chest and arms, falling to the floor, flying away and extinguishing themselves into the air.

I last saw him at the Veteran's Hospital in Jamaica Plain, on the trolley route to where I lived at the time. He was there for treatment of prostate cancer that had spread to his spine. The cancer was doing what cancer did, wasting him away. During my visit, our chat was light, the same as if I had dropped by the house at any time over the years. I gave him a first-hand account of myself. He told a story about another patient. Overall, while we'd never been particularly close to each other, we hadn't been estranged. Now, a distance was certain.

To his wake, I brought a small square of fired red clay. It was one of hundreds I had shaped reflexively when I studied ceramics. They were repetitive, dimensional doodles of a sort. My intention was to surreptitiously drop it into his casket — so something from me would always be with him. Earth returned to earth.

Standing before his body, I hesitated, self-conscious. The act seemed trivial, artsy play at a somber occasion. My father noted my awkwardness and I explained my plan. He encouraged me to go ahead. I leaned over and dropped it inside.

3: We pulled his nails

Leo A. Mailloux was born 19 April 1906 in St. Albans Vermont to Beatrice and Harvey Mailloux. He was one of six children who survived infancy in the family, four others dying young. Before settling in Haverhill, Massachusetts — where Leo would grow up — the Mailloux family lived in Burlington, Vermont, then Laconia New Hampshire. The work available in the mills in the Merrimac River valley region attracted many from New England and eastern Canada. Leo's father originally sold furniture but was

also an inventor. One of his inventions used an alarm-clock mechanism to open the draft of a furnace. Harvey died from a stroke while on a trip to Boston to apply for a patent on a new invention.

As a young man, Leo delivered meat throughout the area for a local butcher. One of his stops was at the grocery operated by Blanche Shaw's mother. When he and Blanche married, they took the house across the street from the store. From the back yard of the house, Leo ran a butcher shop, and did his own deliveries. He enjoyed the work primarily because he was his own boss. Maintaining the business, however, was difficult, and he eventually had to give it up. Leo took a job at one of the shoe factories in Haverhill to find regular employment.

The factory work was grueling. Leo operated a heel seat lasting machine, which was large and required repeated pulling of a heavy lever. Hernias resulted from this action. His feet and ankles also suffered exceptionally from standing all day. Other kinds of piecework were brought home, such as making fancy hand-cuts to shoes. These required working quickly and exactly with sharply honed blades. Severe cuts and punctures often occurred, even to those familiar with the work – as he and Blanche were. Compounding the harsh physical labor was problems with his supervisor.

Of these troubles, one thing was certain: it was the boss' attitude at fault. Leo's personality wasn't confrontational or argumentative. Nor did he shirk his duties. Leo had foibles and ideas that would try his family and friends' patience until he died. However, there was unanimous agreement about his kind and generous nature. The meat Leo gave away from his butcher shop was only a small evidence of his spirit.

Spirit may be the key word in understanding Leo, for good and ill. He was deeply religious and vocal about his Catholic faith. Many felt he should have been a priest. Their word had absolute authority for Leo, even when it came between Blanche and him. His obsession with religion, his need to continually speak of it was alienating and the cause of quarrels within his extended family. Other of his brothers were religious but not to Leo's extent. To know him at all was to be aware of his faith. However, it was within the family that he preached.

It was the adults in the family who experienced the full force of Leo's demonstrative creed. His nine grandchildren — by his three children, Richard, Leonard, and Janet — were doted upon. The religious books and artifacts in *pepere*'s house weren't that extraordinary to kids attending Catholic grammar school. Christ seemed to matter more to him than almost everyone else we knew. But we were taught that wasn't a flaw. It was important to us that we mattered more to him than almost everyone we knew. Pepere was a soft touch and could always be relied upon for favors and comfort. One of my earliest memories is of being consoled by him after being frightened by an image on the TV screen.

An eagerly awaited activity for us kids was pulling out nails from the soles of his shoes. He wore heavy-treaded thick-soled shoes at work that collected small tacks. *Pepere* would sit in an easy chair and present the bottom of his shoes so we could pry out the nails with butter knives.

That activity ended with us moving from next door to a block away. The toll the shoe factory took on *pepere*'s health was such that he retired early on disability. In his retirement, he became a shoe salesman of a sort. He discovered a special brand of mail-order shoe that soothed his abused feet. They were godsends — and he quietly tried to convert others. A small sign — unnoticeable unless you were looking for it — on the side of his house identified him as a representative of the shoe company. It's unlikely he sold a single pair.

It didn't matter. The shoes weren't about making money; it was about the spirit — about caring for people. It could have been this spirit, or that of his father — or both — which led to an attempt to patent his own invention. Remembering a common hazard of his early career, he devised a mechanism to allow butchers to lock swinging meathooks in place. Being no draftsman, he enlisted my older brother to draw diagrams of the device from his descriptions and crude sketches. The project, begun in earnest, never amounted to anything.

Pepere always had time for us grandchildren, continuing to be the soft touch for a favor. Usually, this was a ride to somewhere in town we wanted to go. I took advantage but wasn't consistently attentive in the discussions during our drives. One day, he was intent on making me comprehend how

many drops of blood there were in each seed, and the import it had for me. I had no clue how this related to me but nodded assent. By the time I recalled the conversation — years later — and grasped what he was talking about, it was far too late.

When he fell ill and it was learned of the extent of his health problems, it was too late to do anything. Even if he hadn't kept it to himself, little could have been done. His doctor recited a litany of debilitating conditions of which no one was aware. What the adults knew was that his religious obsessions were intensifying, as were his anxiety attacks. A year before his death, he agreed to enter a psychiatric hospital for treatment. A doctor there asked him how he felt: "Miserable." "Then why then are you smiling?" the doctor asked. What had been Leo's almost constant expression left then, never to return.

Every remnant of his personality followed the smile before his body died. He was set in an easy chair when I visited him during his sickness. There was no definite response when I spoke with him. He was gone yet still occupied our space. And as I have a definite first memory of him, I have a last. It's my father leaning in my bedroom doorway one morning to tell me he had died during the night.

Of the things he left, I chose a book: *Saints to Know and Love*. I wanted it for its kitsch-value, thinking of it as *A Field Guide for Spotting Saints*. That joke wore thin fast but I kept the book. I realized the joke was my excuse for sentimentality. I now keep two images of *pepere* simultaneous in mind. Both have me sitting before him. One is at his feet plucking out tacks; the other next to him during the visit before his death.

They interlace in my memory. Like those lenticular portraits of Christ that can be turned to see different pictures. Look one way for his life, the other for his redemption.

Spinarette

I was in my doctor's waiting room leafing through a science magazine. In the letters to the editor, a respondent pointed out an oversight in an article from the previous issue. The story announced that researchers had established that everything in the universe spun, from micro to macro. However, claimed the writer, the author neglected to answer an obvious question: *why?*

The editor suggested that it hadn't been so much an oversight as a deliberate — though benign — omission. *Observations are easy to make,* began the reply, *but determining causes is tough.* In an "are-you-sure-you-want-to-get-into-this?" tone, the editor then ran down an inventory of physical forces ending with quantum mechanics. Any and all of these might play a role in universal spin. No one could say with any certainty which or in what combination. The response concluded with a kind of shrug: *everything spins because it does.*

Science's failure to find a first cause here isn't a fail. It's inaccurate to even consider it a downfall. Beyond (or before) a certain point in physics, we're into metaphysics. Not knowing *why* something's happening doesn't mean it's *not* happening. On a personal level, though, origins require more assurance. Like describing *your* origin, and spin.

While I was present for every moment, I didn't observe your birth. I was caught up in it. This may affect my spinning *this* tale. A parenting book

we got during pregnancy warned that a child often develops an insatiable desire to hear the story of her birth. Take notes as it happens, the book counseled, get the facts straight. *But how would she know if I made it all up?* I wondered. It's not as if you creditably recall it in adulthood – never mind when you're a child. But I know your response when I deviate from the text while reading you a favorite book. Embellishments between the printed words go unchallenged — as long as I keep talking. (A pause of more than one second prompts your imperious command: "Read.") But alter a word, and you're on me like a proofreader.

It hasn't mattered. You've never called for the birth account. Perhaps that's yet to come, when you have a better grasp on the concept of origins. By then, the details may entangle with those of your brother's nativity. I was better prepared for his birth and considered myself steeled. This time I wouldn't be captivated either by the tedium of anticipation or the rush of activity. Shortly after we settled into our room at the midwifery and your mother tried to sleep, I wrote a paragraph or two. That was it, *fin*. Steel I was, though fashioned into a sieve. Particulars poured through me like so much breaking water.

Reconstructing the timelines of both yours and your brother's births can only happen now in collaboration of your mother and me. Are we remembering or manufacturing? It's a mix, then a remix, with every telling. That memory is actually a confabulation, an interpretation, alternately distresses and comforts me.

This telling is wound around two images. The first imprinted itself through prolonged viewing. Our hospital room window looked out onto Lake Superior and a freighter that lay anchored just off shore. Ships often floated outside the harbor, sometimes for a week or more, waiting for their docking time. As they tarried, ships anchored further out in the bay would turn slowly in circles like nautical clocks marking out their own time. Many summer days we sat on the lake beach with you, looking out at one of these ore carriers. On occasion, as we watched, a ship halted its rotation and headed in to dock. This sea-going horizontal building would maneuver itself between the twin jetties jutting out into the lake. It seemed impossible that the largest of them could squeeze through. Reverse birthing to

their berth, each navigated the channel straight and true.

We witnessed enough of these passages with you *in utero* that you might have sought to emulate them. Instead, you bumped, twisted, toiled, roiled and moiled into this world. Your birth was an interminable coda tacked onto a *sempiternity*. We found ourselves trapped in true life within a thought-problem. The one with the arrow progressively covering the half-distances to a target yet never reaching it. I wanted to insist to the nurses that we were calling you off. We'd try again when we were rested and better able to handle the stress. Forced to recognize this wasn't an option, I considered fleeing the room. But since your mother couldn't join me, I fixed myself beside the bed, trying to imagine the unimaginable: you.

There was no running away, no looking away. The doctor probed, determined dilation, and asserted progress. I needed a more tangible sign. A limb, perhaps. Then the doctor announced she could see you. For hours, you'd pressed on your mother's spine, out of position. Now you were moving, rotating for the literal final push. *Come look*, the doctor instructed me, *you can see the top of her head!* And I could, I did. Part of your mother had a mind of its own, absolutely.

Within a small circle, I witnessed your slow circuit, turning one way then back, in space. At the top of your skull was a thin, matted spiral of hair. A whorl within the whirl. I observed, then returned to the effort of interrupting your irregular, solo orbit. And suddenly, so abruptly, you were here. A fast, fluid reentry, borne up by the doctor, describing an arc from earth to sky. Blue, slimy, impossibly folded. An expectancy was now a person.

You kept the momentum. Then conveyed it.

Why does the world spin? Why do I? Because you do. At this point, you'll accept that. When you twirl, everything blurs and becomes mutable. Anything's possible. I know if I gathered the many details omitted in this telling, you'd accept an alternate version of your birth story — that parenting book notwithstanding. You embrace every new rendition of *The Little Mermaid* or *The Nutcracker* or Rapunzel that we provide. For you, they all exist in parallel universes through which you slide effortlessly. Then you turn and return. *Good night.*

"(extended play)" is an epilogue, coda, postscript, postlude, peroration, envoi for «Process Music». It consists of one text, "Six secrets of the hexahexaflexagon" originally published as a limited-edition, letterpress booklet.

Six secrets of the hexahexaflexagon

▲

The hexahexaflexagon was discovered by a slightly tipsy graphic designer (she stumbled back to the studio after a professional mixer) that half-forgot what she'd learned in a night class in origami. She spent hours folding paper this way and that with no clear goal in mind while the paying work languished unfinished and deadlines loomed. Upon stumbling on the hexahexaflexagon, she imagined it might serve as a novel marketing gimmick. It would be the next iteration after those redolent perfume strips in magazines. Six scents! However, as she nursed a small hangover the next day, she realized it would be impossible to mechanize the construction of the object, making them impractical to produce.

The hexahexaflexagon was the result of contemporary investigations into a unified field theory of physics. Specifically, to secure government funding for said investigations. The hexahexaflexagon was developed as a visual aid for reviewers of a particularly abstract grant proposal. In comparison, string theory was conspicuous. When operated, the hexahexaflexagon would demonstrate how the basic forces interacted. The reviewers were intrigued. They played with the hexahexaflexagons long after. But they rejected the proposal due to an egregious typo.

The hexahexaflexagon is thought to be the protrusion of a six-dimensional object into our three-dimensional space-time. Speculation is that were we able to perceive the hexahexaflexagon in its entirety, our notions of reality would be wondrously transformed. Meanwhile, the occupants of that protruded-from six-space regard our universe as magnificently uncomplicated. For them, the hexahexaflexagon is the key to a simpler life.

The hexahexaflexagon was the crowning glory of six years of dedicated, meticulous research and development by a fussy but forward-thinking geometer. He had set himself the task of developing an engaging amusement for his sextuplets' birthday party. He wanted something more competitively challenging and educational than Pin the Tail on the Donkey. At the celebration, the hexahexaflexagon was found amusing for six seconds then ripped.

I created the hexahexaflexagon while under the influence of a powerful psychoactive drug prescribed to treat an inexplicable and debilitating condition that affects my ability to comprehend spatial relationships (no sense of perspective). The hexahexaflexagon came about when I attempted to fold a paper airplane.

The hexahexaflexagon was found in the debris of the 1952 test "shot" of the first hydrogen bomb on Eniwetok Atoll. Also among the remains of the blast was element number 99. Some scientists wanted to call the element "pandamonium" after Project Panda, the program that developed the thermonuclear device. It was rejected in favor of "einsteinium."

[T]his is the "end matter" of «Process Music», the material that follows the main text of a book. Typically, the index would appear here, however, it has been placed on the inside front and back covers. The following is known as the colophon, which provides information about a book's production. The design of «Process Music» was devised by Jiwon Lee, then realized and adapted by Kenneth FitzGerald with suggestions from Freek Lomme. The texts are set in Bunita Swash, designed by Petra Niedernolte and Ralf Sander, published by Buntype; and Mr. Eaves Sans, designed by Zuzana Licko, distributed by Emigre Fonts. The book was published by Onomatopee Projects. Printing by KOPA, Kauno, Lithuania.

This is an Ephemeral Statesment
www.ephemeralstates.com

Process Music : songs, stories, and studies of graphic culture